YOUR WILL BE DONE

A Biography of Sister Mary Samuel Coughlin

Alice O'Rourke, O.P.

KENDALL/HUNT PUBLISHING COMPANY
4050 Westmark Drive Dubuque, Iowa 52002

Library of Congress Catalog Card Number 94-79690

ISBN 0-7872-0191-X

Printed in the United States of America

10 9 8 7 6 5 4 3 2 1

To the Sisters of the Sinsinawa
Dominican Congregation of the
Most Holy Rosary

Sister Mary Samuel Coughlin

Contents

Preface ix

Chapter One: *Minnesota Background* 1

Chapter Two: *Interlocking Destinies* 19

Chapter Three: *Preparation for Leadership, 1901–1910* 37

Chapter Four: *Decade of Outreach, 1910–1920* 53

Chapter Five: *Challenges of the 1920s* 79

Chapter Six: *The 1930s: Decade of Depression* 113

Chapter Seven: *World War II and Its Immediate Aftermath* 139

Chapter Eight: *Years of Retirement, 1949–1959* 167

Chapter Nine: *Her Legacy* 191

Appendices:

Appendix A: Genealogical Table 197

Appendix B: Funeral Sermon for Mother Samuel Coughlin by the Most Reverend William P. O'Connor, Bishop of Madison 199

Bibliography 205

Index 209

Illustrations

Maps

Native Americans in Minnesota, 1850s-1860s 2
Railroad Plans in Minnesota, 1857-1862 2
Father Samuel Mazzuchelli's Missionary Territory, 1830-1843 9
Southwestern Cork County, Ireland 15

Tables

I. Schools Conducted by Sinsinawa Dominican Sisters, 1900 51
II. Schools Accepted by Sinsinawa Dominicans, 1901-1910 52
III. Schools (Missions) Accepted by Sinsinawa Dominicans, 1911-1920 75
IV. Schools (Missions) Accepted by Sinsinawa Dominicans, 1921-1930 112
V. Missions Accepted by Sinsinawa Dominicans, 1931-1940 137

Photographs

Sister Mary Samuel Coughlin iv
Bishop Mathias Loras 9
Father Samuel Mazzuchelli 9
Bethlehem Academy 22
Graduating Class of 1885 22
Sister Gertrude Power 23
Ellen Coughlin at an early age 23

View of Mound Buildings in 1890s 23
Mother Emily Power 39
Sister Benetta Coughlin 39
John Ireland 39
John Lancaster Spalding 39
Coughlin Family 40
Sr. DeRicci and Mother Samuel 68
Mother Samuel and Sr. Ruth Devlin 68
Mother Mary Joseph (Maryknoll) 68
Sr. Louis Bertrand Droege 68
Sr. Grace James, Thomas à Kempis Reilly, O. P. and Sr. George Adamson 69
George Cardinal Mundelein 69
Archbishop John T. McNicholas 69
Villa des Fougères 70
Bishop Thomas Esser, O.P 90
Joseph Cardinal Pizzardo 90
Rosary College, 1924 90
Reigning Pontiffs during Mother Samuel's years of leadership 91
Honorary Degree Presentation at the White House, 1937 130
Mademoiselle Boulanger's Class, 1944 147
Villa Schifanoia, Florence 158
John Coughlin 178
Brigid, Dan, Angela 178
Mary Hunt's Family 178
Father Bernard Coughlin and Kathleen Hunt 179
Bertrand and Barbara Coughlin 179
Bishop O'Connor at Mother Samuel's Funeral 186
Mother Samuel's Memorial Tablet 187

Preface

The title of this biography of Sister Mary Samuel Coughlin—*Your Will Be Done*—paraphrases her response in 1910 and every six years from 1913 through 1943 to the call through election by the sisters to lead the Sinsinawa Dominican Congregation as Mother General. With the ten months as acting Mother General from October 1909 to August 1910, she served God in this capacity for forty years.

My acquaintance with her began in September 1949 when I entered the Congregation shortly after her final term had ended. My reverence for her started at that time, nourished by the reports of the sisters and others who knew her. The history of the Congregation by Sister Mary Eva McCarty, *The Sinsinawa Dominicans: Outline of Twentieth Century Development, 1901-1949*, published in 1952, acquainted me with the remarkable developments that she helped bring about through her leadership.

This biography serves primarily to reveal the personal life of Mother Samuel, particularly the price she paid in suffering. My involvement in the research and writing has deepened my appreciation of her sometimes to the point of tears.

The major resource used is her diary, which she kept sporadically from 1905-1910 and regularly from 1910 until a few months before her death in 1959. Her correspondence with Sister DeRicci Fitzgerald, who served with her on the General Council throughout thirty-nine years of elected leadership, was the next most valuable record. Matters relating to congregational developments covered by Sister Mary Eva McCarty are summarized whenever relevant to her personal journey or when new information on them has become available since Sister Eva's book was published.

I have been aided by ready access to the Sinsinawa Dominican Archives and by interviews with Sister Mary Benedicta Larkin, former Mother General, Mary Ann Randall and Kathleen Hunt, grandnieces of Mother Samuel, and Molly Coughlin, her sister-in-law. Marie Mahoney Fitzgerald of South Dartmouth, Massachusetts, a distant cousin of Mother Samuel, shared her work on the Coughlin ancestry and current family relationships. My visit to Faribault, Minnesota, Mother Samuel's home town, brought valuable information and insights through the guidance of Sister Zacchaeus

Ryan, Educational Resource Person at Bethlehem Academy. The sisters at Sinsinawa, Wisconsin, where I am in residence, provided informal details through their daily reminiscences.

Kaye Ashe, O.P., outgoing Prioress of the Sinsinawa Dominican Congregation, and Clemente Davlin, O.P., member of the Department of English at Rosary College, River Forest, Illinois, edited the chapters as they were drafted, providing valuable advice on content and style, as well as spotting grammatical and typographical errors. Pauline Ingram, O.P., helped in the selection and placement of photographs. For the opportunity to engage in the remarkable experience of learning about Mother Samuel's life, I am grateful to Kaye Ashe, O.P., Jean McSweeney, O.P., current Prioress of the Sinsinawa Dominican Congregation, and Marise Barry, O.P., Prioress Provincial.

It is my hope that *Your Will Be Done: A Biography of Sister Mary Samuel Coughlin* will extend knowledge and appreciation of Mother Samuel among all who read it as the Sinsinawa Dominican Congregation, which she led for so many years, enters its period of celebration of its sesquicentennial in 1997.

Alice O'Rourke, O.P.
Sinsinawa, Wisconsin
August 1994

Chapter One

Minnesota Background

By a conjunction of circumstances the Coughlin family and the Dominican Sisters of Sinsinawa, Wisconsin, arrived in Faribault, Minnesota, in the summer of 1865 within a few weeks of one another. Minnesota had become a hospitable environment for new settlers; the Coughlins had found their way by a series of stages from their birthplace in County Cork, Ireland, to the upper Middle West; and the Dominican Sisters responded to a family need that brought them north from their motherhouse in southwestern Wisconsin. This chapter deals with the interlocking circumstances that brought the Coughlin family into contact with the Sinsinawa Dominicans: political evolution, including conflict with Native Americans; emergence of Church structures; and organization of the Sinsinawa Dominican Congregation.

The development of Minnesota from a wilderness area into an environment that encouraged migration from the eastern states and northern European countries began in earnest in the second quarter of the nineteenth century. The acquisition of lands from the Native Americans was promoted under the protection of United States military forces based at Fort Crawford near Prairie du Chien, and Fort Snelling located at the junction of the Minnesota and Mississippi Rivers. A series of treaties in the 1830s and 1850s alienated lands from the Sioux and Chippewa tribes under terms much in favor of white settlers (see map, p. 2).[1]

Political organization was given impetus by the admission of Wisconsin as a state in 1848. Minnesota's political leaders—Henry Hastings Sibley, Henry Mowrer Rice, and Joseph R. Brown—devoted

---

[1]Theodore C. Blegen, *Minnesota: A History of the State* (Minneapolis: University of Minnesota Press, 1963), pp. 114, 129, 166-175.

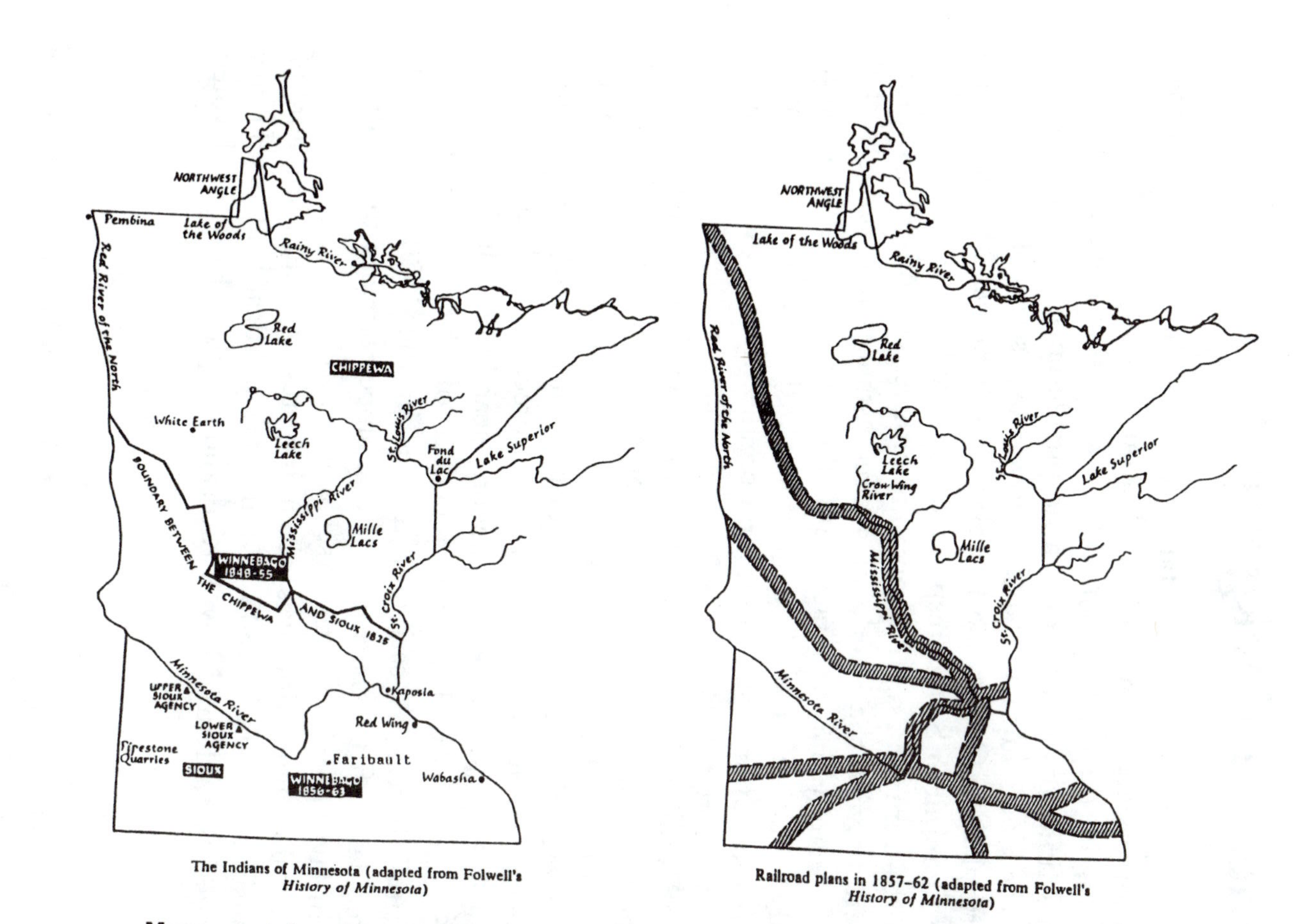

The Indians of Minnesota (adapted from Folwell's *History of Minnesota*)

Railroad plans in 1857–62 (adapted from Folwell's *History of Minnesota*)

Maps are taken from Theodore C. Blegen, *Minnesota, A History of the State*, pages 22 and 196.

their talents toward gaining territorial status for Minnesota through the process initiated under the Land Ordinance of 1785 and the Northwest Ordinance of 1787.[2] Following their success in this with the passage of the bill in Congress on March 3, 1849, the three men turned their attention towards measures necessary to achieve statehood, a goal accomplished by vote of Congress on May 11, 1858.[3]

The acquisition of land through treaties with the Native Americans and the provision of governmental structures spurred rapid migration into Minnesota in the 1850s. Most of the influx came from already established states including those in New England, the upper tier along the Great Lakes, and the Middle West. Foreign born settlers, encouraged by formal colonization efforts, such as those of Father Francis Pierz with German immigrants in Stearns County and General James Shields with Irish immigrants in Rice County, became more numerous as the decade closed. Shields, a veteran of the Mexican War and a former senator in Illinois, had arrived in Minnesota in 1855.[4] By 1860, more than thirty per cent of white Minnesota settlers were foreign born.[5] The sections benefiting most from the growth in population were the capital, St. Paul, which had 10,000 residents in 1860, and several centers with between 1,000 and 5,000 each in the southeastern quarter of the state.[6]

Faribault was one of the latter group. It was established in the early 1850s, beginning with a frame house built in 1853 by Alexander Faribault. This man, born in 1806, was the son of Jean Baptiste

---

[2]*Documents of American History*, Edited by Henry Steele Commager, Seventh Edition (New York: Appleton-Century-Crofts, 1963), pp. 123-124, 128-132.

[3]Blegen, pp. 161-164; 220-229.

[4]"James Shields," *Dictionary of American Biography*, Vol. IX, 106-107; William H. Condon, *Life of Major-General James Shields: Hero of Three Wars, and Senator from Three States* (Chicago: Blakely Printing Co., 1900), p. 267.

[5]James Michael Reardon, P.A. *The Catholic Church in the Diocese of St. Paul: from earliest origin to centennial achievement* (St. Paul, Minnesota: North Central Publishing Company, 1952), pp. 94-95; Blegen, p. 175.

[6]Blegen, p. 177.

Faribault, renowned fur trader. By the age of twenty, Alexander had established a trading post on the Cannon River, near the present site of Faribault. The land ceded by the Sioux under the Treaty of Traverse des Sioux in 1851 included this area, which soon was opened to white settlers. Faribault became one of the proprietors of the town named for him, as did General Shields, who, as noted above arrived in the area in 1855. In addition to his connection with Faribault, he was also responsible for the establishment of Shieldsville shortly after his arrival in Minnesota. He and Alexander Faribault were among the collaborators in the organization of Rice County in 1855, which encompassed Faribault as county seat, Shieldsville, Northfield, Morristown, Dundas, Canada, Millersburg, Webster, Warsaw, Wheatland, and Cannon City.[7]

The Panic of 1857 interrupted the growth experienced in the mid-Fifties, but by 1860 Minnesotans were expecting a return to prosperity, with the development of railroads being a significant element in the economic revival (see map, p. 2). These expectations met with setbacks due to the Civil War and the Sioux Wars.

Minnesota rallied patriotically to render support to the Union from 1861-65. Because of its remoteness from the fields of battle, normal life was not disrupted to a severe degree.[8]

The Sioux Wars, beginning in August 1862, caused much more havoc because of their concentration in settled areas of central Minnesota. A combination of Federal troops and state militia sufficed to end hostilities by late fall of 1862. The following year brought occasional skirmishes and operations leading to the expulsion of Native Americans to reservations and territories to the west. By the mid-Sixties, political, economic, and social conditions were conducive to the expansion of settlement.[9]

---

[7]*History of Rice and Steele Counties, Minnesota*, compiled by Franklyn Curtiss-Wedge (Chicago: H.C. Jr. & Co., 1910) 2 vols., Vol. I, 87; *Portraits and Memories of Rice County, Minnesota* (Dallas, Texas: Rice County Historical Society, 1987), Chronology.

[8]Blegen, pp. 248-249.

[9]Blegen, pp. 260-275.

The progress of religion was also significant in providing a hospitable environment for newcomers. Catholic missionary groups, especially Jesuit and Recollect priests, had been present in the Lake Superior region of Minnesota beginning in the seventeenth century. Their work was interrupted in the late eighteenth century with the suppression of the Jesuits, first in France and later world-wide.[10]

Formal jurisdiction of the Catholic Church was extended to the new American nation with the organization of the diocese of Baltimore in 1789. As settlers moved westward, so did Church organization and activities.[11] By the 1840s, under the leadership of Bishop Mathias Loras, Minnesota began to benefit from these developments. Because of the importance of their faith to the Coughlin family, the story of the establishment of Church structures in Minnesota is told in some detail below.

Bishop Mathias Loras was ordained in Mobile on December 10, 1837, as bishop of the newly created Diocese of Dubuque, which encompassed all of Minnesota. Asking the Dominican priest, the Reverend Samuel Charles Mazzuchelli, who was serving the area of southwestern Wisconsin, northwestern Illinois, and eastern Iowa (see below, p. 9), to serve as vicar general, Loras departed for Europe to seek priests to work in his diocese and funds to support the many needs to be met in organizing the new diocese. He succeeded in recruiting two ordained priests, the Reverend Joseph Cretin and the Reverend Anthony Pelamourges, and four seminarians: Lucien Galtier, Augustine Ravoux, Remigius Petiot, and Jacques Causse to join him. All these men would serve the Church in Minnesota.[12]

Loras and his entourage left LeHavre at the end of August 1838. Upon reaching the United States, they journeyed by way of Baltimore, where the four seminarians were enrolled in a seminary to

---

[10]Sister Alice O'Rourke, *The Good Work Begun: Centennial History of Peoria Diocese* (Chicago: Lakeside Press, 1977), pp. 7-8.

[11]Reardon, p. 62.

[12]*Ibid*, p. 69.

learn English. Loras, Cretin, and Pelamourges continued the slow trip to St. Louis. A severe winter blocked their passage to Dubuque, so they spent several months with Bishop Rosati as their host, occupying themselves in priestly functions near St. Louis. Mazzuchelli joined them on March 23, 1839, in order to accompany them to Dubuque. On April 21, Loras took possession of his cathedral church, the nearly-completed structure that Mazzuchelli had begun to erect in 1835.[13] Assisting the Bishop on that occasion were Cretin, Pelamourges, and Mazzuchelli.

Towards the end of June 1839, Loras, accompanied by Pelamourges, made the first official visitation of a bishop to the area of Minnesota. He offered Mass at St. Peter's (now Mendota) for the traders and soldiers of the garrison of Fort Snelling. He found 185 Catholics in attendance. He promised to send a priest to take up residence at St. Peter's. On their return trip to Dubuque, the Bishop and Pelamourges visited Native American villages along the Mississippi and spent eleven days among French families at Prairie du Chien. Here, too, they promised to provide a priest.[14]

Loras was quick to fulfill his promises of providing priests for those places he had visited. On January 5, 1840, he ordained three of the seminarians he had brought with him from France: Lucien Galtier, Augustine Ravoux, and Jacques Causse. Galtier left for St. Peter's four months later. During the following year, he built a small chapel on a bluff near Fort Snelling, dedicating it to St. Paul on November 1, 1840.

Ravoux was assigned briefly to Prairie du Chien from January 1840 to September 1841. He then was transferred to work at Parle and Chaska (Little Prairie). At this latter mission, where Jean Baptiste Faribault had a trading post for the Sioux and where he built a small chapel, Ravoux struggled for three years under appalling

---

[13]*The Memoirs of Father Samuel Mazzuchelli, O.P.* Translated by Sister Maria Michele Armato, O.P. and Sister Jeremy Finnegan, O. P., (Chicago: The Priory Press, 1967), pp. 148-149.

[14]Reardon, pp. 39-40.

physical conditions but with encouraging results in the form of sacraments administered. In 1844, he replaced Galtier at St. Paul in what he thought would be a temporary assignment. Instead, it proved to be an extended one, in which he was still serving when the new diocese of St. Paul was organized on July 19, 1850. Joseph Cretin was appointed to serve as bishop and chose to hold his ordination on January 26, 1851, in Belley, France, where he had been ordained to the priesthood in 1823. One of Cretin's earliest appointments was of Ravoux as vicar general on July 5, 1851.[15] The political, economic, and social developments previously described and increase in population provided opportunities for the Church of St. Paul Diocese to advance toward maturity during the 1850s and early 1860s.

Another track of development that converged with others sketched above to provide the setting for the coming of the Coughlin family was the establishment of the Sinsinawa Dominican Congregation of Sisters. Their founder was the Dominican missionary, Father Samuel Charles Mazzuchelli, previously mentioned for his association with Bishop Mathias Loras (see above, p. 5).

Mazzuchelli, a native of Milan, Italy, who had entered the Dominican Novitiate at Faenza in 1823, was recruited by Edward J. Fenwick, O.P., Bishop of Cincinnati, a diocese established in 1821. Still a seminarian, Mazzuchelli arrived in the United States in 1828. Following his ordination in Cincinnati in 1830, Mazzuchelli was assigned to the northernmost area of what was then the Diocese of Cincinnati. He was based at Mackinac Island and served other places in northern Michigan, including settlements, such as Arbre Croche on the northwest shores of Lower Michigan, and Green Bay, which was then part of the Territory of Michigan, in the lands served by Jesuit missionaries in the seventeenth and eighteenth centuries. His travels took him through the Wisconsin portion of the Michigan Territory as far as the Mississippi River at the site of Prairie du Chien in 1832 (see map, p. 9).

---

[15]*Ibid.*, pp. 41-46, 51-59, *passim.*

The death of Fenwick from cholera on September 26, 1832, and changes in diocesan structure helped to redirect Mazzuchelli's ministry. Following the organization of the diocese of Detroit in 1833, he retained his affiliation with the Michigan missions until 1835, collaborating frequently from 1830 onward with Father Frederic Baraga, another of Bishop Fenwick's recruits. Baraga's area of service overlapped those of Mazzuchelli at Arbre Croche and other settlements in the northern part of Lower Michigan. After 1835, Baraga personally served and also supervised other missionaries among the Chippewa tribes of the Lake Superior region, with its old mission locations at La Pointe and L'Anse. In 1843, he was appointed Vicar Apostolic of Upper Michigan and in 1857, first Bishop of the newly established diocese of Sault Ste. Marie (now the Marquette Diocese).[16]

Meanwhile, Mazzuchelli had become interested in the plight of European immigrants, chiefly of German and Irish origin, with whom he came into contact in his missionary journeys into southwestern Wisconsin and northwestern Illinois. The latter area, formerly of Bardstown Diocese, was being administered by Bishop Joseph Rosati since the organization of the Diocese of St. Louis in 1826.[17] Early in 1835 Father Mazzuchelli decided to travel to Somerset, Ohio, to consult with his Dominican superiors on where he should continue his ministry. En route by river, he visited Galena, Illinois, and Dubuque, Iowa, where Catholics who had long been without benefit of the sacraments urged him to remain. He could not do this without proper authorization, so he continued his journey by way of the Mississippi River to St. Louis where he met Rosati. Entering the Ohio River at the southern tip of Illinois and stopping at Cincinnati on the way, he eventually reached Somerset. His superiors

---

[16]Sister Alice O'Rourke, *Sown on Good Ground: Centennial History of St. Mary Cathedral Parish, Gaylord,* (Gaylord, Michigan: Privately Printed, 1984), pp. 3-4.

[17]O'Rourke, *The Good Work Begun,* pp. 14-15.

Bishop Mathias Loras

Samuel Charles Mazzuchelli

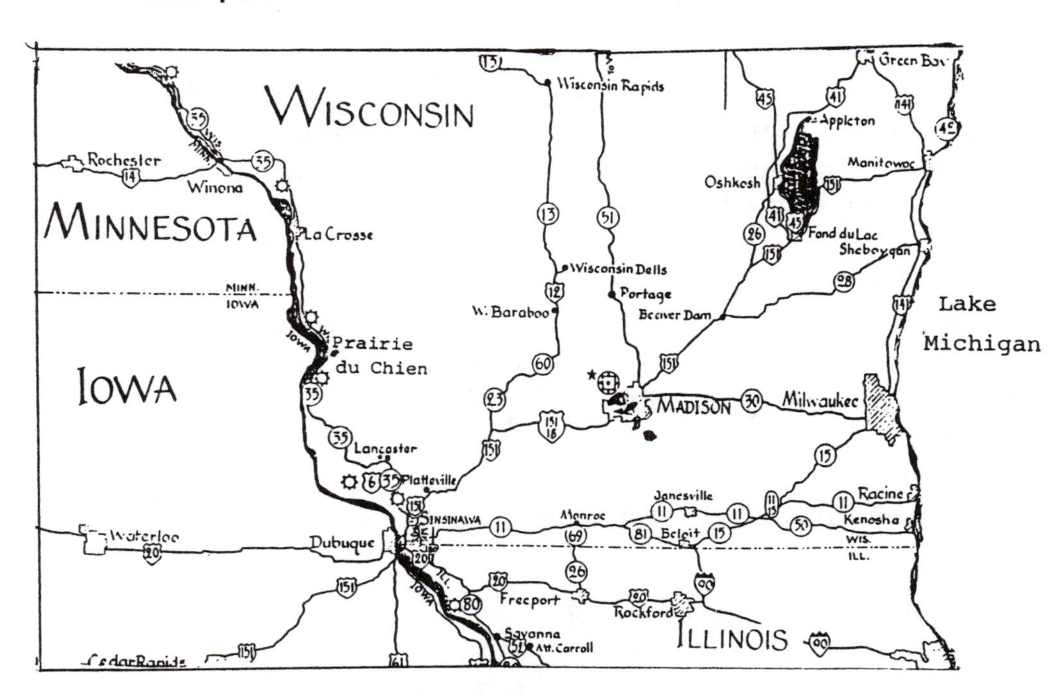

Mazzuchelli's Missionary Areas

concurred with his opinion that he should respond to the call to labor in the above mission.[18]

For the next eight years, 1835-1843, he ministered to the Irish and German immigrants in the lead-mining regions of southwestern Wisconsin, northwestern Illinois, and eastern Iowa. For six of these years, 1837-1843, he served as vicar general for Loras. This position brought added responsibilities to an already impossible schedule. On both sides of the Mississippi and on both sides of the border between the State of Illinois and the Territory of Wisconsin, Mazzuchelli organized parishes, built churches, schools, and parish houses, and entered into civic activities. He has been credited with building sixteen churches in this region, many of which are still standing, and organizing fourteen other church communities where buildings were later provided. He found time to visit Joseph Smith, the Mormon leader, at Nauvoo, in 1843.[19]

Mazzuchelli spent the year from June 1843 to the late summer of 1844 in Europe, chiefly in Milan, enjoying a much-needed break from his labors, visiting his family, and writing a report, known as *Memoirs*, of his thirteen years of missionary work in the United States. This constituted his report to the Dominican Master General. He also raised funds from relatives and the French Society for the Propagation of the Faith for some projects that he would undertake when he returned to America.

As location of the contemplated projects, Mazzuchelli, on his return to Wisconsin in 1844, purchased 800 acres of property with Sinsinawa Mound as the center. The following year he established a new province of the Dominican Order, which he named in honor of his patron, St. Charles Borromeo, permission for which he had been given the preceding year both by officials of the Order and of the Church in Rome. In 1845, he began building a school and relocating

---

[18]18 Mazzuchelli, *Memoirs*, pp. 141-143.

[19]*Memoirs*, pp. 210-243; Sister Mary Nona McGreal, O.P., *Positio, Samuel Mazzuchelli, O.P., a Missionary to the United States: A Documentary Account of His Life, Virtues, and Reputation for Holiness* (Rome, 1989), pp. 252-400, *passim*.

and rebuilding a church. Closely following upon this came the organization of a college for men, the latter being named in honor of St. Thomas Aquinas. He constructed a stone building in 1846 to house some of these activities, a structure still in existence today.

Another institution was added in 1847 when, on August 4, he received two women into a newly organized religious community of the Third Order of St. Dominic. Two more women joined in December 1847 and another two in April 1848. Four of these women professed on August 15, 1849—Sister Ignatia Fitzpatrick, Sister Clara Conway, Sister Josephine Cahill, and Sister Rachel Conway—are regarded as the four cornerstones of the Sinsinawa Dominican Congregation. In anticipation of their ministry of teaching, Mazzuchelli arranged in August 1848 for the incorporation of Sinsinawa Female Academy.[20]

The new province for men did not prosper, and the men's college was slow in developing. Thinking that the fault was his, Mazzuchelli in September 1849 renounced his authority and the control of the property in favor of Dominicans from the St. Joseph Province based in Somerset, Ohio. He took up residence at Benton, Wisconsin, serving as pastor of St. Patrick, Benton, and St. Augustine, New Diggings, both of which parishes he had organized and for which he had built churches.

The remaining fourteen and one-half years of his life were spent at Benton, to which in 1852 he welcomed the four Sisters from Sinsinawa whom the prior there had suggested be placed under his direction. When the Sisters opened St. Clara Academy in 1853, Mazzuchelli served as superintendent and teacher in addition to pastoral responsibilities at several new locations. As in years gone by, his gifts as builder of institutions and structures to house them were put to good use. He was educator for the Sisters as well as spiritual

---

[20]Sister Mary Paschala O'Connor, O.P., *Five Decades: History of the Congregation of the Most Holy Rosary, Sinsinawa, Wisconsin, 1849-1899* (Sinsinawa, Wisconsin: The Sinsinawa Press, 1954), pp. 13-39, *passim*.

director, instructing them in secular subjects and in the spirit and practices of the Order of Preachers as adjusted to the active life of the Third Order in America. He incorporated a description of this spirit and these practices in the *Rule of 1860*.[21]

Because he had spent more time at Benton than at any other place of ministry, Mazzuchelli was perhaps more deeply loved and appreciated there than elsewhere. It was with profound grief that the Sisters, students, and parishioners faced his death on February 23, 1864. Their unanimous conviction of his holiness was shared by all who knew him in all of the phases of his ministry. Stories of his kindness and virtue and events regarded as miraculous began to circulate before the year was out; thus a foundation was laid for initiating the Cause of his beatification that would be undertaken in the mid-twentieth century.

Though feeling bereft at the loss of Mazzuchelli, the group of twenty Sisters and two novices continued with their labors, picking up the many tasks that their Founder had formerly managed. To commemorate his memory they continued to celebrate November 4 as Founder's Day. As a sign of renewed vitality, they were ready to open a new mission in the summer of 1865. The new venture was the establishing of Bethlehem Academy in Faribault, Minnesota.

At the southernmost tip of County Cork, Ireland, is a small peninsula sixteen miles long and six miles wide, bordered on the northwest by Dunmanus Bay and on the southeast by Toormore Bay (see map, p. 15). Within its boundaries branches of the O'Mahoney clan had lived for centuries. The fortunes of the members waxed and waned as rival groups contended for control. From the time of the Tudor monarchy at the end of the fifteenth century, when the entry of the English brought even more violence and impoverishment into Ireland, the O'Mahoneys retained a tenuous hold. A succession of rebellions within the extended family or between branches of the family and the English overlords kept the area in turmoil. The

---

[21] *Ibid.*, pp. 54-86.

descendants fought for James II in 1689-1690, meeting defeat and exile at the hands of William of Orange, who had been proclaimed co-ruler of England and Scotland with his wife, Mary, the daughter of James II. Count Daniel O'Mahoney, one of James' supporters, who had been exiled to France, was head of the branch of the family from which the O'Mahoneys of the nineteenth century were descended.[22]

Mother Samuel Coughlin's parents were children of families in this remote area of County Cork. Her mother, Ellen, the daughter of Jeremiah O'Mahoney of the above family and of Honora Burns, was born at Malavogue on December 3, 1837; her father, Daniel, the son of Timothy Coughlin and Mary Mehigan, was born on December 4, 1834, in nearby Dhough. John Coughlin, an older[23] brother of Daniel by two years, and Catherine O'Mahoney, older by nine years than her sister, Ellen, married in 1855 and soon emigrated to America, two among the million persons who did so during that decade.[24] They settled at Long Branch, New Jersey. Daniel migrated to New Jersey at a later date and found employment on the farm of Mr. Wardell, a wealthy seaside resort owner. Ellen left Ireland on March 11, 1861, and after a rough, six-week voyage reached New York. Her brother-in-law met her and took her to his home in New Jersey. Shortly thereafter, she found work in the home of the Wardells, where she experienced great kindness and where she met Daniel.

Ellen O'Mahoney and Daniel Coughlin were married on June 24, 1862, in St. James Church, Jersey City, New Jersey. The following is a description of the event as recorded by Brigid Coughlin:

---

[22]"An Almost Forgotten Sept," Copied from *The Southern Star*, Cork, Ireland, Saturday, November 13, 1909, Sinsinawa Dominican Archives, Papers of Mother Samuel Coughlin; Charles-Marie Garnier, *A Popular History of Ireland*. Translated and adapted by Hedley McCay (Baltimore: Helicon Press, 1961), p. 47.

[23]The information in this and succeeding paragraphs is taken from reminiscences of Brigid Coughlin prepared in the 1950s and found in the SDA. The date given for Daniel Coughlin's birth is taken from his tombstone in the cemetery in Faribault; other sources give it as December 6, 1834.

[24]Garnier, p. 132.

It was a very simple ceremony—so different from the long requirements of today's weddings. They merely went to the priest's house, told him they wanted to be married and of their plan to go west. Father Kelly took them to the church, heard their confessions, and married them with his housekeeper and sexton as witnesses. He gave them some advice for their journey, wrote out their marriage certificate, and that same afternoon they were on their way by train to Aurora, Illinois.

Their first child, Mary Anne, was born in Aurora on October 15, 1863; she died at ten months of age from whooping cough. In the late summer of 1864, they moved to Chicago, where Mr. Coughlin found work in the railroad yards. Still not settled, they responded to a suggestion of Mr. Coughlin's uncle, Patrick, that they join him in moving to Montgomery, Minnesota, where he had purchased land.

In late April 1865, they boarded a train draped in mourning for the death of President Lincoln. Arriving in St. Paul, they took a boat to Hastings and then a stage coach to Faribault. Here they remained instead of going on to Montgomery, which was about twenty miles away. Though no reason is identified in the archival material, the decision may have been reached due to accessibility of land near Faribault. After renting a house for a couple of months, the Coughlins on July 1, 1865, purchased from a Mary Evans 22.5 acres of land a short distance north of Faribault at a cost of $400.00.[25] The property had on it a log house that would later be replaced with a frame dwelling.

Soon also to begin residence in Faribault during that summer of 1865 were five Sinsinawa Dominican Sisters. The members of this Congregation founded by Father Samuel Mazzuchelli (see above, p. 11) were called to Faribault by Bishop Thomas L. Grace, a Dominican priest who had succeeded Bishop Joseph Cretin as

---

[25] Book M, page 327, July 6, 1865, Recorder of Deeds, Rice County Court House, Faribault, Minnesota.

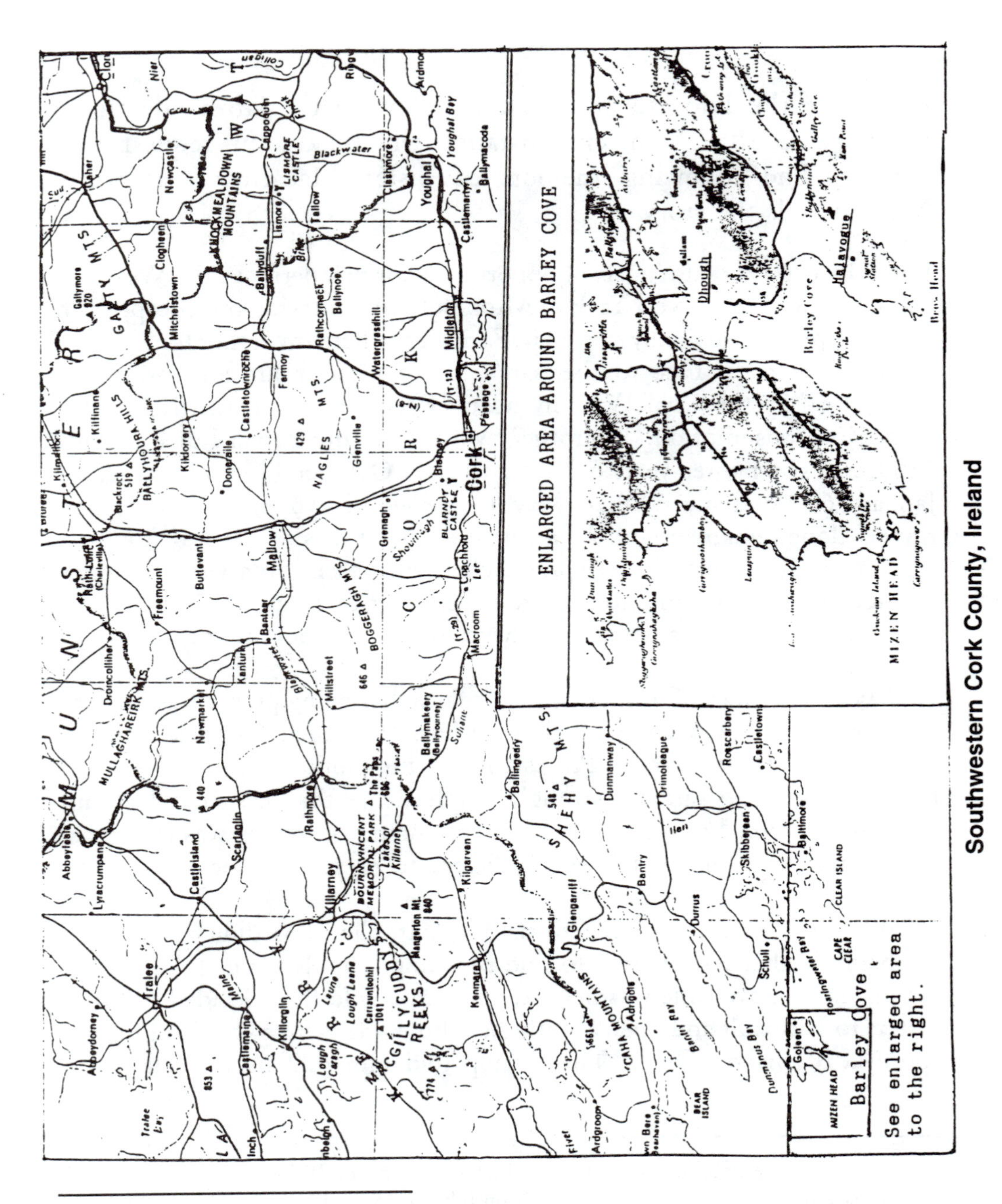

Map of Cork County with inset enlargement of area of birthplaces of Ellen O'Mahoney and Daniel Coughlin. Permission of use for portion of Cork County granted by National Geographic Society, publisher of Revised Sixth Edition of National Geographic Atlas of the World.

Bishop of the Diocese of St. Paul, following the latter's death on February 22, 1857.[25] The circumstances which led to his request were unique. The following memoir of Sister Macarius (Catherine) Murphy tells the story.

Lured by extravagant reports of opportunity for prosperity in the West, my parents moved from New York to Minnesota. After trying our prospects in different places, we finally settled in Faribault, where my father took charge of stone quarries. Due to the hardships of pioneer life and privations brought on by the Civil War, my relatives fell into what was then called "galloping consumption." A brother two years younger than I died August 1863. My sister three years older than I died October 1863; my father on January 6, 1864; my mother, May 12, 1864. My youngest brother and myself alone remained without a single relative this side of New York.

The parish priest, Rev. George Keller, was absent on a visit to France and returned just in time to prepare my mother for death. While she was receiving the last sacraments, the lawyer was in the next room waiting to draw up her will.

My mother was a Catholic of strong faith; her dying prayer was that my brother and I would enter religious orders. It seemed probable that we would fall under the care of Protestants, so my mother asked the Rev. G. Keller to be our guardian, strongly emphasizing that we should attend Catholic schools. I never heard just what amount of money was left to us, but I have been told that it was sufficient to prepare us for earning our living.

At that time, since there was no Catholic [boarding] school in Faribault, Father Keller tried to find boarding schools for us [elsewhere]; but any school available was beyond our means. He then decided to bring Sisters to Faribault and open a Catholic school. He went to St. Paul for the approval of Bishop Grace. The Bishop told him that he himself was a

---

[25]There was a lapse of almost two and one-half years between Bishop Cretin's death and the ordination of Bishop Grace in St. Louis on July 24, 1859. The reason for this was the resignation of Father Anthony Pelamourges, who had originally been appointed. Father Augustine Ravoux, who had served as missionary among the Indians, as pastor of several parishes, and as vicar general of the Diocese (see above, p. 7), served as administrator during the interim.

Dominican and that Father Samuel Mazzuchelli (a Dominican missionary) who recently passed away had established a community of Sisters at Benton, Wisconsin. The Bishop said he wanted to help these Sisters and that he wanted to introduce them into the St. Paul Diocese. Providing Father Keller agreed to take these Sisters, the Bishop gave his promise to furnish the home and buy their first piano. Of course, Father Keller at once accepted this proposal. I recall this for I was present at the conference.

The Bishop, true to his word, purchased Major Fowler's residence. For that time it was quite a large and comfortable building, but a long distance from the church and parish school. The Bishop also gave their piano. Edward Ayde, the church sexton, brought it from St. Paul on a lumber wagon. . . .[26]

Accompanied by Mother Regina Mulqueeny and the Rev. Herbert J. Nuyts, O.S.C., pastor and chaplain at Benton, the following Sisters left Benton, Wisconsin, by stage coach at 5:00 on Monday morning, July 31, 1865: Sisters Josephine Cahill, superioress; Gertrude Power, prefect; Imelda Hertzog, directress of music; and Veronica Power and Benevenuta McCullough, who were to teach in the parish school. They boarded a boat in Dubuque, which brought them to St. Paul on Wednesday afternoon, August 2. They stayed with the St. Joseph Sisters until Friday morning, August 4. Leaving by stage coach at 4:00 a.m. in the company of Bishop Grace, they reached Faribault at 7:00 that evening, the Feast of St. Dominic. They were greeted by several women of the parish and escorted to their home, where, at Father Keller's suggestion, some of the young women had prepared dinner.

---

[26]27 SDA, Annals of Bethlehem Convent.

Chapter Two

Interlocking Destinies

The stories of the Coughlin family and the Dominican Sisters in Faribault continued to be intertwined during the remainder of the nineteenth century. Their political, economic, social, and cultural settings were favorable. Except for brief economic setbacks in 1873 and 1893, and the grasshopper plague of 1873-77, which was especially devastating in Rice County,[1] earning a living was generally within reach for those who were willing to work hard. The Coughlins were of that type and filled their early days in Faribault with clearing their newly purchased land, planting, harvesting, and all the other tasks associated with subsistence farming. Mr. Coughlin supplemented farm work with a job as a section hand on the Chicago, Milwaukee, and St. Paul Railroad. In the late 1860s they were able to purchase an adjoining 16-acre tract of land.

Their second child and first son, John, was born on December 22, 1865. He was followed on April 7, 1868, by Ellen Theresa, named for her mother. Daniel Murphy and his wife, who served as midwife for the birth of all but one of the seven Coughlin children born in Minnesota, were godparents at Ellen's baptism by Father Keller on April 18, 1868. Other children and their birthdates were: Mary (later Sister Benetta), August 2, 1870; Joseph, January 7, 1872; Angela, May 20, 1874; Brigid, April 26, 1876; and Daniel, August 13, 1878.[2]

Paralleling these developments in the Coughlin family, the Dominican Sisters established their convent and academy. The Fowler residence was renovated to provide classrooms, dormitories for sisters and students, and a chapel. By September 1865, the building was ready to accommodate a few boarders and day pupils. Sisters

---

[1]William Watts Folwell, *A History of Minnesota, 1833-1929* (St. Paul: The Minnesota Historical Society, 1921-1930), 4 Volumes, Vol. III, pp. 93-111.

[2] Annals of Bethlehem Academy, p. 2.

Veronica Power and Benvenuta McCullough took up their duties as teachers in classrooms in the basement of the parish church, a mile north of the convent. This was the school established by Father Keller in 1858 and staffed by lay teachers until the coming of the sisters.

During school terms for the next four years, Sisters Veronica and Benvenuta made the trek to the school, often under difficult conditions as described in the annals:

> In those days there was no sidewalk, only the wagon road, or a shorter trail over the hills through the thick underbrush, which had to be traveled in single file, holding aside the branches and bending under the heavier boughs. Yet, daily for those first four years Sisters Veronica and Benvenuta made this journey through the heavy snows of January when the temperature was thirty-five degrees below zero, or through the drenching rains of April.[3]

The sisters of both schools suffered other hardships, including lack of food, fuel, and clothing. They survived despite these dire problems, at times through what they regarded as providential occurrences. One such occasion is recorded as follows in the annals:

> It is told that on one bitter cold night in 1868 the fuel had given out and there was no way of procuring any even for the morrow. The Superioress, Sister Gertrude Power, requested the boarders to retire earlier than usual, while she and the other Sisters went to the chapel to pray. Soon a loud knock was heard at the door. Sister Gertrude, though startled, went bravely to answer the call. On opening the door she found a large, burly-looking man who asked her where he should unload the wood which was outside. After Sister had given him directions as to what he should do, quickly and without a word of explanation, he unloaded the wood and drove away. To this day no one knows who the benefactor was.[4]

---

[3] Annals of Bethlehem Academy, p. 2.

[4] *Ibid.*, p. 2.

Aware of the difficulties the Sisters experienced, Father Keller in 1869 purchased a house one block from Immaculate Conception Church to serve as convent and boarding school. The nearness to the church was a great advantage, but the space for the sisters and boarders was limited. Further improvements would come later.[5]

Another transition came the following year: Father Keller— "the Sisters' best friend"—left Faribault to return to France. Appointed temporarily to replace him was Father Emile Reville, O.P. Early in 1871, Father Clement Scheve became pastor. One of his first projects was the erection of a new parish school, which was ready for occupancy in September 1872.[6]

Further accommodation was needed for housing and classes as enrollment increased in both parish school and Bethlehem Academy. In 1874, Sister Gertrude purchased for the Sinsinawa Dominican Congregation some property next to Immaculate Conception Church and contracted for the building of a three-story brick structure, which would serve as convent and academy for ninety years. A curricular development soon followed, as in the early 1880s the sisters began offering high school courses for young women who had completed the elementary grades. By 1884, a full curriculum was available, consisting of the following subjects:

four years of English;
ancient, modern, medieval, and American history;
algebra I; plane geometry, advanced algebra, and solid geometry;
physical geography;
physiology, physics, and astronomy;
art and music;
religion.

---

[5]*Ibid.*

[6]*Ibid.*, pp. 3-4.

***Left*: Graduates of 1885: Mary McManus, Emma Conlin, Ellen Coughlin, Mary Jane O'Brien, Julia Delehanty**

Sister Gertrude Power

Ellen Coughlin as a child

View from Mound in 1890s: Exhibition Hall; Stone Building; Academy and College Building

During that school year the sisters applied for and received a charter for the Academy from the State of Minnesota.[7]

The Coughlins were associated with the Dominican Sisters during these years chiefly through the schools. When John was ready to enter first grade, his mother learned that the nearby public school had poor discipline. She chose to teach him at home to read, write, and spell. At the age of seven, his parents decided to send him to Immaculate Conception School, despite the distance of almost three miles. All of the children followed the same pattern: instruction at home by their mother followed by enrollment at the sisters' school at approximately age seven. Most of the time, they walked to school, braving the elements except in the worst weather when their father would provide transportation by lumber wagon or sleigh drawn by horses.

In the 1950s, Brigid Coughlin recalled some of the content of their formal education and the conditions under which it was provided:

I'm sorry I don't know what text books were used, but I'm quite sure McGuffey's Readers were not among them. I associate that name with public school texts. In my time we had Sadlier's Readers. As to methods of teaching there were, of course, no visual or audio aids. Much stress was placed on memorizing. We were drilled on the multiplication tables, on the names of the states and capitals, on names and dates in history. We had frequent "spell-downs." The Coughlins were good spellers. I remember hearing John's college-graduate son, who worked with him in the office, saying: "When we don't know how to spell a word, we don't look it up. We just ask Dad."

Our school year started the first week of September and ended the last week of June. The morning session began at 9:00 o'clock with prayers, which we said on our knees. It ended at noon with the saying of the Angelus. The afternoon session lasted from 1:15 to 4:00. There were fifteen-minute recesses at 10:30 and 2:30. . . .

---

[7] *Ibid.*, pp. 3-5; SDA, Papers of Mother Samuel Coughlin, School Catalog and Programs, Bethlehem Academy, Faribault.

There was a high board fence between the girls' and boys' playgrounds. . . . In the shade of the high board fence was a long wooden bench on which in good weather the girls who lived at a considerable distance from school sat to eat their noon lunch. Almost uniformly it consisted of bread and butter sandwiches—some had bread and molasses—a slice of pie or cake or some cookies, and, occasionally, an apple. . . . We all used tin pails for our lunch and set them on a shelf in the unheated first floor corridor, and more than once we bit into a frozen sandwich.

In winter the girls ate in one school room, the boys in another, and, as I recall, we had no supervision nor seemed to need it.

In addition to their formal schooling, the Coughlin children profited from informal education provided by the reading in the evenings of English masterpieces. They had few playmates but found enough activity within their own family circle. They had their assigned household, gardening, and farming tasks; and there was time left over for games typical of that age.

The parents set the example for the children's religious upbringing, including regular attendance at Sunday Mass, evening devotions, family rosary, night prayers, and attendance at week-long missions when those were held.[8]

By the time Ellen had completed the courses comprising the elementary curriculum, the sisters of Bethlehem Academy had organized the advanced program of high school work referred to above. She and four classmates—Mary Jane O'Brien, Emma Conlin, Mary McManus, and Julia Delehanty—were the first graduates of the newly chartered institution on June 30, 1885. Ellen was awarded two gold medals, one for mathematics and the other for superior good conduct. Attending the ceremonies on this occasion were Bishop Grace, recently retired Bishop of St. Paul, Bishop John Ireland, who had been coadjutor bishop since 1875 and Bishop Grace's successor

---

[8]Reminiscences of Brigid Coughlin.

in 1884, and Michael Lilly, O.P., Provincial of the Dominican Order in the United States.[9]

In September 1885 following her graduation, Ellen entered the Sinsinawa Dominican Congregation. She was received as a novice on August 15, 1886, being given the name "Samuel," the first time the Founder's name was used by one of the sisters. During her novitiate year, she taught for several months at St. James, Rockford, where classes for private students were offered in the convent. After her profession on August 15, 1887, she remained at the Motherhouse, where, among other assignments, she took a special course to prepare her for teaching in the primary schools conducted by the Congregation.

In 1888-89 she joined the other sisters assigned to St. Patrick's School in Lemont, Illinois, where the sisters of another congregation who had staffed the school had withdrawn. The following fall of 1889 brought an assignment to Holy Rosary Convent in Minneapolis, Minnesota, where she remained for twelve years.[10]

The foregoing information, covering the years from 1865 to 1901, was told in a remarkably delightful form by Mother Samuel herself in an essay written as an assignment for a correspondence course in English composition taken from the University of Chicago in 1903. Because of its significance, it is reprinted in full in the following pages.

---

[9]Annals, Bethlehem Academy, p. 5.

[10]Annals, St. Clara Convent, St. James, Rockford, St. Patrick's, Lemont, Holy Rosary, Minneapolis.

ONE OUT OF MANY

Sister Samuel Coughlin

On the southern slope of a wooded hill, north of the now flourishing town of Faribault, there stood in the late sixties a log house which has long since gone the way of its companions, the Red man, the great oaks and maples, the mink and the rabbit, the quail and the partridge. A clump of lilacs and a few shoots of asparagus and horseradish still mark the place where the modest garden repaid the toil of the pioneer's wife, while nearby the deep well sunk in those early days supplies the coolest water to be found for miles around the country.

Memory makes no picture of this, my first home. My earliest impressions record in half dreamy characters a day of unusual activity, when every one was engaged in "carrying things" to a new house some rods farther west on the hillside. This was the first frame house in the neighborhood, a very plain and old-fashioned one at the present, but one which received many admiring glances in those days of strenuous western life.

One picture of that day of "moving" is more vivid in my mind than the rest, perhaps because it occupied the largest canvas—my father and some two or three other men struggling with a large press which resisted all their efforts for a long time, but was finally established in new quarters where it still does service in the kitchen.

In the five years which followed, the chief influences at work in the evolution of me were those of my parents. First and chiefly, there was my mother whose striking characteristics were a strict adherence to a lofty code of moral rectitude, and indifference amounting almost to contempt for the luxuries of life and the ways of modern progress. She lived wholly in the past of her once-renowned family in Ireland, and the assured hope of an eternity of happiness hereafter. The present and its needs gave her thought only for contrast. The world could wag as it pleased, she cared only to have the necessaries of life and to make each of her seven children as far as possible, a perfect copy of herself. She was, notwithstanding, sensitive, tender, full of beautiful sentiment. She loved books, and keenly felt the lack of a well stocked library. She often used the money allowed for a new dress or bonnet to purchase books or other intellectual treats for her children. I know of no woman who made greater personal sacrifice for the education of her children.

My father's character was almost an entire opposite—silent, more timid than grave, matter-of-fact, yet lacking in the enterprise and push which go to make the successful pioneer, he found the world "too many for him." He never manifested affection by word, though he slaved incessantly for his family and did a thousand sweet things, which, if accompanied by the words of love, would have made him a sentimental husband and father. Truly, his was a strange, inarticulate love entertained for a life time in a kind of automatic heart. A certain strain of humor occasionally escaped from him, as much apparently to his own confusion as to the surprise and delight of his children. How much would I not give to know what were the thoughts which occupied his mind from the earliest dawn when he arose and lit the fire and half prepared our modest morning meal before awaking the household, through the long day as he felled the trees, or followed the plow, or worked at the harvest in the scorching August days, or tended the stock with unvarying, seemingly mechanical regularity!

He cared as little for society as did my mother, although like her, he was warm-hearted and hospitable towards the very few friends who broke the forbidding walls of his manner. To the world at large he was passively antagonistic, regarding all strangers and business men with suspicion. Of the two, my mother's was the stronger character, and the one most felt in the development of her children.

Visitors were almost unknown at our home. The day's work was finished late; an hour or so of reading aloud or of reminiscence of the "old land" followed our simple supper; then family night prayers, and all went to bed except my mother, who prayed much longer, and before seeking her own rest came to each bed to bless her children, and, in winter, to see that we were snug besides.

Of both my parents' natures I am no slight degree a partaker. When a wave of tenderness suffuses my eyes with pity for others (or for myself, as sometimes happens), as well as when the fire of indignation is kindled in me by the ways of the world, or when the desire for higher and better life thrills me, I know that I am my "mother's daughter": while silent mistrustful moods and melancholy timidity declare my father.

To this simple and almost primitive home life of my childhood, the closest and fullest contact with nature was added. Wide range of wooded hills and newly broked fields, daily association with birds and domestic fowl and animals, wild flowers and the living creatures of the forest gave to my life a charm which I learned only too late to value at its proper worth. As I write, the scents of the clover and new mown hay in the meadow, byt [sic] breath of the cows, the maple sap in the spring time, the newly threshed straw stack where I played in childish delight—all come freshly blown by the winds of memory.

The district school was little in harmony with my mother's projects for the education of her children. Between the ages of seven and eight, each of us entered the Parish School in the town of Faribault. This meant an early breakfast, a cold lunch at noon, and a walk of two and one-half miles twice a day, to the good effects of which I attribute my excellent health even to this day. Inclement weather usually found our father ready to drive us in of a morning, and a welcome, half-expected surprise it was, on coming out of school on a winter evening to have the dismal prospect of miles of slowly conquered snow drifts banished by the sight of a horse and sleigh and the dearest man in the world patiently waiting for us.

This school into which my timid figure entered was conducted by the Dominican Sisters, ladies of much culture and refinement. My first impression of my teacher, a handsome woman, so filled me with admiration and reverence that I fancied her to have been the model for the Madonnas in my copiously illustrated second reader. (We all were in "second reader" and could write and "figure" well after one year of our mother's training given at intervals in her pressing household duties.) This awe and reverence inspired by the personality of my teachers was never dissipated, and now, though I am a member of that same Sisterhood, no nearness of association nor force of familiarity can dispel the ethereal glow which envelops for those of my teachers who survive.

My excessive timidity and my lack of sympathy with my school mates kept me more or less isolated, while my old-fashioned dress and manners gave the children much amusement which sometimes degenerated into ridicule and caused my sensitive nature much pain. Happily, for me, I was gifted with a fertile constructive imagination, and once the sharpness of the first pang of impotent anger was over, my fancy was away building situations and incidents to soothe my wounded feelings and too often to revenge myself on my tormentors. Added to this doubtful comfort was my great love for study and a proficiency in my lessons which gained the approval and praise of my teachers; and my school life was not really unhappy.

Indeed, I must confess that I was vain of my ability, and something occurred early in my school life which frightened my vanity. When I was eleven years old, a cousin of ours, a young man of finished education, visited us for a few days. He questioned me about my studies, and could not be convinced that I had already mastered the difficulties of "cube root," until with my slate and pencil and clear explanations I had removed all doubt. Immediately, he told my mother that it would be nice to keep me out of school for a year or two, as I was too far advanced for my age.

How my heart hung upon my mother's reply! "A child who can walk five miles and eat four meals a day cannot be in danger from over study. Her head is not being developed at the expense of general exercise. There is good balance." So I was permitted to continue at school and usually stood first in my classes. How my feet bounded over those miles of country road on such evenings (and they were many) as I had some triumph of the day to relate—spelling down the school, being the first to solve a problem on which my class had worked for a week, winning the prize for composition, or for observance of the rules of discipline!

My mother heard all these with grave pleasure, never such as to foster vanity; and though my father rarely made a comment upon these occasions, I knew he was the prouder of the two. Our mother expected us to be intellectually quick; to our father, our excellence was a matter of silent wonder.

I do not remember that any particular study had the strongest attraction for me. Each new subject fascinated me. My enthusiasm for the natural sciences was somewhat less than for the others, but this was doubtless due in a great measure to the meager apparatus we had for experiments. The study of literature gave me great delight, and before I reached the age of seventeen, I had already planned several masterpieces which were to bring me fame and wealth. Later, my lessons in painting and drawing made me wish to be a follower of Raphael and Murillo.

However, a stronger force than these ambitions was determining the character of my future. The home life of serious thought and high spiritual ideals had made its impression. I was drawn to consider deep truths from many standpoints. The austere home discipline, the absence of material luxury, the total separation from the little fashionable world of the town, had made me at the age of seventeen something not only of a philosopher but an ascetic as well.

Besides this, the beautiful lives of the Sisters appealed to me in unmistakable language. In them I saw the ideals which my being demanded. Sister Gertrude, in particular, one of my teachers in my year of graduation at the Academy was a remarkable woman. Scholarly, simple, inspiring, ever cheerful, ever enthusiastic for something which made quickly and sweetly for nobler living, she won all hearts.

She visited and brought sunshine to the home of the sick washerwoman, delighted the banker or lawyer by her clear grasp of technicalities, cheered the Sister in the kitchen by a humorous anecdote or by a helping hand at the dishes or the peeling of potatoes, interpreted the pages of Shakespeare or Milton, discussed questions of philosophy or theology with the parish priest—all with equal pleasure to herself. She was one of the gentlest and most unobtrusive of women. Next after my mother, she was my ideal of a noble woman. She was my mother's ideal of a saint.

Inspired by so beautiful an example, and knowing considerable of the spirit of the Dominican Order, its devotion to the education of youth, its obligation of life-long study, its many means of satisfying the cravings of the soul, and feeling convinced, moreover, that Providence was leading my steps, I knelt a few evenings before the day of my graduation at the feet of my mother, where I had learned to say "Our Father," and poured out my heart to her, and asked to be permitted to follow what I felt to be that Father's voice. Nor was she wanting with her sympathy and encouragement. She was happy rather than grieved, and embraced me with a tenderness the memory of which will never depart from me.

It were better to pass over the scenes of parting from father and mother, brothers and sisters and home, the only world I knew. It will be enough to say that I have never regretted the step, and that all that I hoped for—and much more—has been given to me—verily the hundred-fold.

Accompanied by two other young ladies, one a student of the Academy, the other, like myself, a candidate for the Order at St. Clara, I arrived in Dubuque, on a rainy night early in September. The next morning we ordered a carriage and set out for Sinsinawa Mound, Wisconsin, where St. Clara Convent and Academy was situated. The rain continued to fall. At that time there was no bridge over the Mississippi, and we crossed on the old platform ferry. The drive of six miles which followed our landing in

Wisconsin was indeed rough, but interesting as well. The road was narrow, and wound in great curves to avoid breasting the hills which have been flung pell-mell into this part of the country. Occasionally, however, a steep ascent had to be made, and the corresponding descent on the opposite side. The hills were well wooded. The great branches of the oaks and walnuts and elms often splashed their dripping burden against the sides of the carriage as we moved with difficulty through the defiles.

Many times the driver showed us the Convent in the distance, standing out in the red and white relief against the leafy background of the Mound, but soon we lost sight of it as we went down on the levels, and when it next appeared it was in a different part of our horizon, and apparently as far off as before. The freshness of all nature around, where the many ripe things were taking their last bath on the parent stems, gave an impression of strength not unmixed with sadness.

We arrived at the convent grounds about eleven o'clock and drove up the winding avenue on either side of which Nature and Art held joint dominion over a wide range of sloping ground. Here the sturdy oak looked approvingly down upon the catalpas, snowball trees, and syringas; there the walnut threw its protecting arms over the lilacs, roses, and hydrangeas, which had taken the places of the shrubby undergrowth of its early association; farther on a pine forest in miniature challenged the passerby to decide whether it was or was not the product of art, while the Mound itself, grand in its wealth of natural beauty, bore upon its breast a succession of artistically rounded terraces and carefully planned beds of brilliant geraniums, asters, and bright foliages.

The three buildings fronted the longest terrace, one a white frame structure, one of light yellow stone, and one of red brick. On entering the brick building, to which the driveway led first, we were welcomed by a tall, brown-eyed Sister, whose tender Celtic sympathies, as I have since learned, make her an ideal portress and win her the first place in the heart of many a timid, homesick girl whose entrance to boarding school is made through "Sister Rose's Hall."[11]

My first few days at St. Clara were passed in visiting with my old teachers, several of whom were then at the Motherhouse, in inspecting the buildings—the convent, the academy, the auditorium, the church, the

---

[11]The Sister was probably Sister Rose McSweeney.

chaplain's cottage, the post office, the barn; in climbing the Mound and in viewing from all sides the great expanse of rolling land half wooded, half tilled fields. Away to the south rose a line of blue, the bluffs along the Mississippi. The hills which we had avoided or climbed on our way out from Dubuque had all lost their individuality in a mass of green which stretched westward to the horizon.

Then, the life of the postulant was begun. It was a novel experience for me to be thrown into close relationship with young women from all parts of this country and from many parts of Europe, from the ranks of society—all drawn to the same goal by the same motive. Community of hearts and of interests, no less than community of goods, soon united all, and made the name "Sister" truly expressive of the mutual relations and affections established. Nor is the development of the individual lost sight of in the plan of religious life. The spirit of the order aims to direct and purify the natural tendencies, not to strain or crush them. I can truly say that my individuality is as strongly marked as is that of either of my sisters who remained at home.

Even dearer than the association of "sister" is that of "mother" which is preserved in convents of women. The Sisterhood at Sinsinawa has been signally favored in this regard. At the time I entered the Community, Mother Emily Power had been elected Mother General annually for twenty successive years by the unanimous vote of the Sisters, and by the same suffrage she has continued in office ever since. This fact alone speaks for the power of her character; but to estimate this remarkable woman at all thoroughly, one must be brought to feel the charm of her personality. The tones of her voice are heart tones and always touch the heart of the listener. Her clear blue eyes search and read one like a book, and probe with a half omniscient sympathy which nothing can resist. She has made this Community what it is, financially, intellectually, spiritually. Her executive ability is marvellous. She has a perfect grasp of the management and details of the forty convents under her jurisdiction, and a personal interest in each of the six hundred Sisters, of whose individual abilities and characters she has a thorough knowledge. She is tender without weakness, and strong without a shadow of hardness. The Sisters love her as they love no one except their own natural mothers.

Having passed the term of novitiate under the supervision of this gifted woman, and afterwards taken a special course of training, I began the work of teaching in the primary schools. In the inexperience of my younger days, I was somewhat intolerant of the short-comings of my pupils, but deeper study and observation, and above all, my own failures to realize many of my ideals, have broadened my sympathies. I dare say that my experience in schools during the past fifteen years has been that of every other earnest teacher—objectively considered, a series of hopes realized and hopes disappointed, sunshine and shadow; subjectively, one great yearning to clasp the young to my heart and shield them from the evil consequences of much of their environment, of heredity, or of their own folly. They will go on their way without me; yet He who ordains or permits all, loves those souls infinitely more than I do; and if I have made some few more conscious of His love, my work has not been utterly fruitless.

Thus far, my relations with my fellow beings and with the world have been on the whole most happy. I may, indeed, say with Brutus:

> My heart doth joy that yet in all my life
> I found no man but he was true to me.

My earliest friendships have stood the test of time and varying fortunes. Because of a certain proud reserve and a streak of seriousness approaching melancholy which run through my disposition, everyone would not enjoy me as a close companion, nor do I make friends at sight; yet I am not lacking in a kind of simple brightness of manner, and a hearty appreciation of the humorous. I have had as close friends many choice and gifted women, who have never given evidence of having tired of me. Perhaps my love of solitude and books has prevented me from wandering to the limits of friendship and into the realm of boredom. I am not easily influenced even by my dearest friends. The foundations of my character were so firmly laid by my mother exclusively when little or no other formative force had as yet acted upon me, that I cannot change much even if I would. One of many influences that has made me what I am is that I am a compound product of all the elements which have been wrought into my life—"one out of many."

This sketch would not be complete without a pen picture of myself at the age of eighteen when I assumed the Dominican habit: a tall, very slender girl, with the least tendency to round shoulders, a large head, a forehead wide rather than high, a round face, heavy dark eyebrows perfectly arched, brownish gray eyes, a mouth rather small with a faint suggestion of a smile at the corner; a well-formed nose, neither large nor small; reddish auburn hair combed smoothly back; my complexion blends with a fair sprinkling of freckles, a form and face neither beautiful nor ugly, but just "one of many." The graceful white folds of the Dominican habit have somewhat idealized me, as they do every one whom they enfold.

When I finished the last paragraph, I stepped to the window. The early moonlight is reflected from the snow covered Mound which rises smoothly but rather abruptly from the driveway behind our convent. It is still early evening, but December is impatient for the night. Four naked apple trees raise their branches to the clear unpitying sky. Here and there on the slope other black lines in various compositions mark individual trees, while an intricate fringe of dark lines marks the woody outline of the Mound against the sky. A few stars peep behind the bare trees and smile a bright "Good evening."

The strains of piano music fill the air. The novices are practicing in the music rooms along the corridor. A weak odor of something savory steals up from the kitchen two floors below, and reminds me that supper time is near. I run over the events of the day: the office in the Chapel in the early morning where row on row of white figures bowed or stood or sat in unison chanting the words of the Hebrew Prophet with their complement of Christian praise; the Mass which followed, that central vivifying principle of Catholic belief where young and old, teachers and pupils drank in spiritual nourishment for the day; the breakfast eaten in solemn silence; my walk around the buildings in the crisp air with Sister M— who can never get enough of exercise out doors; the assembling of the teachers in the corridor outside the classrooms and their morning greetings in bright, mirth-provoking strains which still echoed when the students filed out from the assembly halls, and the serious work began; my own classes in elementary English,—how one group brightened at the prospect of a Christmas story!—then my lone girl in arithmetic, and my disappointment in her test in bank discount after our doing so much make-believe banking; my visit of an hour with Mother in her room and the refreshment and inspiration given me; the dinner hour with its welcome relaxation; another walk in the noonday sun and the world of dazzling snow; our envy of the children who tied their sleds on the back of the coal sleigh and had a fine ride; the hour in the library with my class; the evening office with its usual temptation to mark the poetic in the psalms; my return to my writing. I run over to the college building where our two hundred young women are bending over their books at evening study, the thoughts of home and Christmas intruding everywhere. How few of these dream of the destinies which wait them, the trials, the tears, perhaps the tragedies! The stars twinkle, "It is better so."

Now I turn from the window and see my white bed in the corner, my desk with its pile of unanswered letters awaiting the vacation; my row of friendly books, my crucifix dearest of all, and I say from the depth of my heart, "It is well for me to be here."

Chapter Three

Preparation for Leadership: 1901-1910

On August 10, 1901, at the Third General Chapter of the Congregation of the Most Holy Rosary, Sinsinawa, Wisconsin, Sister Samuel Coughlin was elected Bursar General. This same Chapter reelected Mother Mary Emily Power for a third six-year term as Mother General under the Constitutions approved in 1889. The Sisters had been assured beforehand that the dispensation from the limitation to two terms in the Constitutions would be readily granted.[1]

The transition to the Motherhouse from Holy Rosary, Minneapolis, where she had taught for twelve years, 1889-1901, was made at a time of significant change in the world, the nation, and the Church. The nations of Europe from which so many millions of immigrants had come to America during the nineteenth century had not yet resolved their rivalries, though wars and revolutions had produced new configurations of power by the late nineteenth century.[2] The United States had become a new player on the world stage with its expansion into the Caribbean, the central Pacific, and the Far East during the Spanish American War of 1898-1900. Internally, the industrial revolution had been given impetus in the United States by the Civil War, and the latter third of the nineteenth century had brought spectacular advances in technology. Unfortunately, it had also brought economic, social and political problems.[3]

---

[1]Sister Mary Eva McCarty, O.P., *The Sinsinawa Dominicans: Outlines of Twentieth Century Development, 1901-1949* (Dubuque, Iowa: The Hoermann Press, 1952), pp. 6-7.

[2]R.R. Palmer and Joel Colton, *A History of the Modern World* (New York: Alfred A. Knopf, 1965), pp. 421-548, *passim.* (Copyright now the property of McGraw-Hill, Inc.)

[3]John M. Blum, et al, *The National Experience: A History of the United States* (New York: Harcourt, Brace Jovanovich, Inc., 1977) pp. 490-407, *passim.*

The Catholic Church felt the impact of such changes and problems, most directly in its efforts to accommodate the needs of the immigrants. The Sinsinawa Dominicans[4] shared in the responsibilities and worries of the Church. Among developments during the closing years of the nineteenth century that brought opportunities and challenges to the Congregation as the twentieth century opened were: requirement by the Third Plenary Council of Baltimore in 1884 that parishes should establish Catholic schools if at all possible; the Faribault Plan of 1891-93; Irish colonization projects; establishment of the Catholic University of America, approved at the Council of Baltimore in 1884 and opened in 1889; organization of parishes for immigrant groups; anti-Catholic movements; and the creation of a permanent Apostolic Delegation.

The first-mentioned of these developments—the requirement of the Third Plenary Council of Baltimore—gave impetus to the establishment of parochial schools, for which bishops and pastors sought teachers from religious congregations. Before the century ended, requests for teachers exceeded the number of sisters available for assignment to the schools. Although membership in the Sinsinawa Dominicans and in other congregations progressively increased, the number of sisters available for assignment could not meet the requests. This situation would be a continuing reality in the years to come.[5]

Other developments occupying the interest and concern of the bishops of the United States were brought to the attention of the Sinsinawa Dominicans through the involvement of two staunch friends among the hierarchy, Bishops John Lancaster Spalding of Peoria Diocese and John Ireland of St. Paul. The two collaborated closely on Irish colonization projects and the establishment of the

---

[4]The term, Sinsinawa Dominicans, will be used henceforth in this book instead of the full title, Congregation of the Most Holy Rosary.

[5]McCarty, pp. 24-35.

Mother Emily Power

Sister Benetta Coughlin

John Ireland

John Lancaster Spalding

Coughlin Family in front of family home: *Front Row*: John, Joseph, Angela; *Middle Row*: Daniel Coughlin, Sr.; *Back Row*: Brigid, Ellen Coughlin (Mother), Daniel, Jr.

Catholic University but parted company on the Faribault Plan, the organization of national parishes, and the establishment of a permanent Apostolic Delegation. The friendship between the two bishops suffered from the friction these issues generated, though eventually the rift was healed.[6]

Problems associated with the implementation of the decree of 1884 regarding the establishment of parochial schools culminated in disagreement over the Faribault Plan. Bishops and pastors who dealt with real-life situations in the Midwest and West did not find it simple to comply. In addition to the financial burden that building and staffing schools entailed, the charge by "native Americans" that Catholic schools were divisive worried some prelates. Ireland was particularly sensitive to the latter charge, and his plan for meeting educational needs sought to answer such criticism as well as to find financial support. The Faribault-Stillwater plan, named for two towns in Minnesota where it was initiated in 1891, provided for the leasing of the parochial school building to the public school district. The district paid the salaries of teachers, most of whom were members of religious orders, and covered the cost of maintenance. Religious instruction was provided before or after regular school hours. The idea, though receiving lukewarm approval from Rome, pleased neither extreme in America. Protestant ministers saw it as a plot on the part of Catholics to take over American public schools; Spalding and other bishops feared it would undermine Catholic education. The experiment in Faribault was terminated after two years. It left a residue of hard feelings among Protestants and adversely affected enrollment in Catholic schools for several years.[7]

The issue of "Faribaultism" became entwined with controversy over the establishment of a permanent Apostolic Delegation in the

---

[6]Information on these matters is taken from Sister Alice O'Rourke, *The Good Work Begun: Centennial History of Peoria Diocese* (Chicago: The Lakeside Press, 1977), pp. 38-44, *passim.*

[7]William Watts Folwell, *A History of Minnesota, 1833-1929* (St. Paul: The Minnesota Historical Society, 1921-1930), 4 Volumes, Vol. IV, 174-183.

United States, a project that Spalding and most of the other bishops opposed. Spalding felt that Ireland had capitulated to Rome on this dispute as the price of Rome's endorsement of his plan. Even after the matter had been settled in 1893 with the appointment of Archbishop Francesco Satolli as the first permanent delegate, Spalding did not give way gracefully.

Conditions peculiar to America gave rise to still another debate in which Spalding took sides and was again ranged against Ireland. The issue was "Cahenslyism," named for Peter Paul Cahensly, a German merchant who organized societies in Europe and America to protect the religious, social, and material interests of Germans and people of other nationalities who migrated to America. European directors of these societies, thinking that the American Church was not doing enough to safeguard the interests of non-English speaking groups, met at Lucerne, Switzerland, in December 1890. They drew up a memorial to Pope Leo XIII recommending the establishment of separate churches for each nationality, served by priests of the same nationality; the setting up of separate parochial schools for each group, with courses in the language of that group as a part of the curriculum; and the appointment to the American hierarchy of bishops representing various national elements.

Reports of the affair alarmed many American bishops who saw it as a conspiracy to establish separate National Churches rather than national parishes. Spalding thought the reports were exaggerated, and he himself appreciated the contributions of the German people to America. He defended their loyalty and praised their frugal and industrious habits as contributing to the strength of the nation and the Church.

By the last decade of the nineteenth century, the immigrants became greatly diversified. While the number of people from Northwestern Europe—England, Ireland, Germany, Belgium, and the Scandinavian countries—continued to be high, a greater number came from Eastern and Southern Europe during the decades from 1890-1910. Among the new immigrants were Austrians, Hungarians, Poles,

Slovakians, Lithuanians, Italians, Croatians, Serbs, and Russians.[8] Most of these immigrants, largely peasant in origin, settled in cities stretching from the Eastern seaboard through the industrial corridor of the states bordering on the Great Lakes. Chicago, Milwaukee, and the northern half of Illinois became known for their national neighborhoods and their national parishes and schools. The Sinsinawa Dominicans would be among the religious congregations responding to requests for teachers in schools of non-English speaking nationalities, though such missions were few in number compared with those of Irish nationality or native-born.

Sister Samuel must have anticipated a significant change in her life as she moved from the grade school mission of Holy Rosary, Minneapolis, to Sinsinawa Mound, where her responsibilities would be much different. That fall of 1901 coincided with the beginning of planning for a college. Steps toward this had begun in 1899 with the offering of postgraduate courses to St. Clara Academy graduates. The corporate title of the institution was changed by amendment of the charter on April 25, 1901, from "St. Clara Female Academy" to "St. Clara College." Over the next several years additional classes were added yearly until a full four-year program was available in 1910.[9]

There was great bustling around the Mound during those September days of 1901 as the Academy students moved into their newly alloted space in the recently completed convent. The first floor was originally planned for academy use; due to an excess in registrations over that anticipated, the third floor that was to have been a "Novitiate Studio" was taken over for use as an academy dormitory.[10] Sister Samuel's major responsibility in addition to her duties as Bursar General was teaching English for Academy students and for the few students taking postgraduate courses. As had become common for the sisters assigned to the Academy, she shared in the

---

[8] Blum, pp. 444-445.

[9]9 McCarty, pp. 49-52.

[10]*Ibid.*, p. 5.

supervision of the students at times when they were not in class but in study hall, at recreation, at meals, or in the dormitory.

Anticipating greater professional demands from the post-graduate courses, Sister Samuel sought and received from Mother Emily permission to undertake preparation through courses from the University of Chicago and the University of Wisconsin. She matriculated at the former institution in the late fall of 1902, registering for a correspondence course in English composition taught by Edith Foster Flint, at a cost in tuition of $21.00. In response to her request that no envelopes with University insignia be used in returning her manuscripts, Mr. Hervey F. Mallory, Secretary of the Correspondence-Study Department, suggested that she enclose a return envelope with each assignment she mailed.[11]

The first assignments were daily short essays, usually a page or two long, followed by longer essays and short stories as the quarter progressed. Mrs. Flint proved to be an exacting teacher, carefully guiding her student by means of frequent comments to help improve her style. On one paper, for example, Mrs. Flint wrote: "I wish you would think it worth your while to write a little more of what you see in the people about you and what you think about them . . . a little more of dealing with the real world, as you see it in your school, would strengthen and inform your style, I think!"[12]

As the quarter continued, the teacher's assessment became more and more favorable. Towards the end of the course, Mrs. Flint appended this comment to one of the essays: "Your writing has certainly gained in ease and naturalness and individuality. I am glad you are thinking of going on, and I shall be happy to see your name again among those of my students." Over the next year and one-half, Sister took two more composition classes, one of which was probably on campus during the summer of 1903. It was during this course that

---

[11]Correspondence, Hervey F. Mallory to Sister Samuel, October 11 and November 2, 1902.

[12]SDA, English Course Notes, 1902-1903.

she wrote the autobiography that is reproduced in Chapter Two. To the final copy of Sister Samuel's manuscript, Mrs. Flint wrote: "I congratulate you on having accomplished what is much more difficult than an excellent first draft—an excellent revision!" It seems that she had one correspondence course in English literature from the University of Wisconsin during this same time; her course notes do not have a date to identify the time.

Sister Samuel's reflections in the autobiography presented in Chapter Two show the great affection that she had for Mother Emily. The impression gained from this document is strengthened in Sister Samuel's diary for which there are fairly regular entries in 1905 and 1906, which indicate that the relationship was one of mutual love, trust, and respect.[13] They show what joy Sister Samuel found in having time with Mother Emily, especially on walks around the grounds. The days and weeks of Mother Emily's absence were times of loneliness for Sister Samuel.

Mother Emily's confidence in Sister Samuel was manifested in a very tangible way in the summer of 1904. On a July day, Mother called her into the Bay Window Room outside the Chapel to tell her of the decision to appoint her prioress of St. Clara Convent. The position carried with it the responsibilities of Directress of Academy and College. The announcement was a shock to Sister Samuel, one that she recalled frequently on the anniversary of that day and on August 24, the day of the actual appointment. Throughout her diary she has notations such as: "a painful anniversary;" "an awful anniversary;" "the beginning of my real cross in religion—1904." The duties as Directress of the Academy and College brought many episodes of concern over enrollment and disciplinary cases.[14]

Another change in responsibilities for Sister Samuel occurred in 1907 when she was elected by the General Chapter as First Councillor. She was reappointed to her position as prioress of St.

---

[13]Diary, Sister Samuel, 1905-06, *passim.*

[14]*Ibid., passim.*

Clara Convent with its attendant duties as Directress of the Academy and College. Mother Emily was reelected and, having received the necessary dispensation from Rome, began serving her fourth term under the 1889 Constitutions. During the preceding fall, Mother Emily had suffered the loss of her half-brother, the Reverend Louis Power, who died on October 20, 1906, at Sparkill, New York. She attended his funeral and burial at Newark, New Jersey, where he had lived for eighteen years. During her railroad journey she was slightly injured from a fall when the train started while she was still on the steps. The jolt resulted in her falling off the steps.[15]

Mother Emily's strength began to decline early in 1908 following a slight paralytic stroke. The doctor advised a period of complete rest. Appointing Sister Samuel as Vicaress of the Congregation, Mother Emily left in early June for Denver, Colorado, accompanied by her sister, Sister Adrian Power.[16] After three months in Denver and several weeks in Anaconda, she returned to the Mound on October 26, 1908. However, she asked the mission sisters to continue sending their business letters to Sister Samuel for a while.[17] Her strength did not fully return and her condition was a source of concern for Sister Samuel at the time of the St. Clara Alumnae Reunion in mid-June 1909.[18]

During the fall months, Mother Emily called upon the members of Council to help implement the examination program for the sisters designed to equip them better as teachers, a program that had been in existence for several years. While making visitation to the convents to which Mother Emily assigned them, Sister Samuel and Sister Bonaventure Tracy would administer tests to the sisters enrolled in the program. Thus it happened that Sister Samuel was in Oshkosh when Mother Emily became critically ill of pneumonia. When the

---

[15]Mission Letters, Sister Samuel to Mission Sisters, October 29, 1906.

[16]16 McCarty, pp. 94-95

[17]Mission Letters, Mother Emily to the Sisters, November 9, 1908.

[18]*Ibid.*, Mother Samuel to the Sisters, June 30, 1909.

word reached Oshkosh on Saturday, October 16, Sister Samuel left immediately, journeying by way of Madison. There she received the word of Mother's death; joined by Sister Reginald Kean, she returned to the Mound, arriving Saturday evening.[19]

The Most Reverend Peter J. Muldoon, Bishop of Rockford officiated at Mother Emily's funeral on Tuesday, October 19, 1909. All of the missions except Anaconda, Montana, and Plattsmouth, Nebraska, were represented. Archbishop John Ireland delivered the funeral sermon, a long, tenderly sketched portrait of her life and works that could not have left a dry eye in the assembly. Probably no one was more deeply touched by it than Sister Samuel, who loved her so deeply. She must have taken especially to heart the following paragraph near the end of the sermon:

> Not for Mother Emily, you say, but for ourselves, do we sorrow and weep; a void that naught can fill is around us; the sadness of our loneliness—what can wrest us from it? Yes—the Apostles on Mount Olivet sang chants of joy as the triumphant Christ went up to the skies; yet, as the clouds closed upon Him, they sorrowed remembering that He was gone—He whose love had been so tender, Whose voice had been so sweet. Time was needed before comfort came in the realization that still He was with them in grace and in blessing. And so with you, dear Sisters; the loss of Mother Emily is apparent, not real. The just live forevermore: Mother Emily is in Heaven; she prays for her Sisters; she prays for her Congregation; she takes part in your saddenings and in your rejoicings; she comforts you in your trials and your labors. The Congregation of the Most Holy Rosary is still, and always will be, the cherished love of Mother Emily, now more powerful than when she was on earth to obtain for it happiness and prosperity. Would you honor her, as she now wishes you to honor her? Would you love her as she now wishes you to love her? Hearken to the inspirations of her life; copy into yourselves her virtues; dedicate yourselves in renewed fervor to the work and welfare of her Congregation.[20]

---

[19]McCarty, pp. 97-100.

[20]John Ireland, *Tribute to Mother Mary Emily Power, O.P.*, October 19, 1909.

In the event of the death of the Mother General without a vicaress having been appointed, the Constitutions of 1889 provided that the Prioress of the Motherhouse serve as acting mother general until an election could be held. Sister Samuel informed the Sisters on October 25, 1909 of the decision of the Council to comply with this statute and schedule the election at an Extraordinary Chapter to be held in August 1910, which would have been the time for an Intermediate Chapter.[21]

With courageous yet heavy heart, Sister Samuel continued her responsibilities as Prioress of the Motherhouse and Directress of the Academy and College, to which were added the new duties as Acting Mother General. These included duties associated with the presidency of the St. Clara College Board of Trustees, to which she was elected on October 21, 1909. Her four months as Vicaress during 1908 had given her some experience with the role, but the new reality was understandably more burdensome.

As part of the preparation for the Chapter, the Reverend John T. McNicholas, O.P., preached the retreat preceding it, an arrangement made by Mother Emily the year before because of her satisfaction with his conferences at that time. Bishop James Schwebach, Ordinary of the Diocese of LaCrosse, delegated authority to preside over the election to the Reverend Edward S. McGinnis, O.P., Chaplain of St. Clara.

Sister Samuel's apprehension as the Chapter approached, something she had surely felt at various times during the year, is expressed in her diary entry of August 5, 1910: "I am most unhappy in anticipation of tomorrow. Prayed and sought counsel; but my mind is set on safety, refusal. Yet, I fear God."[22]

The following day, after the preliminary ceremonies, the election for the three years of Mother Emily's uncompleted term took place.

---

[21]Sister Samuel to the Sisters, October 25, 1909.

[22]Diary, August 5, 1910.

Of the fifty-seven sisters who voted, "vocals" as they were called, fifty-five cast their ballots for Sister Samuel Coughlin. The satisfaction with this outcome was recorded in the St. Clara Annals as follows: "The selection of one to fill the place of their beloved Superior General, Mother Emily, could not be to the Sisters an occasion of joy, but the guidance of the Holy Spirit earnestly invoked since October last was manifest in the unity of spirit which pervaded the Chapter and was an occasion of deepest heartfelt gratitude."[23] Sister, now Mother Samuel, had misgivings as evident in her diary entry for that day: "A day of awful import. My soul is full of fear, lest I have done wrong in taking a responsibility for which no one is fit. Yet in many ways it seemed God's will. I shall never know till my death whether I have done the Community a great wrong. God pity it and me. Fr. McGinnis was kind; the Sisters beautifully tolerant, but my heart is full of fear."[24]

A few weeks later, on September 4, 1910, the General Council, as prescribed in the Constitutions, elected a new member of Council to complete the term vacated by Mother Samuel. The choice fell upon Sister DeRicci Fitzgerald. Thus began her thirty-nine-year period of close association with Mother Samuel as colleague on the Council, including thirty years as Vicaress General, and as trusted confidante. She had been born Mary Fitzgerald, daughter of Bridget Carroll and John Fitzgerald, immigrants from County Limerick and County Cork, Ireland, respectively, on March 5, 1866, in Atlanta, Illinois, a small rural town near the center of the state. The family later moved to Arcola, Illinois, about fifty miles south of Champaign. She was introduced to the Sinsinawa Dominicans through meeting the sisters at Bloomington, Illinois, and entered the Congregation in 1887. She was received on April 5, 1888, and made first profession on August 4, 1889. Her places of mission were: Bethlehem Academy, Faribault, Minnesota, 1888-1893; Immaculate Conception,

---

[23] Annals, St. Clara Convent, August 6, 1910, pp. 70-71.

[24] Diary, August 6, 1910.

Waukegan, Illinois, 1893-1895; St. Mary, Appleton, Wisconsin, 1895-1899; St. James, Kenosha, Wisconsin, 1899-1901; and St. Brendan, Chicago, 1901-1910.[25]

Two younger sisters of Sister DeRicci entered the Sinsinawa Dominican Congregation later: Elizabeth (Bernardus) and Nora (Marita).

Part of Mother Samuel's previous responsibilities, that of Prioress of St. Clara Convent, was lifted by the appointment on August 11, 1910, of Sister Reginald Kean to that office.[26]

Thus Mother Samuel spent nine of the first years of the twentieth century at St. Clara, often involved with matters related to the whole Congregation. During those years, the number of professed members grew from 389 to 617.[27] She saw a growth in the number of foundations as well, twenty being added between 1901 and 1910. The charts on the following pages show the missions in existence when the century opened and those that were established during the first ten years.

---

[25] SDA, Papers of Sister DeRicci Fitzgerald, Biographical File.

[26] Record of Council Meetings, p. 71.

[27] Sister Paschala O'Connor, *Five Decades* (Sinsinawa, Wisconsin: The Sinsinawa Press, 1954), p. 330; SDA, Statistics on Professions and Deaths, 1900-1910. Added to the 389 sisters who were members at the close of 1899, 276 more made profession between then and August 4, 1910, not counting those who did not persevere. Among the total of 665, there were 48 sisters who died during that period from 1900 through August 4, 1910.

Table I

Schools Conducted by Sinsinawa Dominican Sisters, 1900

Name of School	Place	Year Opened	Type of School
St. Clara Academy	Benton, WI	1853	Private Academy
	(Sinsinawa)	1867	
Im. Conception	Faribault, MN	1865	Parish Gr. School
Bethlehem Academy	Faribault	1865	Private Academy
St. Mary	Portage, WI	1866	Parish Gr. School
Im. Conception	Chicago, IL	1868	Parish Gr. School
St. James	Kenosha, WI	1869	Parish Gr. School
Im. Conception	Waukegan, IL	1870	Parish Gr. School
St. Michael	Galena, IL	1870	Parish Gr. School
St. Regina	Madison, WI	1871	Private Academy
(St.Raphael)	Madison, WI	1880s	Parish Gr. School
St. Mary	Freeport, IL	1873	Parish Gr. School
St. Jarlath	Chicago, IL	1873	Parish Gr. School
St. Mary	Evanston, IL	1874	Parish Gr. School
St. Patrick	Dixon, IL	1874	Parish Gr. School
St. Joseph	Bloomington, IL	1876	Private Academy
Holy Trinity	Bloomington, IL	1879	Parish Gr. School
St. Mary	Bloomington, IL	1879	Parish H. School
St. Peter	Oshkosh, Il	1878	Parish Gr. School
Holy Rosary	Minneapolis, MN	1879	Parish Gr. School
Edgewood Academy	Madison, WI	1881	Private Academy
Sac. Heart of Mary	Washington, D.C.	1882	Private Academy
St. Dominic	Washington, D.C.	1882	Parish Gr. School
St. James	Rockford, IL	1886	Parish Gr. School
St. Thomas Apostle	Chicago, IL	1886	Parish Gr. School
St. Lawrence,	Faribault, MN	1887	Parish Gr. School
Sacred Heart	"	"	" " "
(Srs. lived at Bethlehem Academy)			
St. Patrick	Lemont, IL	1888	Parish Gr. School
St. John	Plattsmouth, NE	1888	Parish Gr. School
Im. Conception	Spring Valley, IL	1888	Parish Gr. School
St. Mary	Appleton, WI	1889	Parish Gr. School
Holy Rosary	Kansas City, MO	1890	Parish Gr. School
St. Dominic	Denver, CO	1890	Parish Gr. School
Visitation	Chicago, IL	1891	Parish Gr. School
St. Rose	Milwaukee, WI	1893	Parish Gr. School
St Catherine	Jackson, NE	1893	Parish Gr. School Private Academy
St. John	Milwaukee, WI	1895	Parish Gr. School
Visitation	Kewanee, IL	1895	Parish Gr. School

Source: Book of Foundations, Sinsinawa Dominican Archives.

Table II

Schools Accepted by Sinsinawa Dominicans, 1901-1910

Name of School	Place	Year Opened	Type of School
St. Brendan	Chicago, IL	1901	Parish Gr. School
Sacred Heart	Rockwell, IA	1901	Private Academy
Sacred Heart	Eagle Grove, IA	1901	Parish Gr, H. Sch.
St. Thomas Aquinas	Milwaukee, WI	1902	Parish Gr. School
St. Patrick	Bloomington, IL	1902	Parish Gr. School
St. Joseph	New Hampton, IA	1904	Parish Gr. School (closed, 1910)
St. Bernard	Peoria, IL	1904	Parish Gr. School
Sacred Heart	Omaha, NE	1904	Parish Gr. School
St. Rose	Omaha, NE	1904	Private Academy
St. Cecilia	Omaha, NE	1907	Parish Gr. School
(Convent Provided)			1910
Sacred Heart Acad.	Washington, D.C.	1905	Private Academy (1931: Became Parish H.S.)
St. Basil	Chicago, IL	1905	Parish Gr. School
St. Joseph	Sioux Falls, SD	1905	Parish Gr. School
St. John	Milwaukee, WI	1905	Parish H. School
St. Patrick	Green Bay, WI	1905	Parish Gr. School
St. Peter	Anaconda, MT	1907	Parish Gr,H.Sch.
St. Gall	Milwaukee, WI	1908	Parish Gr. School
(Convent Provided)		1910	
Epiphany	Chicago, IL	1910	Parish Gr. School
St. Matthew	Milwaukee, WI	1910	Parish Gr. School
St. Thomas Aquinas	Rockford, IL	1910	Diocesan H.Sch.

Source: Book of Foundations, Sinsinawa Dominican Archives

Chapter Four

Decade of Outreach, 1910-1920

Though Mother Samuel Coughlin expressed in her diary some reservation about her fitness for congregation leadership, the host of well-wishers who wrote to her after receiving word of her election had none. From New York and New Jersey to Portland, Oregon, from New Orleans to Minnesota and the Dakotas came letters of congratulation. Represented were bishops, pastors, Dominican priests and brothers, religious of other congregations, laymen and laywomen of various professions, including former students. Perhaps the most prophetic of the messages was the one from John T. McNicholas, O.P., who had preached the pre-election retreat and who would remain a close friend and spiritual advisor for the rest of his life. He wrote:

Thank God that the Divine Will has been manifested in your behalf for the government of your Congregation. Personally, I feel sorry for you. They say honor and dignity are attached to these positions, but I know you are so constituted that you will never be able to see either the honor or the dignity. I feel you are to be an instrument in God's hands. However much you may think yourself unfitted, do not worry about the unfitness. It is God that has chosen you. Your great, generous, and self-sacrificing spirit and your love for the Order will bring God's blessing and the protection of our Mother and of Father St. Dominic.

Do not trouble yourself to reply to this. I know how busy you'll be in the weeks and months to come. Remember your strength and remember that God does not wish you to tax yourself beyond your strength.

I shall continue to remember your mother daily in Holy Mass. I will also remember you and the needs of your congregation. I shall always be grateful for every Hail Mary that you may give me and the Holy Name Work.

With every best wish and earnest prayer that God will bless you and all the efforts of your administration,

Very Sincerely in St. Dominic,[1]

The first decade of Mother Samuel's elected leadership encompassed her election to a full six-year term in August 1913 and re-election to a second full term in August 1919. Regular responsibilities of the office and several significant new ventures occurred against the backdrop of World War I, the great watershed of modern history. Some description of its causes and outcomes seems in order.

During the first decade of the twentieth century, the armed camps in Europe—the Triple Entente comprising Great Britain, France, and Russia, and the Triple Alliance formed by Germany, Austria-Hungary, and Italy—competed for resources and prestige backed by build-ups in land-based armaments and naval construction. Confrontation in 1905 between Britain and France on the one hand and Germany on the other concerning Morocco was succeeded by crises in the Balkans. Here the disintegration of the Ottoman Empire opened the way for rival powers to assert territorial claims. Efforts of statesmen to maintain peace were eroded by emotional strains generated by nationalism in Southeastern Europe.[2]

The powder keg was ignited by the assassination in Sarajevo, capital of Bosnia, on June 28, 1914, of Archduke Francis Ferdinand, heir to the throne of Austria-Hungary. The perpetrator was a member of a Serbian secret society, and Austria demanded that its officials be permitted to investigate and punish those responsible for the assassination. Germany supported the ultimatum; Russia, fearing attack by Germany, issued orders for mobilization. Germany responded by declaring war on Russia on August 1, and on France, Russia's ally, on August 3. England wavered briefly on whether or not

---

[1]SDA, Correspondence with John T. McNicholas, August 8, 1910.

[2]R.R. Palmer, *A History of the Modern World*. New York: Alfred A. Knopf, 1965, pp. 665-667. (Copyright now the property of McGraw-Hill, Inc.)

to honor obligations to France. The German military plan to attack Paris from the North and West led to the violation of the neutrality of Belgium, an act that tipped the balance in favor of an English declaration of war on Germany on August 4.[3]

Within two years, other European powers had joined—Turkey and Bulgaria on the side of Germany and Austria-Hungary, the new alignment now known as the Central Powers; and Italy on the side of Britain, France, and Russia—the Allies—who had promised a more favorable post-war settlement than Italy would have had under the Triple Alliance. In the Far East, Japan declared war on Germany in 1914, promptly seizing German-held islands in the Pacific and German concessions in China.[4]

Although the general reaction in the United States was a conviction that America should not become involved, there were situations that pulled the nation gradually toward war. Some "hyphenated" Americans—Irish-Americans and German-Americans—opposed an Allied victory and most Americans did not want to become associated with despotic Russia. Despite this, propagandists were more successful in stirring anti-German than anti-British sentiment. President Wilson insisted on the observance by the warring powers of America's traditional policies on neutral rights, which included the right to trade with belligerents and not suffer attacks in international waters. This led to crises over the use of submarines by Germany to stem the flow of munitions and other supplies from the United States to the Allies. American lives were lost in the sinking of the British passenger liner, the *Lusitania*, in May 1915 and of the French ship, the *Sussex*, in March 1916. The United States drew closer to war early in 1917 when the Germans announced their intention to sink all ships at sight, including those of neutral nations. To this was added in February 1917 the revelation of a plot to involve Mexico in war against the United States in return for reacquisition of its "lost

---

[3]*Ibid.*, pp. 667-669.

[4]*Ibid.*, p.676

territories" in Southwestern United States. In March 1917, Germany acted upon its threat of unlimited submarine warfare by sinking three American ships. The change of government in Russia in that same month removed the appearance of despotism for the time being. As Wilson weighed all of these developments, he came to the conclusion that "no one was immune from German aggression, and there could be no real peace while it went unpunished." On April 2, 1917, he asked Congress for a resolution "recognizing the existence of a state of war with Germany." The Senate complied on April 4 and the House of Representatives on April 6.[5]

America's entrance into the war tipped the balance in favor of the Allies. Within twenty months, including several that brought great loss of American lives, the war ended with the signing of an armistice on November 11, 1918.

To the carnage of the battlefields was added an unsatisfactory peace settlement, contributing further to the world-shaking impact of the war. The outcome is summarized by R. R. Palmer as follows:

> The First World War dealt a lasting blow to the ancient institutions of monarchy and aristocratic feudalism. Thrones toppled in Turkey, in Russia, in Austria-Hungary, in the German Empire and the individual German states; and with the kings went the courtly retainers and all the social preeminence and special advantage of the old landed aristocracies. The war was indeed a victory for democracy, though a bitter one. It carried further a process as old as the French and American revolutions. But for the basic problems of modern civilization, industrialism and nationalism, economic security and international stability, it gave no answer.[6]

America's entry into the war brought added burdens to Mother Samuel. She felt a responsibility for guiding the sisters in their

---

[5]John M. Blum, et al., *The National Experience* (New York: Harcourt Brace Jovanovich, Inc.), pp 551-559.

[6]R.R. Palmer and Joel Colton, *A History of the Modern World* (New York: Alfred A. Knopf, 1965), p. 703. This material is reproduced with permission of McGraw-Hill, Inc.

reaction to the crisis. Her letter during Holy Week contained the following observations and admonitions:

The Alleluias of Easter are broken 'by the sounds of war and rumors of war.' May God's blessed Will be done by us in this critical time of the world's history. I wish to remind you of our duty now in this national crisis. No matter what may have been our private opinion as to the wisdom of the nation's declaring a state of war, we must keep them *absolutely to ourselves*. It is our duty now to follow our leader, the President, by our prayers and by speaking of patriotism to our pupils, in season and out of season, urging always that loyalty to country comes next to loyalty to God. Let no word of criticism of the government escape our lips. Pray in School, pray privately, pray in community, that God may send peace soon to the world for whose ransom He died and rose again from the dead. . . .

The Government asks that all our people try to economize as never before. I know that you will all respond generously to this appeal. Let us put away from us all superfluity, and do even more than our Rule prescribes in the way of poverty, offering every privation to God for His honor and the welfare of the Nation. . . .[7]

She wrote periodically throughout the year to urge the sisters to pray and to practice mortification, not only of the spirit but also of the body in cooperation with the President's call for saving food and other resources. Her letter of November 26, 1917, was especially strong:

The call of our country to save food has a solemn warning for us all. We are poor. Our revenue, our salaries are but a pittance; the cost of food is great. To end the war soon, prompt sacrifice is needful. None should obey more devotedly than we Sisters who teach the young the lessons of patriotism in school. Our example will now crown our teaching. Let us therefore, in the name of God and country, go heart and soul into this campaign of saving and sacrifice. It is good to suffer privation now, that we may the sooner rejoice with a nation-wide joy that will come of our having,

[7]Mission Letters, Mother Samuel to the Sisters, Holy Week, 1917.

under God, brought victorious peace to mankind. Our country is in the war for principle, Christian principle, not profit. . . ."[8]

Other concerns that arose because of war-time conditions were the worry over the sending of sisters to Fribourg in July 1917 and over how they would fare when they arrived; the delay in starting the new college building; the interruption of work once started due to labor troubles and scarce building materials; and the illnesses and deaths that resulted from the influenza epidemic in the fall of 1918 and winter of 1919. More will be said below about these and other major developments that occurred during the second decade of the twentieth century.

Mother Samuel's regular routine was governed largely by seasonal duties. Council meetings occupied a considerable portion of her time, including meetings to approve postulants for reception into the novitiate and novices for admission to simple vows and final profession, and to approve the election of prioresses and appointment of vicaresses. Assignment of sisters to their summer work and "fixing the missions" for fall consumed weeks during the spring and summer. During the school year there were many substitutions to be approved as sisters suffered illnesses. Other responsibilities calling for action by the Council included approval of new missions and matters of building and finance of a substantial value. A special project undertaken in 1919 required many hours of council time as well as work by a special committee established by the General Chapter of that year. The assignment was to bring the Constitutions into conformity with portions of the newly published Code of Canon Law related to Religious Congregations.[9]

In addition to Council meetings, handling of correspondence with Roman officials, bishops, pastors, and sisters was an on-going activity that Mother Samuel found burdensome.

---

[8]*Ibid.*, November 26, 1917.

[9]Sister Mary Eva McCarty. *The Sinsinawa Dominican: Outlines of Twentieth Century Development, 1901-1949* (Dubuque: The Hoermann Press, 1952), pp. 277-278.

She and the council members who assisted her in making visitation of the convents were "on the road" during the interims between council meetings. Several major railroads with connections in Galena, East Dubuque, and Cuba City, provided passes for Mother Samuel and Companion.[10] In her diary she nearly always recorded the time of her arrival home; it could literally be at any hour of the day or night.

While the service available for long-distance traveling was adequate, local transportation was a problem. Travel to and from East Dubuque was seriously hampered by poor roads and inadequate vehicles. This became a major problem not only for Mother Samuel's own travel but also for recruitment of students for the Academy and College and led to consideration of various propositions for solving the difficulties. Rumors of extensions to be built by major lines proved false. A plan begun in 1903 to provide a private electric road from Dubuque to Platteville via Sinsinawa failed to obtain adequate financing. Two other efforts from 1905 to 1908 met similar fates. A project involving an electric line from Freeport to Galena with a spur to Hazel Green and Sinsinawa, proposed in 1911, petered out in a few years. In 1912, the Congregation even considered financing its own line from East Dubuque to the Mound. Consultation with Bishop Schwebach of LaCrosse on obtaining necessary permission for the outlay of money for such a project was not encouraging.[11]

Although the transportation problem seemed destined to affect student recruitment adversely, the enrollment in the Academy in 1910-1911 reached 125, the highest it had ever been, and there were more than 40 College students. Dormitory space was inadequate and some areas used for dining and recreation were reduced in size to accommodate the need for classrooms and laboratories. About 1911, Mother Samuel began considering the need to expand the College

---

[10]Those roads were: Illinois Central; Chicago & North-western; Great Western; Chicago, Milwaukee, St. Paul; and Chicago, Burlington, & Quincy.

[11]McCarty, pp. 66-73, 180-181.

with the assumption that it would remain at Sinsinawa and that railroad transportation would improve. A small nest-egg of funds for expansion was already at hand. In her letter to the sisters on September 19, 1907, in which she announced the confirmation by Roman authorities of Mother Emily's re-election, Mother Samuel had asked the sisters to start a fund in anticipation of Mother Emily's Golden Jubilee of profession in 1911.[12] The St. Clara Alumnae Association voted in June 1911 to add donations for a Mother Emily Power Hall. The following March, Mother Samuel asked the sisters to collaborate with the alumnae in this new fund-raising activity.[13]

Just shortly before Mother Samuel gave this instruction to the sisters, she was asked to consider moving the College to a new location. Francis X. McCabe, C.M., President of DePaul University in Chicago, met with her and Sister Reginald Kean in Chicago in early January, 1912, to ask their consideration of a plan to establish a college for women that would affiliate with DePaul. The offer had first been made to the Sisters of Charity of the Blessed Virgin Mary, Dubuque, Iowa, who, after agreeing, later were obliged to withdraw.

Mother Samuel asked the advice of the mission superiors and other sisters whom the latter wished to consult. The consultation resulted in both practical and visionary responses and paved the way for future support for moving the College from Sinsinawa. Mother Samuel and Father McCabe corresponded for a few weeks about the working out of plans. Before any commitment was made on the part of Mother Samuel, Father McCabe notified her that his Provincial Superior had directed him not to go any further with the project unless the religious community of women would assume full responsibility for building the institution. This turn of events made it fruitless for the discussion to continue, as Father McCabe well

---

[12]The convents were to set aside $1.00 per month per sister and all gift money. By the time of Mother Emily's death, this fund had reached $3,800.

[13]Mission Letters, Letters to the Sisters, August 15, 1911; March 2, 1912.

understood.[14] The time spent on the matter was by no means a waste, however, for the emergence of the option of moving the College proved to be highly significant. Among the special concerns and responsibilities of Mother Samuel for the remainder of the decade, the location and building of the College was paramount.

For more than four years after the DePaul proposal failed to materialize, Mother Samuel weighed the options regarding the location of the College. By early 1914 she was clearly open to the possibility of moving away from Sinsinawa. In January 1914 she addressed letters to Archbishop Sebastian G. Messmer of Milwaukee and Archbishop James E. Quigley of Chicago, asking permission to investigate possible sites within their archdioceses where the Congregation might build a college. Archbishop Messmer's reply was warm and inviting: "Yes, dear Mother, not only do I grant to you and your community permission to come and establish a convent and college in or near the city of Milwaukee, but I shall be most happy if you will succeed in doing so. . . ." He went on to emphasize the need for such an institution. Archbishop Quiqley's response was more business-like as he stressed the need to know more exactly the location where the sisters might choose to build, so he could present the request to the Archdiocesan Council.[15] Mother Samuel sent Sisters Peter Connor and Constantia Leamy to Madison and Milwaukee to look at possible sites.[16] In a letter to the missions on February 24, 1914, she asked the sisters to begin a novena on February 27 in honor of Our Lady of the Rosary for help in building the College "near some city such as Madison, Chicago, Milwaukee."[17]

Extended and serious consideration was given in 1915 to an Omaha site. Mother Samuel wrote to Bishop Richard Scannell on

---

[14]McCarty, pp. 181-184.

[15]SDA, Correspondence with Bishops, Messmer to Mother Samuel, January 31, 1914; Quigley to Mother Samuel, January 12, 1914.

[16]Diary, January 9, 1914.

[17]Mission Letters, Mother Samuel to the Sisters, February 24, 1914.

January 8, 1915, proposing a college in Omaha provided there would be help among local businessmen in finding property and raising funds. The Bishop quickly concurred in regard to the Congregation's establishing a college in his diocese, but added:

> As to your getting a gift of a site, I am afraid to offer you any encouragement. There is now within a radius of six miles of our City Hall a population of over two hundred thousand people, and our business is about twice as large as most American cities of the same size. Such a community does not often give a bonus to establish school buildings. However, you can try, and if you can succeed you will have my congratulations.[18]

Despite this less than encouraging response, an Omaha location remained under consideration. Mother Samuel and Sister Catharine Wall visited some properties there in May 1915 and discussion of the viability of purchasing land continued in the General Council. That body voted on August 29, 1915, to accept the offer of the businessmen of Omaha of 20 acres of land valued at $20,000 for a college site.[19] However, a conflict of expectations regarding the financing of the project led eventually to its cancellation. The businessmen did not fulfill what Mother Samuel and her Council members understood had been agreed upon—that they would assist in acquiring a site and raise $20,000 in partial payment. A note appended to the Council minutes of November 13, 1915, reads: "Jan. 13, 1916: Up to the present, the businessmen of Omaha have not secured any site for a Young Women's Catholic College, nor, as far as we know, collected any money for the purpose." The death of Bishop Scannell on January 8, 1916, added further doubt about the feasibility of the project.[20]

---

[18]Correspondence with Bishops, Mother Samuel to Bishop Scannell, January 8, 1915; Scannell to Mother Samuel, January, 12, 1915.

[19]Diary, May 21, 1915; Council Meeting, August 29, 1915.

[20]Diary, October 18-29, 1916, *passim*; Minutes of Council Meetings, November 13, 1915, January 13, 1916.

Although no decision had yet been reached on location, Mother Samuel and her Council had in January 1915 engaged Ralph Adams Cram, a nationally-known architect, to begin drawing up plans. Presumably, these would be adaptable to a variety of locations, including Edgewood in Madison, which was under consideration for this or for some other educational projects. At the direction of the Council, Mr. Cram assigned his associate, Mr. Hoyle, to study the site, a task undertaken in July 1915.[21] For reasons that are not evident in the records, neither the Edgewood site nor any in the Milwaukee area were pursued after 1915. With the collapse of negotiations about locating in Omaha, Chicago seemed the most viable option.

The death of Archbishop Quigley on July 10, 1915, and the lapse of time before the installation of Archbishop George Mundelein on February 9, 1916, delayed permission for the steps necessary to pursue the project in the Chicago area. Mother Samuel paid a visit to the new Archbishop at the Chancery Office on April 7, 1916, finding him "most gracious."[22] On April 24, 1916, the General Council in special session voted to submit to Mundelein the proposition of transferring St. Clara College to the Chicago area. Thus began the dialogue between Mother Samuel and Mundelein, sometimes fraught with misunderstanding and disagreement, that culminated in the opening of Rosary College in River Forest in October 1922.

One matter in particular was disputed initially: Mundelein wished to have a college for day students in the city; Mother Samuel preferred a residential college in a suburban location. Negotiations on the issue took place through personal conversation, particularly during a series of meetings held during the week of June 19-23, 1916, in Chicago. Mother Samuel recorded the progress of the discussions in her diary:

---

[21]Council Meeting, May 4, 1915.

[22]Diary, April 7, 1916.

June 19: ". . . Went to see Oak Park 'find' [16.5 acre tract of land at corner of Oak Park Avenue and Division Street]. Much pleased. . . ."

June 20: ". . . I called on Abp. Mundelein 6-7:15 p.m. Gracious, but not satisfied to let us pay $37,000 for property in Oak Park."

June 22: Went to Chancery Office with Fr. McGuire & Sr. Peter. Saw Abp. Mundelein twice. Advised waiting, if possible. Later he sent telephone [message] by Dr. Hoban [chancellor] to buy property. . . ."

June 23: "An anxious day. Fr. Madden called. Ed McG. brought contract and I signed it 'Ellen T. Coughlin.' Left on night train."

Mother Samuel had excellent advice from several sisters, priests, and laymen. In addition to those mentioned in the above diary entries, William S. Hefferan, who served as lawyer for the Congregation throughout the project, was especially trustworthy. The choice of Charles W. Kallal as associate architect to Mr. Cram was fortunate. He donated his services during the time he could give from his position as City Architect of Chicago. He became a close friend of Mother Samuel, who later welcomed two of his daughters to St. Clara Academy, one of whom continued at Rosary College and entered the Congregation as Sister Mary John.[23]

Although the location of the College seemed to have been resolved by the June 1916 negotiations, an episode in October upset Mother Samuel. On October 9, she received a clipping from a Chicago newspaper sent by Sister Catharine Wall, reporting an address made by Mundelein to the Catholic Women's League. He spoke of the need for "one, or perhaps two first class Catholic *Day* Colleges [italics added] for women right here in Chicago." He outlined plans for bringing a women's college to Chicago without naming the college or the congregation in charge of it. Mother Samuel was startled and disappointed to receive the communication and wrote to Mundelein about it that same day.[24] He responded with

---

[23]McCarty, p. 208; Sister Mary John taught violin at Rosary College for more than 50 years. Diary, June 19-23, 1916.

[24]Diary, October 9, 1916.

a letter that brought reassurance that the arrangements worked out in June still stood.[25]

Mother Samuel wrote to the sisters of the Congregation on October 16, 1916, informing them that: "We can now announce to you that we are really committed to the project of building our College in Chicago. . . . We hope to begin to build in the spring. . . . We need $300,000. Where can we get it? . . ."[26] Despite this concern, one that would continually plague the enterprise, planning went forward rapidly. On January 19, 1917, *The New World*, the Chicago Archdiocesan Newspaper, published an official announcement, written by Mother Samuel and approved by Mundelein, of the pending establishment of the new college.

Overlapping negotiations leading to the implementation of plans for Rosary College, Mother Samuel participated in an episode that typified her concern for the needy and her desire to cooperate with Church officials. On February 9, 1917, Mundelein addressed a letter to the Catholics of the Archdiocese of Chicago, informing them of a decision of the Circuit Court of Cook County on January 25 declaring child-caring institutions under Catholic auspices ineligible to receive state aid. After a lengthy analysis of the injustice and lack of wisdom of such a decision, he asked for help from Catholics of the Archdiocese to care for some of the children through monetary donations or adoption.

In consultation with Mundelein and with the approval of the General Council, Mother Samuel worked out an arrangement with the administration of the Chicago Industrial School for Girls at Des Plaines, Illinois (also known as Saint Mary's Training School), for the care of four girls. Three were from one family where the father had died and the mother was hospitalized with a terminal illness. The plan was to place each of the children at one of the academies conducted by the Congregation: Mary Keating, aged twelve at Bethlehem

---

[25]McCarty, p. 190.

[26]Mission Letters, Mother Samuel to the Sisters, October 16, 1916.

Academy in Faribault; Margaret, aged eleven at Edgewood Academy in Madison; and Josephine, aged nine at St. Joseph Academy in Bloomington. Mother Samuel had offered to place a child from another family at St. Catherine Academy in Jackson, Nebraska, a plan that was dropped when a member of the girl's family assumed responsibility for her. Two of the Keating children entered the Congregation as professed sisters after graduating from the academies: Mary, known as Sister Eymard, and Margaret, as Sister Marie Thomas.[27]

Meanwhile, between the time of the October developments and the announcement in *The New World*, an opportunity arose to acquire property in River Forest. Frequent consultations with advisors and many trips to River Forest led Mother Samuel to the conclusion that the purchase of the River Forest property was feasible and advantageous, particularly if the Oak Park property could be sold at a good price. The General Council voted approval of the transaction on May 5, 1917. Mundelein had no objection when Mother Samuel informed him on May 22 of the opportunity. The sale of the 16.5 acres in Oak Park and the purchase of 27.5 acres in River Forest were concluded on May 28, 1917.[28]

The story of the next six years regarding the College is one of hope, worry, and frustration for Mother Samuel. It involved great sacrifice among the sisters and creative efforts among students and benefactors to provide funds; war-time and post-war conditions led to delays in construction. Mundelein gave support to fund-raising through his personal and official contacts and by personal donations. Through his suggestion, a War Savings Stamps Campaign was adopted by schools and parishes where Sinsinawa Dominican Sisters served, a venture of benefit to the nation as well as to the College.

The enormous amount of work required of Mother Samuel by the College project led her in the summer of 1917 to seek help from

---

[27]Correspondence with Archbishop Mundelein, February 1917; Council Meetings, February 17, 1917.

[28]Diary, October 18,1916 - May 28, 1917, *passim*.

Sister Ruth Devlin and Sister DeRicci Fitzgerald. She asked Sister Ruth to serve as vicaress of the Congregation, a position that gave her authority to act as Mother General in case of Mother Samuel's absence. She pleaded with Sister DeRicci to accept the responsibilities as prioress of St. Clara, a position that became vacant when Sister George Adamson was assigned to Fribourg (see below, p. 72). The combination of this office with that as member of Council was one that Mother Samuel herself had had from 1907-1910, which she had found almost overwhelming (see Chapter Three, p. 45).[29] After showing some reluctance, Sister DeRicci agreed to assume the office of prioress for three years.

In July 1920, when the term was nearly completed, Mother Samuel wrote to Sister DeRicci to thank her for all the improvements at St. Clara during her term and to express the wish that she could continue in office. However, Mother Samuel also acknowledged that the Constitution assumes that a Councillor should be free to serve the whole Congregation. The letter concludes with a touching passage of appreciation:

> . . . Please dearest Sister DeRicci, forgive me for my many failings towards you. I have been overburdened in addition to my natural weakness and I have not been considerate often. But believe me to be deeply grateful, and to have hope that you can do much for the Congregation when you can put your mind entirely on the general good of all the Sisters and the problems of the entire congregation.[30]

---

[29]Correspondence of Mother Samuel with Sister DeRicci, August 1917; Diary, August 14, 1917.

[30]Correspondence with Sister DeRicci, Mother Samuel to Sister DeRicci, July 21, 1920.

Sister DeRicci and Mother Samuel

Mother Samuel and Sister Ruth Devlin

Mother Mary Joseph

Sister Louis Bertrand Droege

Sister Grace James,
Thomas à Kempis Reilly, O. P.,
Sister George Adamson

George Cardinal Mundelein

Archbishop John T. McNicholas

Villa des Fougères

Despite her reluctance to do so, Mother Samuel reappointed Sister DeRicci to another three-year term.

Two other major episodes requiring Mother Samuel's careful attention had long-range consequences. Intimately involved in both stories was John T. McNicholas. First was the assistance rendered by the Sinsinawa Dominican Congregation in the foundation of the Maryknoll Congregation. Cardinal Farley of New York had asked McNicholas to organize a group of Dominican Tertiaries, formerly known as Teresians, as a sisterhood for work in the Foreign Missions. McNicholas apppealed to Mother Samuel to send one of her sisters to give assistance in the spiritual formation of the women as they waited for approval from Rome of formal status. The Reverend James A. Walsh, founder of the men's branch of the Maryknoll Society, assisted McNicholas in the negotiations with Mother Samuel. The latter agreed to help in the project by sending Sister Ruth Devlin to Maryknoll in April 1917, where she served for several months. Responding to another appeal from Walsh after formal approval had been received from Rome, Mother Samuel sent Sister Fidelia Delaney in June 1919 to help in formal novitiate training according to the Dominican Constitutions. Her stay lasted five years, a time much treasured by her and by the Maryknoll Sisters. The passage below from Penny Lernoux's book, *Hearts on Fire*, captures some of that appreciation:

> Among the blessings received by the Maryknollers during the trying time of rejection and waiting for Vatican approval was the arrival of a Dominican nun from Wisconsin [June 1919], Sister Fidelia. A gentle and kindly person, she continued the instruction begun by the IHM Sisters, only hers was less rigid, and there were none of the earlier constraints. . . . Sister Fidelia was able to distinguish between the essentials of religious life and unnecessary formalities. . . . Sister Fidelia loved Mollie

[Mother Mary Joseph, the Maryknoll Superior], and the affection was returned.[31]

The second episode was the acceptance of the offer to establish a foundation in Fribourg, Switzerland. The first word about the project came in a letter from McNicholas dated February 13, 1917. He was writing from Rome where he had recently begun serving as Socius of the Master General. The latter had asked him to suggest a congregation of American sisters that might be willing to purchase the Institute in Fribourg founded by the Reverend Joachim Berthier, O.P. The school and the property were owned by two lay women. McNicholas immediately suggested the Sinsinawa Dominicans. In his first letter on the subject and in succeeding ones to Mother Samuel in April, he strongly advocated her acceptance of the proposal. Among his arguments were the likelihood of the venture being profitable and the advantage for the sisters of attending lectures at the University of Fribourg and of working for degrees there. He urged prompt action on the part of the Congregation, including a visit to Fribourg, and offered to assist in the transactions needed to conclude an agreement, a matter that would be highly complicated because of wartime conditions.[32] The possible advantages of the new foundation convinced Mother Samuel that she should seriously consider it. In May 1917 she decided to send Sisters George Adamson and Grace James to inspect the property, cabling McNicholas to that effect on May 23. She agonized over the necessity of placing the sisters in possible jeopardy, since she herself could not go: "The question of the morality of sending the Sisters in war-time worried me, but Bishop [Schwebach of LaCrosse] and priests say that the end justifies the risk.[33]

---

[31]Penny Lernoux, *Hearts on Fire: The Story of the Maryknoll Sisters* (Maryknoll, New York: Orbis Books, 1993), p 38.

[32]Correspondence with McNicholas, McNicholas to Mother Samuel, February 13, April 15 and 20, 1917.

[33]Mission Letters, Mother Samuel to the Sisters, July 8, 1917.

Matters moved quickly after that. With advice and assistance from Raymond Meagher, O.P., Provincial of St. Joseph Province, and Thomas à Kempis Reilly, O.P., who was also traveling to Europe, passage was arranged for the sisters on the *Montevideo*, a Spanish liner believed to be safe from German submarine attack. They sailed on July 17, 1917. The journey proved to be safer than anticipated. On July 21, Sister George recorded in her diary: "We have not seen a single ship of any kind since we left New York Harbor." Landing at Cadiz on July 28, they made their way, sometimes under precarious conditions, through Spain and France and arrived at Fribourg on August 17. McNicholas, who had traveled from Rome, was there to greet them and to assist in the inspection and arrangements for purchasing the property.[34]

Sisters George and Grace felt great anxiety from the necessity of making a decision about the purchase, the price of which was to be about $60,000, almost twice what had been originally estimated. They arrived at their decision on August 25, later informing Mother Samuel: "I hope you and the Council will be pleased with what we have done; if not, please break the news gently, for I'm not sure how much more we shall be able to bear. . . ."[35]

Mother Samuel, who had first informed the sisters on July 8 of the evolving Fribourg venture, wrote to them on October 11 about plans to defray the initial costs. She asked twenty-five of the larger missions to provide an average of about $500 each to cover the down payment, as she could not divert funds that had already been collected for the College. The response was encouraging, as $10,000 was quickly subscribed.[36]

Thus was launched a project that would evolve into a highly successful venture for the Congregation, fulfilling many of the

---

[34]Diary, April-August, 1917, *passim*; Mission Letters, Diary of Sister George Adamson, July 17, 1917; McCarty, pp. 253-259.

[35]Sister George, Fribourg, to Mother Samuel, August 31, 1917.

[36]Mission Letters, July 8 and October 11, 1917.

expectations expressed by McNicholas in his advice to Mother Samuel. The first year was fraught with many worries about finances and the inadequacy of communications between Sinsinawa and Fribourg. Most tragically, the death of Sister George on August 20, 1918, due to causes not fully determined, was a great burden to Sister Grace and a great sorrow to Mother Samuel and the other sisters of the Congregation. The Diary entry for August 24, the day Sister Grace's cable was received, reads:

> The saddest day of the year. Cable came at 1:30 a.m., received by Sister Maura: 'Fribourg—Sister George died. Signed Grace.' Sisters overwhelmed with grief. Mass for Sister George's soul."[37]

To bring comfort to Sister Grace and assistance for the work, Mother Samuel assigned Sister Evelyn Murphy as vicaress at Fribourg and Sisters Teresita Hessian, Laserian Doran, and Rosemary Crepeau as participants in the mission. After a hazardous voyage on the *Rochambeau*, which left New York on September 18, 1918, the sisters arrived at Bordeaux, France, on September 28 and made their way to Fribourg by October 4. The development of the ministry during the next two years before Mother Samuel herself was able to visit Fribourg is described in further detail by Sister Eva McCarty.[38]

Between 1911 and 1920, Mother Samuel established sixteen new grade schools, two new high schools, and added high school classes at five places where grade schools already existed. (See list on page 75.) The latter development paralleled the expansion of public high school education and met a need very much of concern to the Church, and, consequently, of great interest to Mother Samuel. Ordinarily, the sisters would offer freshman level courses to which were added the other levels in succeeding years. The following places were accommodated with the new high school ministry from 1911 to 1920:

---

[37]Diary, August 24, 1918.

[38]McCarty, pp. 260-271

Table III

Schools (Missions) Accepted by Sinsinawa Dominicans, 1911-1920*

Name of	Place	Year Opened	Type of School
St. Mark	Peoria, IL	1911	Convent Built
Incarnation	Minneapolis, MN	1911	Parish Gr. School
St. Joseph	Baraboo, WI	1911	Parish Gr. School
St. Joseph	Sioux Falls, SD	1913	Began High School
St. Patrick	Ottawa, IL	1913	Parish Gr. School
Holy Angels	Omaha, NE	1913	Parish Gr. School
St. Peter	Oshkosh, WI	1914	Began High School
St. Clement	Sheboygan, WI	1914	Parish Gr. School
St. Robert	Milwaukee, WI	1914	Parish Gr. School
St. Joseph	Sinsinawa, WI	1914	Parish Gr. School
St. Thomas	Rockford, IL	1915	Convent Built
St. Vincent	Denver, CO	1915	Convent remodeled for Sanitorium
Visitation	Chicago, IL	1915	Began High School
St. Thomas	Kenosha, WI	1916	Parish Gr. School
St. Rose	Cuba City, WI	1916	Parish Gr. School
St. Thomas	Chicago, IL	1916	Began High School
Sacred Heart	Faribault, MN	1916	Convent Built
Villa des Fougères	Fribourg, SWI	1916	Institute Estab.
Our Lady of Mercy	New York, NY	1917	Parish Gr. School
Rosary (Trinity)	River Forest, IL	1918	Began High School
St. Cecilia	Omaha, NE	1919	Began High School
St. Bernard	Wauwatosa, WI	1919	Parish Gr. School
St. Sabina	Chicago, IL	1919	Parish Gr. School
St. Patrick	Madison, WI	1920	Parish Gr. School
St. Philip Benizi	Chicago, IL	1920	Parish Gr. School
St. Patrick	Imogene, IA	1920	Par. Gr. and High School
St. Luke	River Forest, IL	1920	Parish Gr. School

*This information is taken from SDA, Book of Foundations.

St. Joseph, Sioux Falls; St. Peter, Oshkosh, 1913; Visitation, Chicago, 1915; St. Thomas the Apostle, Chicago, 1916; St. Cecilia, Omaha, 1919. New institutions were organized at Rosary House, River Forest, 1918 (later to become Trinity High School) and at St. Patrick, Imogene in 1920.[39]

A change in a previously established foundation occurred in 1915 with the remodeling of St. Dominic Convent in Denver, Colorado, to serve the needs of the sick. It was renamed St. Vincent Sanitorium. The Congregation purchased another house to serve as convent for the sisters teaching in St. Dominic Grade School.[40]

The regular and extraordinary responsibilities of Mother Samuel, such as those described above, took a heavy toll on her physical, mental, and spiritual resources. It is chiefly through her diary that this is revealed. She was frequently ill, often for days at a time, sometimes requiring hospitalization. Begining as early as November 1913 she had spells that she attributed to heart weakness, a self-diagnosis that would later be confirmed by physicians. In June of 1914 she spent 10 days at Mercy Hospital in Dubuque and in October required several days of bed rest at the Mound. She suffered a frightening illness the following June of 1915—"Came down from play to go to bed. Great illness came on. Was near to death. Sr. Peter and Sr. Maura kind beyond words. A fearful night." The illness persisted throughout most of July and August that year. A year later, in July 1916 she experienced another several days when she was unable to be at work. Her concern about her heart was confirmed by a physician in August 1917. She records the episode as follows: "About ten I became so weak I had to go to bed. Feared death. Went in to see Dr. Killeen after dinner. She says I have acute dilation of the heart."[41]

She expresses sadness and worry over school problems: "A cruel day. School opens with only 60 acad. & Preps. My heart is sad and

---

[39]*Ibid.*, pp. 143-153.

[40]*Ibid.*, p. 289

[41]Diary, November 1913-August 1917, *passim.*

sick;" "College girls return—few in number."[42] She mourned the death of her mother on September 17, 1911: "My beloved mother died at 6:00 p.m. Oh! this sad night and the nights to come." This sentiment was repeated on the first anniversary of her mother's death and on many more to come: "Anniversary of the saddest loss of my life." She worried about the illnesses of the sisters and mourned their deaths, especially that of Sister Reginald Kean on April 30, 1917: "Found Mother Reginald near death; she knew me, lingered a few minutes, and died looking into my eyes. I cannot weep, my heart is numb. My good helper is gone. . . ." The death of Sister Peter Connor, one of the victims of the influenza epidemic on January 27, 1919, was also a burden: "My best helper and friend dead." Sister Richard Barden succeeded her as bursar general in March.[43]

On a brighter note, Mother Samuel was delighted to greet her niece, Mary Coughlin, oldest daughter of her brother John, when she came on September 13, 1916, to enroll in St. Clara College. The two of them had visits when schedules permitted and they sometimes prayed together in Chapel. After Mary's graduation on June 3, 1920, the bond of affection was maintained through letters and visits.[44]

The most poignant of the Diary entries during these years are ones she wrote at the time of election. On August 8, 1913, the entry was: ". . . Rumors of the Community's probable action . . . drives me to seek advice I resolved never to seek. 'My God, if it be possible, let this cross pass from me. . . .'" The following day, she wrote: "Election this afternoon. Only God knows whether I did right in accepting the cross. If a choice of being burned alive in the furnace—and accepting this office were given me—I should gladly choose being burned . . ." At the time of her re-election for a second full term in August 1919, she entered these words: ". . . Tractatus held, humiliating. Have been Sister Samuel, free from the cares of the Mother General since 12:30

[42] *Ibid.*, September 6 and 13, 1911.

[43] *Ibid.*, April 30, 1917; January 27 and March 2, 1919.

[44] Diary, 1916-1920, *passim*; Correspondence with Mary Coughlin, 1920-1929, *passim*.

p.m. today. Comforting relief. May God save the Congregation from the punishment I deserve." This was followed on August 9 by: "An awful day! Election of Mother General. Election of Council—Sisters De Ricci, Clare, Ruth, Hyacintha. All my fears returned." The vote in both elections was unanimous.[45]

At this time, her close friend and spiritual advisor, John T. McNicholas, who had been appointed Bishop of the Diocese of Duluth, Minnesota, sent her a telegram that read as follows:

> May St. Dominic be interested, direct, approve every act of your administration for the next six years. Personally I am pleased and grateful to God that the choice has fallen on you. You have but one motive—the good of religion. You also have my sympathy; shall remember you daily in Mass. [Punctuation marks added.][46]

As Mother Samuel faced her second full term of office, which would overlap the beginning of a new decade, she had overwhelming support from her sisters, then numbering 849, whose sentiments closely reflected those of Bishop McNicholas.

---

[45]Correspondence with Bishop James Schwebach, Bishop of LaCrosse Diocese, August 13, 1913, and August 11, 1919.

[46]Correspondence with McNicholas, McNicholas to Mother Samuel, August 11, 1919.

Chapter Five

Challenges of the 1920s

As the decade of the 1920s opened, Mother Samuel Coughlin could look back upon some remarkable accomplishments during the first ten years of her leadership. The preceding pages catalog those developments. This chapter will describe continuing activities associated with long established and recently assumed ministries and explore new challenges facing the Sinsinawa Dominican Congregation and demanding the attention of Mother Samuel. The demands of leadership, as always, were determined in part by the environment in which the Congregation functioned. World and national affairs helped to shape the responses.

In Europe, the high expectation of the people that the policies of Woodrow Wilson, as expressed in his Fourteen Points, would prevail in the postwar settlement was not realized. The Treaty of Versailles with the League of Nations as its centerpiece was adopted by the European powers but not by the United States. The Bolshevik Revolution in Russia in 1917 opened the way for a Communist dictatorship in Russia and Communist infiltration into other nations. The concept of national self-determination was flawed by the geographical reality of dispersion of national groups. The demand by France that Germany pay for war damages—a policy embodied in the Treaty through the formulation of the "War guilt clause"—and the refusal by the United States to forgive all or some of the loans it had made to the Allies undermined the economic stability of the various nations and opened the way to political and social problems.[1] The hope that the democratic structures created after the war would

---

[1]R.R. Palmer and Joel Colton, *A History of the Modern World* (New York: Alfred A. Knopf, 1966, pp. 694-703, *passim*. (Copyright now the property of McGraw-Hill, Inc.)

take root and flourish was undermined by these problems which bred revolution and led to the emergence of nationalist dictatorships.[2]

The United States underwent profound changes as a result of the war and its aftermath in Europe, though the magnitude of those changes was not fully appreciated until the passage of time gave adequate perspective. The United States replaced Great Britain as the world's leading creditor, a position that demanded new monetary and tariff policies on the part of the United States if stability were to be restored, policies that were not forthcoming. The war gave a new spurt to the Industrial Revolution with technological advances and organizational and administrative practices that stimulated business expansion in the 1920s. The intolerance bred of wartime hysteria increased in the wake of economic and social problems following the war. Communist infiltration following the Bolshevik Revolution reached the United States as early as 1919 and 1920. Agents of the Third International and other "radicals" became the objects of attack as labor disputes and other problems of postwar adjustment disrupted American life. Attorney General A. Mitchell Palmer, an enthusiastic "Red-hunter," launched raids against suspected radicals and anarchists, beginning in November 1919 and continuing into the late spring of 1920; he deported as many aliens as he possibly could until the hysteria began to subside and Americans gradually returned to their senses. Intolerance in other forms persisted throughout the 1920s, however. Campaigns for "100% Americanism," support for stringent immigration restriction, resurgence of the Ku Klux Klan, and Prohibition were the most significant manifestations of the revived anti-foreignism and anti-Catholicism of this decade.[3]

The 1920s saw a decline in idealism, due in some measure to the disappointment of expectations that World War I would be "a war to end all wars," a war "to make the world safe for democracy." Artists

---

[2]*Ibid.*, pp. 752-764, *passim.*

[3]John Higham, *Strangers in the Land: Patterns of American Nativism, 1860-1925* (New Brunswick, N.J.: Rutgers University Press, 1955), pp. 218-243.

and writers, dubbing themselves members of a "Lost Generation," were particularly disillusioned, and their influence contributed to the demoralization of the American people. The stress on material values, prominent in this decade of prosperity (though prosperity did not reach all levels), led to a subordination of human and spiritual values. Social disruption, intellectual currents, and materialistic concerns led to a rebellion against traditional moral values, a rebellion manifested in fads and fashions and an increased degree of libertinism.[4]

Mother Samuel had occasion to comment on incidents and trends that illustrate the general conditions described above. Her first experience in foreign travel, the trip to Europe in the late fall and early winter of 1920 (described in more detail below) introduced her to the poverty and disorder of postwar Europe. She described for some of her correspondents in Rome—Bishop Thomas Esser, O.P., Secretary for the Sacred Congregation for the Affairs of Religious; Thomas Cardinal Boggiani, Cardinal Protector of the Sinsinawa Dominican Congregation; Joseph Cardinal Pizzardo; and others—the conditions of bigotry under which the Church and its institutions in the United States labored. Of the latter, the effort of the state of Oregon to force all children to attend public schools was perhaps the most aggressive. The presidential campaigns of 1924 and 1928, especially the latter, brought anti-Catholicism to a high pitch.[5]

Some of the above conditions had a direct impact on projects with which Mother Samuel was associated. This was particularly true for the construction of Rosary College. The delays occasioned by the war and its political, economic, and social aftermath meant that ground-breaking did not occur until February 2, 1920. By delegation of Mundelein, Monsignor Francis Rempe, one of the Vicars of the Diocese, turned the first spade of dirt. Others present were: the pastors of Immaculate Conception and St. Jarlath Parishes; Mother

---

[4]Frederick Lewis Allen, *Only Yesterday* (New York: Harper, 1957), *passim*.

[5]Correspondence with Roman Officials, 1921-1929, *passim*; Mission Letters, Letter to the Sisters, October 21, 1928; Diary, November 7, 1928.

Samuel, Sisters Richard Barden and Ruth Devlin; the sisters of Rosary House and their 40 students; Mrs. Edward Hines, chairwoman of the Fund Drive, and her associate, Mrs. William S. Hefferan, wife of the college lawyer; and some newspaper reporters. The laying of the cornerstone on June 20, 1920, with Mundelein officiating, brought a large crowd, including 40 priests, 60 sisters, and 3000 lay people. During that same month, some of the women of River Forest organized the Rosary College Auxiliary, "to help promote educational and spiritual needs and play a part in furthering the interests of the Dominican Sisters in their plans for the building of a College in River Forest."[6]

For the next several months, construction proceeded at a fairly good pace. However, a strike in the spring of 1921 by the Chicago Builders' Association set off a string of labor stoppages that seriously delayed the project. A previously announced projection that the building would be ready for the 1921-22 school year had to be withdrawn.[7]

Overlapping the demands on Mother Samuel of the Rosary building project were her concern for the program in Fribourg and the welfare of the sisters there and the need to secure approval from Roman authorities of changes in the Constitutions to bring them into conformance with the 1918 English Edition of Canon Law (see page 84). For these reasons, she undertook a trip to Europe in the fall of 1920, taking Sister Ruth Devlin as her companion and appointing Sister De Ricci as vicaress during her absence. Their trip was made aboard the French liner, *Rochambeau*, which left New York on September 23, 1920, and arrived at LeHavre on October 3. Mother Samuel gave the following description of the trip in her diary: "The people on board have been nice to us. But the ocean experience was terrible for three days." The sisters succeeded in getting train

---

[6]Diary, February 2, and June 20, 1920; Sister Mary Eva McCarty, *The Sinsinawa Dominicans: Outline of Twentieth Century Development, 1901-1949* (Dubuque, Iowa: The Hoermann Press, 1952), pp. 202, 206-210.

[7]*Ibid.*, p. 209.

transportation the night of October 3 and reached Fribourg at 8:40 a.m. on October 4. Awaiting them at the station were Sisters Evelyn Murphy, Grace James, and Teresita Hessian; Sisters Rosemary Crepeau, Winifred Mary Carmody, and Barnabas McTighe were at the gate when they reached the Villa; Sister Laserian was preparing breakfast for them. After a day of rest, Mother Samuel visited the grave of Sister George Adamson in the company of Sisters Evelyn and Grace.[8]

During the next sixteen days, she made official visitation with the sisters, inspected the school, visited the University, met with the governing board, made trips to places of interest suggested by the sisters, such as the Benedictine Monastery of Einsiedeln, and Lucerne, at the latter place to express gratitude to the Dominican Sisters who had sent Sister Mary Charles to be with Sister Grace after the death of Sister George. Mother Samuel also had extended conversation with Mathilde Cortaux regarding the latter's interest in joining the Sinsinawa Dominican Congregation, a desire that was later fulfilled. Agreeing to return to Fribourg after their visit to Rome, Mother Samuel and Sister Ruth departed on October 21. They journeyed by way of Milan, Bologna, Venice, and Padua, visiting tombs and shrines along their route, particularly those associated with Dominican history. At Milan they saw DaVinci's "Last Supper"; at Bologna, the tomb of St. Dominic and the Church of San Domenico. In Venice, they rode a steamer on the Grand Canal and venerated the tomb of St. Anthony at Padua. They arrived in Rome on October 27.[9]

Mother Samuel's business in Rome primarily was to confer with Bishop Thomas Esser, O.P., on proposed changes in the Constitutions, as noted above. Esser's relationship with the Sinsinawa Dominicans reached back as far as the early years of the twentieth

---

[8]Diary, September 23-October 5, 1920; Correspondence with Sister DeRicci, October 2, 9, 1920.

[9]Diary, October 5-27, 1920; Correspondence with Sister DeRicci, October 10-27, 1920.

century, when he occasionally was welcomed to Sinsinawa by Mother Emily and, later, by Mother Samuel. After serving some years in Rome as Secretary for the Congregation of the Index, he had become a Consultor for the Sacred Congregation of Religious. Mother Samuel, the members of her Council, and other sisters appointed by the General Chapter of 1919 to assist them had been working on the revisions for more than two years. During this time they had been in consultation personally with Bishops James Schwebach of LaCrosse and John McNicholas, Mother Samuel's close confidant, who had been appointed Bishop of Duluth in 1918. Mother Samuel had kept Esser informed by mail.[10]

After the committee had completed its proposed revisions during the Christmas vacation of 1919-1920, Mother Samuel sent copies to all of the sisters, asking for their reaction to the proposed changes and what suggestions they would make. There was widespread approval of the proposal, but also some consideration of a more extensive revision. In the following weeks of early 1920, Mother Samuel and the Council began expanding on proposed changes, going beyond those related to conforming to Canon Law, including the addition of governmental changes that would provide representation at General Chapters of the sisters in convents of fewer than twelve sisters. The new projection included the reorganization of content, beginning with admission into the Congregation, followed by periods of training, profession, community life, ministries, etc. There were omissions of sections no longer appropriate, such as those on faults and customs. Material relating to liturgical practices—inclinations, ways of reciting the Office, etc.—was to be transferred to a separate document. Added were the enactments of the new Code of Canon Law and, included in an appendix, three documents of the Holy See on confession and Holy Communion. The section on dispensation was revised to show

---

[10]Diary, April 1918-June 1920, *passim*; Correspondence with Roman Offices, Bishop Esser to Mother Samuel, April 25, 1919.

more clearly its application to teachers and their needs. Provision was made for possible extension to ministries other than teaching.[11]

By the end of June 1920, Mother Samuel was working on proofs of the proposed revision; soon thereafter she sent a copy to Bishop Esser. Unfortunately, the parts of the existing Constitutions being replaced were not copied within the revised document. Instead, they were omitted, thus making it unclear what was new and what was part of the existing Constitutions. This circumstance led to confusion, pain, and worry as the process continued.[12]

Mother Samuel and Sister Ruth, tired as they were when they reached Rome on October 27, spent the first few days sight-seeing. A happy coincidence occurred on October 28 when they met Bishop Muldoon as they were visiting St. Peter's Basilica. Mother Samuel recorded for Sister DeRicci her first impression of Italy:

> . . . This is a sad country—soldiers everywhere, poor young soldiers who ought to be in school, some of them. No one has yet molested or annoyed us, but we have not been abroad in Rome. Travel is awful; people assemble in line two hours before train time to buy tickets; any number are sold regardless of the numbers in the car or off the cars. No one at the car step. 'Every one for himself and the devil take the hindmost.' a perfect scramble at every station. Can you picture us in the midst, with a heavy leather hand-bag each, Sr. Ruth with our roll of shawls, rubbers and umbrellas extra, and me with a lunch box? I have had to laugh outright often, even in the midst of these distresses, we cut such a funny, sorry figure. Travel in Europe! It may have been nice once.[13]

Bishop Esser was gracious, helpful in arranging an audience with Pope Benedict XV on November 10 and in suggesting other persons to meet and places to visit. Despite his busy schedule, he set aside

---

[11]Sister Mary Nona McGreal, O.P., *Concerning Dominican Constitutions*, Sinsinawa, Wisconsin, 1977, pp. 41-46.

[12]Diary, March-August 1920, *passim*.

[13] Letter, Mother Samuel to Sister DeRicci, October 1920.

time on five days to work with Mother Samuel on the Constitutions. The first meeting on November 5 was not auspicious. Esser had not read the copy of the revised Constitutions sent by Mother Samuel; the document he had at hand at the meeting was the revised constitutions of St. Mary of the Springs. When he brought out the Sinsinawa Dominican copy, he realized he had not read it at all. The remainder of the meeting was not encouraging. Mother Samuel reported as follows his observations:

He said the Congregation of Religious has made a law or regulation that Congregations shall present their Constitutions with their *Report*. Ours was not ready with our 1917 report. Rome now requires only reports once in *5 years*. He thinks we may present a report at the end of 3 years again with the revision of our Constitutions. Meantime, since our Institute is approved, we may continue to use our old constitutions, amending for ourselves the chief points required by the Code. However, he believes that the Master General will get out a Constitution for all 3rd Order Conventual Sisters,—the phraseology to be the same for the Sisters according to the work they do, and that we shall all have to use the same. Hence, he says, we may save money by this delay which seems so hard now. He read us some of the corrections he made in St. Mary's constitution. Some of these are also applicable to ours. We shall have another conference with him this week, and perhaps two or three more conferences, if he can spare time later, going over ours in detail. The wording of our Profession and that of the Profession as the O.P.'s have been making it, is not according to the Canons. It can be made *only to God.* I think St. Catherine has the new form. Some other faults he also found in the first part. I fear him; yet I feel he is correct on the Canon Law. The Decrees are not to be in the appendix; they are embodied in substance in the Constitutions. He advises against Intermediate Assembly as useless expense.

I asked what we could do for our Novitiate's immediate needs. He said we might use the one hundred copies we have had printed, noting in each copy the mistakes we have made against Canon Law. He thinks we may have to wait but one or two years.

I think now, that after we have finished these conferences for correction, I shall beg him to try to urge the Sacred Congregation to give us approval out of the regular course, if they will. But they may not listen to him, or he may fear to urge an irregularity. I cannot tell you how this weighs on my heart all the time. But we must keep our trust in God and *pray, pray, pray*. The delay may be providential even if it seems a calamity.[14]

Mother Samuel continued her letter with a question of whether she might extend her time abroad by going to Prouille and Lourdes and perhaps to England and Ireland, or should return as soon as possible to the States to attend to problems associated with the building of Rosary College. She asked Sister DeRicci to cable her in care of Sister Evelyn at Fribourg, using *Wait* if her return could be delayed, or *Hurry* if she should go immediately.

In conferences held by Esser with Mother Samuel on November 9, 11, 18, and 25, he dictated changes and she wrote them on her copy of the revised Constitutions which she sent to St. Clara by registered mail. She prepared a duplicate to carry with her on the trip home, letting Sister Ruth know where to find it if anything happened to Mother Samuel.[15] Word reached Mother Samuel on November 22 of the death of Sister Benedicta Kennedy on November 12. It was not a surprise, since word had come from Sister DeRicci earlier about Sister's serious fall; and she herself had said to Mother Samuel when telling her good-bye at the latter's departure from the Mound in September: "I will not be here when you return,."[16]

Mother Samuel and Sister Ruth left Rome on November 25, going by way of Assisi and Florence with Sister Teresita, who had spent some days in Rome and would be studying in Florence. On December 2, they continued their journey by way of Milan for Fribourg. In Milan they tried to get passage for New York but were

---

[14]Letter, Mother Samuel to Sister DeRicci, Rome, November 8, 1920.

[15]*Ibid.*

[16]*Ibid.*

unable to do so before December 19. Given this prospect, they realized that they could not get home for Christmas; since that meant that they could be with the sisters at Fribourg for the holidays, they took their side trip to Prouille and Lourdes before going on to Fribourg.[17]

When they reached Fribourg the evening of December 13, there was no word from Sister DeRicci in answer to Mother Samuel's instruction about cabling her. The cable finally came on December 15; it read: "Hurry; business needs you."[18] The earliest passage that could be arranged was for Christmas Day aboard the French liner, the *La Lorraine*, leaving LeHavre at 7:30 a.m. Following some rough days on the ocean, they arrived at New York City at 2:00 a.m. on Tuesday, January 4. After staying overnight with the sisters at Our Lady of Mercy Convent, they made their way to Chicago for an inspection of the Rosary building project and to visit sisters who were ill. Sisters DeRicci and Richard met them; late Saturday, Mother Samuel and Sister DeRicci took a train for East Dubuque, arriving at St. Clara at 12:30 a.m. on Sunday, January 9, 1921.[19]

In her letter reporting the above, Mother Samuel spoke of her gratitude: ". . . I have been busy learning all that has transpired and making plans for our needs. Sister DeRicci has told me over and over how good all the Sisters were, how you all tried to cooperate with her. I knew it could not be otherwise. And I wish here to express my appreciation and gratitude to Sister DeRicci for her excellent care of the affairs of the Congregation. Lack of Sisters to meet the needs of the several schools has been an acute anxiety."[20]

In this same letter she reported on what had transpired in regard to the Constitutions, a saga that remained unfinished for more than

---

[17]Diary, November, December 1920.

[18]Correspondence with Sister DeRicci.

[19]Diary, December 17, 1920-January 8, 1921; Mission Letters, Mother Samuel to the Sisters, January 21, 1921.

[20]*Ibid.*

five years, and then not to the satisfaction of Mother Samuel and the sisters of her Congregation. It was not until after Mother Samuel had left Rome that Esser became aware of the nature of the document on which he and Mother Samuel had been working. He was understandably upset, as is clear from his letter of December 5, 1920. In a reprimanding tone, he wrote:

Only now I have compared your new Constitutions with those already approved by the Holy See, and to my amazement I have found that they are not any longer the same, but that you have recast them completely. Why did you not ask me beforehand about the work to be done?

He warned her that the revised document would be viewed as a new set of Constitutions requiring all the steps of petition, provision of twenty copies in Latin, Italian, or French for submission to the Sacred Congregation of Religious. A similar message was given to Bishop Schwebach of LaCrosse, who informed Mother Samuel about it. Further action on the project was delayed because of all the confusion, all the "players," the death of Bishop Schwebach on June 7, 1921, Mother Samuel's illnesses, and the burden of her other work.[21]

Some hope regarding the Constitutions was revived in 1923 when Mother Samuel turned for help to Cardinal Thomas Boggiani, who had been appointed Cardinal Protector of the Sinsinawa Dominican Congregation in 1918. On June 15, 1923, she wrote to him as follows:

We have not yet had our Constitutions revised according to Canon Law. Our Constitutions received the first approval of the Holy See in 1888 and the Final Decree in 1893. When we attempted to revise our Constitutions in 1920, we found that very much must be changed and very much omitted, because there is in our Constitutions much that is obsolete,

[21]Correspondence with Bishop Esser, Esser to Mother Samuel, December 5, 1920, January 25, 1921, April 9, 1922; Diary, 1921-1922.

Bishop Thomas Esser, O.P.

Joseph Cardinal Pizzardo

Rosary College, 1924

Reigning Pontiffs during Mother Samuel's years of leadership. Pius X, Benedict XV, Pius XI, Pius XII.

historical and also much that properly belongs in a ceremonial, and the arrangement of chapter was not logical nor convenient. We sent to the Sacred Congregation a copy of the new tentative Constitutions as revised. We also had Bishop Esser review this tentative copy. The Bishop corrected many errors in it and gave us much valuable advice. The Sacred Congregation also found several errors and so much change from the first Constitutions that they advised us to keep the old Constitutions, but revise only what is necessary. We have tried to do this, but because of the many difficulties mentioned above we are not able to make a satisfactory revision.

We have corrected the other revised copy. I am sending the two different copies to your Eminence. Will you be so good as to present these copies to the Sacred Congregation for us? We beg the Sacred Congregation to reserve in the new book the Decree of First and Final Approbation of the old Constitutions, if this can be permitted.[22]

Boggiani responded promptly to Mother Samuel, expressing his interest in helping but pointing out that she should have included a letter to the Cardinal Prefect of the Sacred Congregation of Religious and cautioning her that the work would be delayed until a year from the coming August because of the holidays.[23] He assigned the task of following up on the status of the revision to Louis B. Nolan, O.P., an Associate of the Master General and a consultor for the Sacred Congregation for Religious with membership on the Commission for the revision of Constitutions. Though Boggiani continued to assure Mother Samuel that the matter was soon to be concluded satisfactorily, the reality was further delay. Father Nolan rejected the extensive revision of the Constitutions that Mother Samuel had initially provided and, instead, made a few changes in the original document of 1888. He explained his reasons in a letter to Mother Samuel on February 7, 1924:

---

[22]Correspondence with the Holy See, Mother Samuel to Cardinal Boggiani, June 15, 1923.

[23]*Ibid.*, Boggiani to Mother Samuel, July 2, 1923.

> . . . I must indeed confess that in revising your present Constitutions, I was very glad to find them so thorough and really needing so little alteration, and this especially because they breathe the spirit of your early days, and for this alone merit respect and veneration; they are besides more redolent of unction and the spirit of piety than those proposed (with all respect for the judgment, etc., of those who composed the latter). . . .[24]

Nolan later conceded that the matter of representation at the General Chapter could be adjusted by a Decree of the Sacred Congregation. His letter to Boggiani of March 6, 1924, explaining the process indicated that it would need the approval of the General Chapter before it could be submitted to the Sacred Congregation. Because it seemed urgent that the new rule on representation at Chapter become effective for the General Chapter of 1925, Mother Samuel renewed her efforts to get *some* reforms, though as the year went on she was forced to concede that the results would be minimal.

After making one last effort to convince Father Nolan that the thorough revision prepared in 1920 was preferable to the limited changes that he was willing to accept, Mother Samuel conceded to the drawing up of a petition for a Rescript that dealt primarily with matters of government. The changes required by Canon Law, such as those in the section on the Novitiate were incorporated into the text of the copies printed in 1924; the others were to be attached on each page where a change was granted. The Rescript was approved by Camillus Cardinal Laurenti, Prefect of the Sacred Congregation of Religious on April 23, 1925. Mother Samuel informed the sisters on May 27, 1925, of the outcome.[25]

The most significant part of the Rescript was the provision for representation at general chapters of sisters living in vicariates, convents of fewer than twelve sisters. Those sisters were to be united by the Mother General and her Council into groups of at least twelve

---

[24]*Ibid.*, Nolan to Mother Samuel, February 7, 1924.

[25]Diary, January 12, April 8, 1925; Mission Letters, Mother Samuel to the Sisters, May 27, 1925.

sisters "who shall elect from among themselves two delegates to the General Chapter . . . one from the Superiors and another not a Superior."[26] Among other changes were the moving of the date of the General Chapter from August to July in the year scheduled; the election by the vocals of the Chapter of the Bursar General and the General Secretary of the Congregation; the election of the Mistress of Novices by the Mother General and her Council instead of by the Chapter.[27]

Returning to her situation at the time of her return from Europe, we find Mother Samuel soon facing a personal worry in the form of the illness of her sister, Sister Benetta, in early March 1921. At that time she was prioress of the Convent of the Academy of the Sacred Heart in Washington, D.C., a position to which she had been appointed after Sister Evelyn Murphy was assigned to Fribourg.[28] Sisters Ruth and Richard accompanied Mother Samuel to Washington on the night train on March 4. The illness required surgery and several days of recuperation in the hospital. In the Annals, the sisters recorded their joy at her return to the convent by St. Patrick's Day.[29]

As had been the case before her trip to Europe, the Rosary building project dominated Mother Samuel's thoughts and emotions. If anything, the worries multiplied because of the increase of delays in construction and the slowness with which donations were being received. The burdens became critical for her in the spring of 1922, coinciding, it seemed, with the decision to take a loan in the form of a bond issue for $300,000, secured by a mortgage on St. Clara. The week following Mother Samuel's letter reporting this decision, Sister DeRicci informed the sisters of Mother's condition: "Mother returned from Chicago last week-end quite exhausted from loss of sleep. The

---

[26]Rescript, Rome, April 23, 1925.

[27]*Ibid.*

[28]Previous to this assignment, Sister Benetta had taught public school students in Jackson, Nebraska, for 25 years.

[29]Annals, Academy of the Sacred Heart, Washington, D.C., March 1921.

Doctor urges that she rests for ten days or two weeks or till such time as she will have recovered her Strength." The sisters were to write to Sister Ruth or Sister DeRicci if there was a need that would ordinarily go to Mother Samuel. Although she remained at the Motherhouse, she handled little or no correspondence and seldom had visitors. Her diary entries were very limited.[30]

A letter on July 7, 1922, to the sisters concerning retreats, started by Mother Samuel, had to be completed by Sister DeRicci with this message: "Dear Mother is unable to finish this letter and requests me to do so. I need only add that her recovery is very slow, you will, I am sure, pray daily that she may soon be restored to health. . . ."[31]

Mother Samuel's letter at the end of August seemed to indicate considerable improvement if not full recovery. She expressed her gratitude as follows:

> It is my duty to thank you humbly and most sincerely for the prayers and Masses offered for me during this past summer. From the beginning, I made the intention of giving all these spiritual helps back to the Congregation.
>
> It is also my duty to express through a general letter what a debt of gratitude and appreciation we all owe to Sister DeRicci for her prompt and efficient assuming of the heavy burdens of administration which this particular summer brought. No one except Almighty God knows the hard work, the constant strain of double responsibility and at times the anxiety and positive anguish of spirit required of her and others because of my illness. Similar gratitude is due to Sisters Richard, Ruth, Clare, Hyacintha, and Vincenza. God, through your prayers and cooperation, sustained them. The dear Home Sisters were a bulwark of support in every way. . . ."[32]

Among the blessings of Mother Samuel's recovery was her ability to be present at the opening of Rosary College. Despite its unfinished

---

[30]Mission Letters, Mother Samuel to the Sisters, May 15, 1922; Sister DeRicci to the Sisters, May 24, 1922; Diary, May-August, 1922.

[31]*Ibid.*, July 7, 1922.

[32]*Ibid.*, August 27, 1922.

state, which is described in vivid detail by Sister Eva McCarty,[33] the College opened its doors to students on Friday, October 6, 1922. Archbishop Mundelein had blessed the College the preceding Sunday, Rosary Sunday, October 1; the convent had been formally established on Tuesday, October 3, with the installation of Sister Hyacintha Finney as its first prioress, an office carrying with it the responsibilities of President of the College. During that week, the only buildings that were in any sense habitable were Mother Emily Power Memorial Hall, which served as the students' residence hall, and the service wing.[34] Still to be completed were the science building, the Mazzuchelli wing with social hall and dining hall on first floor and chapel and library on the second. The completion of the buildings over the next three years paralleled the implementation of the educational program, the receiving of accreditation from several agencies, the addition of religious, co-curricular, and social activities.

One of the reasons that Mother Samuel was able to cope with her responsibilities during the busy years described here was the the gift of a generous assistant. Sister Louis Bertrand Droege first met Mother Samuel on January 21, 1908, when the former entered St. Clara as a postulant. After she was professed, she first taught at St. Thomas High School in Rockford, Illinois. Most of her summers were spent at St. Clara, doing secretarial work for Mother Samuel. When she was assigned to Visitation High School in Chicago during the school year of 1919-1920, she spent week ends at Immaculate Conception Convent in Chicago, taking care of correspondence for Mother Samuel and Sister Ruth related to the Rosary College project. Sister Louis Bertrand concludes her summary of this part of her reminiscences with this observation: "At the close of the school year Mother Samuel said: 'Come Home, and bring your trunk with you.' Thus began an intimate association which lasted throughout the length of Mother Samuel's term of office as Mother General—July

---

[33]McCarty, Chapter XIV, pp. 216-246.

[34]*Ibid.*, pp. 217-223.

1949."[35] Sister Louis Bertrand served as her nearly constant traveling companion, taking care of dozens of errands in addition to her secretarial work. She was a woman of wit, wisdom, and humor, delighting all whom she met, thereby being a welcome visitor to any and all convents where she accompanied Mother Samuel.

There was a respite in the trend of accepting new parish grade and high school foundations during the early 1920s. Among the reasons, no doubt, were postwar building problems that affected parishes as well as Congregation-owned institutions. By 1923, the lull had ended with the opening of parish grade schools at St. Bernard, Wauwatosa, Wisconsin; St. Malachy, Geneseo, Illinois; Annunciation, Minneapolis, Minnesota; and Our Lady of Refuge, New York City. Visitation, Kewanee, Illinois, added high school classes and Freeport Catholic Community High School opened with the sisters who taught there in residence at St. Mary Convent. As is shown in the chart on page 112 in the remainder of the decade, at least one foundation was made each year except 1927.

A ministry new to the Congregation was begun in 1923 with the purchase of a site for a summer camp for girls on the shore of Green Bay near Marinette, Wisconsin. Sisters David O'Leary and Mary Christ initiated the search for this site after an inquiry from a parent. They and Sisters Evangeline Cleaveland and Englebert Dilger served as the "founders" of Camp We-ha-kee, named after Mary We-ha-kee LaBatte, the daughter of a Sioux mother at Faribault, who allowed the sisters at St. Clara to take the child as a ward at age five so she could escape the poverty of her home. She responded well to her educational opportunities and brought joy to other students and to the sisters until her death at age fourteen in 1878. The Most Reverend Paul Rhode, Bishop of Green Bay, was cooperative in providing for the religious needs of the sisters and the children by arranging with the Premonstratensian Fathers at West DePere,

[35]Papers of Mother Samuel, Reminiscences of Sister Louis Bertrand.

Wisconsin, for the appointment of a chaplain.[36] Building on a small foundation the first summer, the summer camp gradually grew in facilities and in number of campers, becoming a popular attraction for young Catholic girls.

Another undertaking of the mid-1920s that became widespread was the teaching of religion classes in rural areas during the summer time. Mother Samuel first began to promote this ministry in the Rockford Diocese in 1924 with the hearty endorsement of Muldoon. Further expansion is described in an address she gave at the Milwaukee chapter of the National Catholic Welfare Conference on October 13, 1926, wherein she also noted some questions that had arisen for consideration. Below are the major points she made:

> Our Sinsinawa Dominican Sisters, in the summer of 1924, conducted four religious vacation schools in the Diocese of Rockford, in 1925, about seven schools in the Dioceses of Rockford, LaCrosse, Milwaukee, and Green Bay; in 1926, eleven schools in the Dioceses of LaCrosse, Milwaukee, Green Bay, Rockford, and Omaha. During the last two years, in the Dioceses of Milwaukee and Green Bay the requests for Sisters came directly or indirectly to us from the women of the diocesan councils of the N.C.W.C. Twice as many and more requests came than we could spare Sisters to supply.
>
> Moreover, we have serious considerations in the following:
>
> 1. Will Rome approve of Sisters being out of their convents for three or four weeks each summer? That is a matter for Bishops to request Superiors to take up with Rome if the Bishops deem the cases warrant the dispensation, and if the Superiors think no laxity of observance will result. We have made a try-out, and found that it would be feasible for us for a limited and varying number of Sisters.
>
> 2. Does it seem necessary in this section of the country where Priests are not notably inadequate in number? While Sisters can reach little children's minds and hearts sometimes more effectively than some Priests can, the

[36]McCarty, pp. 485-486.

teaching of Christian Doctrine, in its essentials, is the province of the Priest.

3. The Sisters who teach in the Parochial Schools need a rest from their labors in summer. Some need to take summer school courses; then all make Retreat, and then comes the preparation for the new school year.

4. Can lay women and lay men, trained catechists, undertake these vacation religious schools?

5. It would seem that surveys conducted by the Right Reverend Bishops and the Priests in their own Dioceses with a view to meeting the problem through lay cooperation, will reveal whether or not the help of the teaching Sisterhoods is required. The needful dispensation or approval from Rome can be sought; and I am certain that the Sisters who daily immolate themselves on the altar of sacrifice for the privilege of helping in the work of the Church, will generously and joyfully assume this added duty at the command of ecclesiastical authority.[37]

In 1927, Mother Samuel took it upon herself to get approval from the appropriate authorities in Rome for the sisters to be out of their convents during the weeks they were teaching religious vacation schools, the Congregation's Cardinal Protector, Thomas Boggiani, facilitating the request. Rather than being a risk to their vocations, the sisters reported just the opposite on forms returned to the Motherhouse following the summer sessions. The ministry grew in number of places served and in geographical area throughout the 1920s and beyond.[38]

The middle years of the 1920s brought personal and family burdens to Mother Samuel at the same time as congregational responsibilities were multiplying. The year 1924 proved to be a difficult one. She seemed to anticipate something momentous as she indicated in her Diary on January 1: "May 1924 be the best of my life, full of repentance for my sins by increasing my sense of God's

[37]Papers of Mother Samuel, Talk Given at N.C.W.C., Milwaukee, October 13, 1926.

[38]McCarty, pp. 494-500.

presence, His justice and His mercy. . . ." She became ill in February and entered the Mayo Clinic at Rochester for a preliminary examination on February 13. One of the doctors advised surgery, but Dr. Charles Mayo did not think it necessary at that time. On this trip she visited her father in Faribault and found him weak and restless.

Her health did not improve when she returned to the Mound on February 17. Several days in bed did not improve her condition and the doctors scheduled an appointment for her again at the Mayo Clinic. Sister Maura accompanied her as they left for Rochester the evening of February 26. The next few days were filled with tests, surgery, radium treatments, all of which brought much suffering and fear, including anticipation of death. Though she knew she needed prayers, she asked Sister DeRicci not to tell the sisters about the surgery.[39]

She had just begun to recover from her ordeal when she received word on March 8 of the death of her father. Dr. Mayo gave her permission to attend the wake and funeral on March 10 and 11; she appreciated the gift of seeing ". . . my dear father in his coffin, peaceful in his Dominican habit."[40]

Mother Samuel returned to St. Clara by late March. She had informed the sisters by then of her surgery and in her letter of March 27 expressed her gratitude for their prayers and for the condolences sent to her and Sister Benetta on the death of their father.[41] By early April, Mother Samuel was back to a regular schedule of duties. She returned to Rochester for two weeks in June for a thorough check-up and a tonsillectomy.[42]

These months of her illness and the death of her father in 1924 overlapped the time of her disappointment with the progress of the

---

[39]Diary, February 26-March 5, 1924; Correspondence with Sister DeRicci, Mother Samuel to Sister DeRicci, Feb. 29, 1924.

[40]*Ibid.*, March 10, 1924.

[41]Mission Letters, Mother Samuel to the Sisters, March 27, 1924.

[42]Diary, June 1924.

revision of the Constitutions. In just a little over a year another general chapter would be held. Were she to serve again as Mother General, it would be necessary to secure a dispensation from the limitation to two terms prescribed in the Constitutions. The Chapter was held in July rather than August and representatives of vicariates were in attendance as well as those of priories, changes that had been approved by the Sacred Congregation of Religious on April 23, 1925.

There had been little if any discussion about reelection and dispensation, but Mother Samuel's Diary indicates it was very much on her mind. On the morning of the election, July 11, 1925, she wrote: ". . . General Chapter election at 9:30-10:00. Excruciating doubt; fear of not doing God's will, yet entirely insecure as to value of surrender. A few minutes peace in Chapel. . . ."

The outcome of the election was a vote of ninety out of ninety-two to postulate the return to office of Sister Mary Samuel Coughlin as Superior General for another term. The request was addressed to the Holy Father, Pius XI, whose permission was given to Camillus Cardinal Laurenti, Prefect of the Sacred Congregation of Religious, for relay by the Cardinal Protector, Thomas Boggiani, to the Bishop of LaCrosse, Alexander J. McGavick. The latter received the word from Boggiani by cablegram on July 30, 1925.[43] In her letter of acknowledgement to Boggiani, Mother Samuel indicated her reluctance to accept the office, writing in part:

> I am grateful to you for your kind offices in this matter; but I had sincerely hoped and prayed earnestly to God that I would not have to take this burden of responsibility again. There are many Sisters in our Congregation immensely better qualified to do this work than I am. I cannot feel entirely sure that it was not a mistake. However, I have tried to accept it in obedience and as from the Church authorities, and I shall trust in God to make up for my many defects and deficiencies. May I beg that

[43]Mission Letters, Report by Sister Ruth Devlin, Secretary of the Congregation, August 24, 1925.

you sometimes pray for me that God may help me to do what would be pleasing to Saint Dominic and to our Blessed Lady?[44]

Among items of unfinished business awaiting action by Mother Samuel following the Chapter, was consideration of a request from senior officials of the Vatican that an American Dominican Congregation of women consider establishing a foundation in Rome to provide housing and instruction for Catholic young women attending the university in Rome. The request that was initiated by Pierre Cardinal Gasparri, Vatican Secretary of State, was relayed by Joseph Cardinal Pizzardo, Assistant Secretary of State, to Bishop McNicholas in April 1925 and forwarded to Mother Samuel; in the same mailing he enclosed a similar request from Cardinal Mundelein (who had been made cardinal the preceding year). Her response showed great interest in such a project, though a decision would be delayed because of the pending General Chapter. The relevant paragraphs in her letter of April 29 are as follows:

Your letter with the two enclosures came as I was about to leave Sinsinawa. The letters from Rome interested me immensely. You know that I have hoped that we may some time have a house in Rome where Sisters could be trained in all the excellencies of the Dominican life and at the same time perfect themselves in the history and spirit of the Church. Then these same Sisters could be the leavening influence for the rest of the Congregation. I should love not only to have our own Congregation trained in this way, but also any other Dominican Congregations who could send Sisters to Rome. The other project of caring for university students could be used as a source of revenue for the maintenance of the Sisters.

Inasmuch as this matter will have to receive some very special deliberation, and especially since our General Chapter will convene perhaps about the first part of July, you will see a decisive answer cannot be given to you; but I am confident that the Chapter and whoever are elected to the various offices will be only too happy to consider the project and, even if

[44]Correspondence with the Holy See, Mother Samuel to Thomas Cardinal Boggiani, August 1925.

we have to beg for resources, I think they will be glad to beg. Do you think that an answer could be delayed until Saint Dominic's Day? Meantime, it is possible that two of our Sisters may be going to Europe and they could get some ideas of the location, etc., etc. I have been trying to visualize the Piazza Minerva. As I recall it, and as some of the other Sisters more definitely remember it, that location is rather congested and perhaps low and damp. Would not a place in the new section of Rome or on one of the hills be more likely to attract students or tourists, etc.? Kindly let me know whether this length of time to consider will be acceptable.[45]

Mother Samuel took up the matter again in August 1925, addressing the subject in the letter to Boggiani referred to above, in which she had thanked him for the confirmation of her election as Mother General. Her information to him was as follows:

Your Eminence knows that a request has come to us from the Secretary of State through Archbishop McNicholas and later through His Eminence George Cardinal Mundelein, requesting us to open a house for the boarding and instruction of Catholic young women who attend the university in Rome. We desire to help the Church and to obey the authorities of the Church with all our strength, and therefore it is my hope to go to Rome in September or October and look over the prospects and try to provide at least three or four Sisters to begin the work next year. I fear that we could not begin in November of 1925. However, we can tell better what to do when we know definitely what is expected of us.

Will you kindly communicate to His Eminence Cardinal Gasparri our humble acknowledgment of his request and our desire to serve the Church according to the wishes of our Holy Father Pope Pius XI? Our chief difficulty will be lack of money. We are very much in debt, as you know from our petitions, and we may have to contract still more debt in order to finish certain buildings. However, if this work in Rome is inspired by Almighty God, and it evidently is, He will provide the means. When I spoke to our Sisters assembled in Chapter concerning the Roman Foundation and told them that it would be difficult because of our need of

---

[45]Correspondence with John T. McNicholas, McNicholas to Mother Samuel, April 29, 1925.

money, one Sister arose and said, 'But Saint Dominic went to Rome without any money, and God blessed his work.' May He do the same for us his children.

Mother Samuel's trip to Europe was delayed until December 2, 1925, when she and her companion, Sister Mariola Dobbin left New York on an Italian liner, the *Colombo*. She had written to the sisters of the Congregation on November 22, informing them of her plans and of the status of the project for a "House in Rome." She asked the sisters to "unite . . . in praying to the Holy Ghost to enlighten us as to what decision will be God's Will for us. Recite each day the hymn, 'Come Holy Ghost,' on page 794 of our Office Book, for this intention and for our safe journey. We ought to be willing to beg and to suffer in order to take our part in the work of the Church for the salvation of souls. . . . The means will come, if this is God's design for us. If it is not His design for us, we want none of it."[46]

The voyage by way of Palermo and Naples was stormy, resulting in seasickness for both Mother Samuel and Sister Mariola. Sister Catharine Wall met them in Naples on December 15, and accompanied them to Rome where Sister Rosemary was waiting for them the following day. Sister Evelyn joined them on December 22. The language skills of the latter two were of great use for the business to be conducted in Rome.[47]

With Sister Rosemary translating, Mother Samuel met with Cardinal Boggiani a few days after their arrival. He brought up the subject of a house in Rome, advising them to proceed with caution and prudence, getting as much information as possible before making any decision. He advised requesting written data, though he was doubtful about obtaining it. He asked Louis B. Nolan, O.P., to assist the sisters in finding buildings to buy or purchase, or property on which to build.[48]

---

[46]Mission Letters, Mother Samuel to the Sisters, November 22, 1925.

[47]Diary, December 2, 1925-January 2, 1926, *passim*.

[48]Mother Samuel to Sister DeRicci, December 19, 1925.

On December 28, Mother Samuel, Sister Catharine, and Sister Rosemary ventured on their own to the Vatican where they met with Cardinal Pizzardo. He was anxious that the regimen be not too restrictive; he suggested that one or two Italian-speaking sisters would be sufficient at the beginning. In response to Mother Samuel's question about the attitudes of the Italians toward American sisters, he said that the students had much admiration for Americans. The university professors, he found, were neutral now, rather than anti-Catholic as they had been before the War. He offered to prepare data to help assess the prospects for a foundation, and he warned the sisters to "be cautious; learn everything possible; keep your eyes open, etc." Mother Samuel was very favorably impressed with him, describing him as follows: "He was precious, gentle, personally retiring like Abp. McNicholas, but eloquent and animated when speaking of the needs of the Church. When I see these animated small Italian Priests, I think of what Father Samuel must have been."[49]

The sisters met again with Boggiani on December 30. He expressed surprise about Pizzardo's offer to prepare data for the project. He himself acknowledged the need for such a ministry but thought Italian sisters would be best suited to undertake it. Their visit brought good results in the form of permission for borrowing $600,000 to support construction of Trinity High School in River Forest and the new high school building at Edgewood in Madison. Bishop McGavick of LaCrosse had advised that, because of the large sum involved, the Congregation would need approval from Rome. Formal documents for this were available within a week. Another favor was the arrangement of a private audience for the sisters with Pope Pius XI at 12:45 p.m. on January 2, 1926.

Mother Samuel spent almost four more weeks in Rome, seeking whatever information might be of help in arriving at a decision. Pizzardo and Nolan provided information about the Y.W.C.A.,

---

[49]*Ibid.*, December 28, 1925.

where some Catholic students were boarding. They also provided some leads on property that might become available. Pizzardo, however, had not yet provided the data he had promised by the time they left for Fribourg. They arrived there on January 27 and spent a month visiting the sisters, taking side-trips, and accomplishing business, such as the reorganization of the governing board of the Institute.[50]

Before going to England and Ireland, Mother Samuel returned to Rome to reassess the prospects regarding the foundation. A letter from Sister DeRicci warned that it would be unwise to invest in the project when the Congregation was already burdened with debt. Mother Samuel agreed that it was risky, but feared that an opportunity might not present itself again. She reported on a site that Father Nolan had found—"a 40-room house now being built, steam heat, gas, electric light, water, nice residence district, 4 stories plus dry basement divided into rooms for help, two blocks from street car, 12 min. ride from heart of Rome, and near the place to which the new plan of Rome places the new University." The price asked was $35,000. She had written Pizzardo to ask for more time to consider and for a letter from him authorizing the Congregation to solicit funds if the Holy See wanted the project to go forward. She suggested that he send the word to Boggiani. If all of this transpired favorably, she would ask Sister Catharine and someone else to be given the task of collecting $50,000 before there was a formal commitment to the undertaking. Pizzardo met with her and Nolan a few days later and promised to obtain a letter from the Holy See and forward it to Boggiani for her.[51]

In the midst of these plans and of arrangements for tickets for the trip to England and Ireland, Mother Samuel received the devastating message by cable on March 7 of the death of Mr. Kallal. He had been away from his work as City Architect for a few days, experiencing what he thought was an earache. During this time he

[50]Mother Samuel to Sister DeRicci, January 1926, *passim.*

[51]Mother Samuel to Sister DeRicci, Rome, March 2 and 9, 1926.

was able to meet with Sisters DeRicci and Richard about plans for the new Trinity High School. His last words to them as they thanked him for his generous giving of time and attention were: "Sisters, your problems are my problems and your interests are my interests." That night he became violently ill about 1:00 a.m. and was taken to the hospital; he remained in a coma for most of the day and night and died at 4:30 Sunday morning, March 7. The illness proved to be streptococcus, a deadly virus for which there was then no cure.[52]

Mother Samuel was deeply shocked, as she revealed in her Diary: "A cable was brought to us stating that 'Mr. Kallal died today.' A most distressing shock. Our best secular benefactor gone, and perhaps death hastened by overwork for us. My heart is sick. . . . Wrote Mrs. Kallal amidst tears." She was prepared to cancel her plans for the trip to England and Ireland and return to the States, but she decided that it would be unrealistic to attempt it.[53]

Mother Samuel and Sister Mariola went by way of Lourdes and Paris to arrive in London on March 27. They made side trips to Oxford and Liverpool as well as seeing landmarks in London. Early in Holy Week, April 5 and 6, they visited the sisters in Stone, England, the Congregation from which Mother Emily had received the Constitutions after which the Sinsinawa Dominicans modeled their document that was approved by Roman authorities in 1889. Their next stop was Dublin at the end of that week, followed by visits to Bantry and other sites in County Cork. Here Mother Samuel had an opportunity to visit her cousin Robert Kelly, whom she had not seen for 42 years. They boarded a small ship at Queenstown in order to make connections on the *Republic*, an American liner, at Cherbourg, where Sister Catharine boarded the ship to join them for the trip home. They docked in New York on April 19.[54]

---

[52]Mission Letters, Sister Theodosia to the Sisters, March 9, 1926.

[53]Diary, March 8, 1926.

[54]Mission Letters, Mother Samuel to the Sisters, May 10, 1926.

There was a surprising turn of events regarding the foundation in Rome a few weeks after Mother Samuel's return. In a letter dated May 24, 1926, which she received on June 11, Pizzardo had written:

> Through Mrs. Kuhn Steinhausen I have been informed that you await a letter from me confirming the invitation to come and establish here in Rome a Hostel for Catholic Girls frequenting the University, and at the same time giving authority to request, for this purpose in the name of the Holy See, financial assistance from the Catholics of America.
>
> I have to say, Reverend Mother, that circumstances in these recent times have necessitated, at least in part, a change in the first project, and an effort to try and meet the needs of these girls by other means.
>
> In any case I feel it a duty to inform you that the issuing of a letter on behalf of the Holy See authorising a collection, even for a purpose so worthy, but which concerns only a particular interest could appear not very convenient as the Holy See usually agrees to such a course only in case of great, general and urgent necessity.
>
> Thanking you for the excellent dispositions shown in your readiness to further our desires, and assuring you of my sincere esteem, I remain, dear Rev. Mother General,
>
> Yours very faithfully in Christ
> J. Pizzardo[55]

Mother Samuel was disappointed, hurt, and baffled, given her personal experience with Pizzardo in Rome. His abruptness and seeming change of mind may have reflected his experience of the preceding year, 1925, during which relations between the Church and Mussolini's Fascist party became tense. Pope Pius XI had declared 1925 a Holy Year, during which the canonization of St. Theresa of Lisieux in May was the high point of celebrations that brought hundreds of thousands of tourists to Rome. The Fascist leaders became nervous at the attention being brought to their efforts to suppress all political opposition, especially that represented by the

[55]Correspondence with the Holy See, Pizzardo to Mother Samuel, May 24, 1926.

Catholic Youth Movement. Pizzardo, appointed by the Pope to oversee all activities related to Catholic Action, had delegated direct supervision of the Catholic Youth Movement to Father Giovanni Battista Montini, the future Pope Paul VI; but the latter felt responsible for keeping his superior informed. In November of 1925, all political parties, except the Fascist, and all democratic groups, including the Catholic Youth Group, were outlawed. Later in the decade the Lateran Treaties supposedly settled outstanding difficulties between the Vatican and the Italian State, arrangements that proved inconsequential and shallow during the 1930s.[56] Mother Samuel still clung to the hope of eventually having a foundation in Rome, as her correspondence shows in the 1930s. But the setback of the mid-1920s was difficult to overcome.

Among major projects needing Mother Samuel's attention upon her return to the States in April 1926 were the building projects for Edgewood High School in Madison and Trinity High School in River Forest. These two projects that had been under discussion for a number of years paralleled one another in their construction from 1925 to 1927. The financing of the buildings was facilitated by the loans authorized through the petitions to Rome with the expectation that support from parishes in Madison and private donors in the River Forest area would defray the costs of borrowing. In return for the promise of financial support the Congregation agreed to admit boys at Edgewood High School. Expectations of such support were not met as fully or as rapidly as Mother Samuel and the members of Council would have liked.[57]

Associated with the expansion of secondary education at Edgewood was the organization of a junior college in 1927. Mother Samuel, Sister Grace James, Principal of Edgewood High School, and Sister Thomas Aquinas O'Neill visited with President Glenn Frank

---

[56]Peter Hebblethwaite, *Pope Paul VI: The First Modern Pope* (New York: Paulist Press, 1993), pp.88-106.

[57]McCarty, pp. 381-391; 404-405.

of the University of Wisconsin on April 6, 1927, about the project; the following day, Mother Samuel and Sister Baptist Sloan consulted Archbishop Messmer of Milwaukee. In both cases the response was positive.[58] Using the facilities of the older building until the new high school building was completed, the College opened on September 14, 1927, with eleven students, eight resident and three nonresident. Five more non-residents enrolled for second semester; the number increased gradually throughout the first decade of the College's existence.[59]

One more significant building project was being planned as the decade of the 1920s drew to a close—the construction of a classroom building at Rosary College through the generosity of Mr. and Mrs. William H. Lewis, in memory of their respective mothers. Mr. Lewis conveyed the news of this substantial benefaction to Mother Samuel in person on February 10, 1929.[60] Mother Samuel continued to follow the activities of members of her family, including nieces and nephews as well as brothers and sisters. She frequently had occasion to travel to Faribault and places further north and usually managed short visits with them. She corresponded regularly with her niece, Mary Coughlin, who taught in the public high schools of Minnesota during the 1920s. Mary's brother, Daniel Martin, taught English and ancient history and coached the athletic teams at the Cathedral High School in Duluth, Minnesota. In one of his letters to Mother Samuel, McNicholas, then the Ordinary at Duluth, proudly reported: "His boys have not lost a game this year."[61] A third member of that same family, Bernard Coughlin, attended the University of Notre Dame from 1922-26, graduating from there before entering the seminary. He played on the football team three of those years as teammate of the famed "Four Horsemen," a metaphor coined by the reporter,

---

[58]McCarthy, p. 426; Diary, April 6 and 7, 1927.

[59]Annals, Sacred Heart Convent, Edgewood, 1927-1938.

[60]Diary, February 10, 1929.

[61]Correspondence with Bishop McNicholas, October 30, 1922.

Grantland Rice, at a game between Notre Dame and Army on October 19, 1924.[62] Mother Samuel sometimes had an opportunity to listen to broadcasts of the Notre Dame games, as she and other sisters would join Father Kavanaugh around the radio in his study.[63]

Early in the 1920s, Mother Samuel began the practice of writing resolutions or reflections in her Diary every New Year's Day or the day before. Her entry on December 31, 1929, was as follows: ". . . 1929 is passing tonight. I have heard perhaps 450 Masses and received 350 Holy Communions. O *how* good is God! What a wretch, a fool, am I!"

The themes of these entries—the majesty and goodness of God, her unworthiness and need for mercy—were echoed again and again during the ensuing years of depression and war.

---

[62]The four players were Harry Stuhldreyer, Don Miller, Jim Crowley, and Elmer Layden.

[63]Sports Information Center, University of Notre Dame; Diary, January 1, 1925.

Table IV

Schools (Missions) Accepted by Sinsinawa Dominicans, 1921-1930

Name of School (Mission)	Place	Year Opened	Type of Mission
Rosary College	River Forest, IL	1922	College
St. Bernard	Wauwatosa, WI	1923	Parish Gr. School
St. Malachy	Geneseo, IL	1923	Parish Gr. School
Freeport Catholic	Freeport, IL	1923	Parish High School
		Srs. Lived at St. Mary	
Visitation	Kewanee, IL	1923	Began High School
Annunciation	Minneapolis, MN	1923	Parish Gr. School
Our Lady of Refuge	New York, NY	1923	Parish Gr. School
Camp We-Ha-Kee	Marinette, WI	1923	Summer Camp
Blessed Sacrament	Sioux City, IA	1924	Parish Gr. School
St. Mary	East Dubuque, IL	1924	Parish Gr. School
Blessed Sacrament	Madison, WI	1924	Parish Gr. School
		Srs. Lived at Edgewood	
St. Barnabas	Chicago, IL	1925	Parish Gr. School
St. Mary (Succeeded Benedictine Sisters)	Champaign, IL	1925	Parish Gr. School and High School
St. Augustine S.	St. Paul, MN	1925	Parish Gr. School
Our Lady of Mercy	New York, NY	1926	Began H.S. Classes
St. Rose of Lima	Baltimore, MD	1926	Parish Gr. School
Trinity	River Forest, IL	1926	H.S., new location
St. Giles	Oak Park, IL	1928	Parish Gr. School
St. Patrick	Rockford, IL	1929	Parish Gr. School

St. Joseph Academy, Bloomington, IL closed in 1924 because Trinity, the Parish High School, was able to accommodate the students.

Source: Book of Foundations, Sinsinawa Dominican Archives.

Chapter Six

The 1930s: Decade of Depression

As Mother Samuel Coughlin entered her third decade of leadership of the Sinsinawa Dominican Congregation, she had little expectation of the radical changes in world and national affairs that would be brought on by the depression. The events of the 1920s—those associated with regular responsibilities and those occurring because of unique developments—had been demanding on her energies; the 1930s would bring no respite. The Stock Market Crash of October 1929, identified in retrospect as the beginning of the Great Depression, was not universally recognized as such at the time. Within a few months, however, Americans watched with growing amazement and discouragement the ricocheting developments that brought the nation and the world to the brink of disaster.

The dimensions of the crisis on a world scale are described by R. R. Palmer and Joel Colton:

> The crisis passed from finance to industry, and from the United States to the rest of the world. The export of American capital came to an end. Americans not only ceased to invest in Europe, but sold the foreign securities that they had. This pulled the foundations from under the postwar revival of Germany, and hence indirectly of much of Europe. Americans, their incomes falling, ceased to buy foreign goods; from Belgium to Borneo people saw their American markets slip away, and prices tumbled.
>
> In 1931 the failure of a leading Vienna bank, the Creditanstalt, sent a wave of shivers, bankruptcies, and business calamities over Europe. Everywhere business firms and private people could not collect what was owed them, or even draw on money that they thought they had in the bank. They could not buy, and so the factories could not sell. Factories slowed down or closed entirely. Between 1929 and 1932, the latter year representing the depth of the depression, world production is estimated to have declined by 38%, and the world's international trade fell by two-thirds. In the United States the national income fell from 85 to 37 billion dollars.

Unemployment, a chronic disease ever since the war, now assumed the proportion of pestilence. In 1932 there were 30,000,000 unemployed persons statistically reported in the world; and this figure did not include the further millions who could find work only for a few hours in the week, or the masses in Asia or Africa for whom no statistics were to be had. The worker's wages were gone, the farmer's income now touched bottom; and the decline of mass purchasing power forced more idleness of machinery and more unemployment. Men in the prime of life spent years out of work. Young men could not find jobs or establish themselves in an occupation. Skills and talents of older people grew rusty, young people found no opportunity to learn. Millions were reduced to living, and supporting their families, on the pittances of charity, doles, or relief. . . .

People were crushed in spirit by a feeling of uselessness; months and years of fruitless job-hunting left them demoralized, bored, discouraged, embittered, frustrated, and resentful. Never had there been such waste, not merely of machinery which now stood still, but of the trained and disciplined labor force on which all modern societies were built. And people chronically out of work naturally turned to new and disturbing political ideas.[1]

By the late fall of 1930, the depression was encroaching on the lives of many millions of Americans, including the sisters, their families, the children they taught and the families of those children. In her letter to the sisters of December 9, 1930, announcing the beginning of the Christmas novena, Mother Samuel pleaded for special concern for the material and spiritual needs of the nation. She wrote in part:

. . . alas, what atmosphere and motives for a fervent novena our time and circumstances provide! Our dear country, the richest on earth, exhibits these days the sad contrast of luxurious wealth and stark poverty in close range of each other, as did the Roman world when Our Infant Saviour came to teach true fraternal charity. God is forgotten, denied, or His

---

[1]R.R. Palmer and Joel Colton, *A History of the Modern World* (New York: Alfred A. Knopf, 1965), pp. 780-781. This material is reproduced with permission of McGraw-Hill, Inc.

greatest truths are unknown to five-sixths of our people. And we ourselves, like His chosen race in Judea, are perhaps too much concerned with perishable ambitions, vain earthly desires and projects, to make room for the Divine Infant in our hearts or to follow the star which through our vows leads us to joy and peace at His crib.

We are now given these unusual though sad opportunities of serving the poor, directly or vicariously. We can beg our pupils who have means, to bring of their abundance to the homes of the poor or to the church for the poor. We can ourselves save and limit even our own modest requirements in material things and ask our Superiors to give that much to some one in want. We can serve our Congregation in its need by mortifying ourselves in like manner. We can come before the Tabernacle each evening, each morning at Mass and plead with the most merciful Heart of Jesus to have mercy on the newly poor, the discouraged honest workmen who daily seek employment in vain, the mothers whose hearts are rent by the prospect of dire want in their homes, the children actually hungry. Children starving in the United States! Can we bear to hear that sentence. Let us beg Our Lord, who was once a child and who probably was hungry even as a child as well as when a grown man, to have pity on these innocent suffering brethren of His, to work miracles for them. . . .[2]

During these years of world and national emergency due to the depression, Mother Samuel also experienced some personal trials. The most serious was the injury she sustained just a little more than a week after writing the above letter. On Thursday evening, December 18, 1930, shortly after her arrival for visitation at St. Robert Convent, Shorewood, Wisconsin, she tripped at the middle landing of the stairs between the second and first floors. Her fall caused the dislocation and fracture of her left shoulder, just below the socket. A doctor who lived in the parish took her to the hospital, had an X-ray taken that revealed only the dislocation, which he reset. After a night of great pain, Mother Samuel had further X-rays on Friday, which showed the more extensive damage. She asked to be taken to Rochester. After consultation by telephone with physicians there, Sister Maura Cotter

---

[2]Mission Letters, Mother Samuel to the Sisters, December 9, 1930.

and Sister Harriet Donoghue took her by train Friday night, arriving the next morning at St. Mary Hospital, Rochester. Surgery was performed over the weekend, and Sister Maura reported by telephone on Monday, December 22, that "the patient was doing as well as could be expected."[3]

Sister DeRicci, who provided the information noted above, closed her letter with these words:

> This is hard, coming especially near the eve of Christmas. The interruption in Mother's work relative to the business connected with the Missions may make for inconvenience, even disappointment. On the other hand, we may be grateful that her accident was not more serious. The delay may be caught up by the new semester, February lst. You will, I am sure, pray for Mother's speedy recovery. If the sentiments expressed in her recent Christmas letter to the Sisters be heeded, then each and every one of us will enjoy a holy, happy Christmas. May this be a reality for each Sister.[4]

Mother Samuel's time of recuperation proved to be much longer than first projected. Sister Harriet was with her throughout her entire stay from December until the end of April, taking the night shift while one of Mother Samuel's nieces cared for her in the daytime during the critical first days. Sister Harriet wrote every day to Sister DeRicci, letters that reveal the pain and worry that Mother Samuel suffered. In addition to the physical discomfort, she expressed concern over the expense, her "uselessness," the extra burden of work for Sister DeRicci, concern about the expense and construction delays in the Lewis Memorial Hall project at Rosary College.[5]

By mid-February, Sister Harriet was expressing optimism in her letters that Mother Samuel's condition was improving significantly. In early March, however, she reported that the doctor was recommending additional surgery. The hope that new bone tissue would

---

[3]*Ibid.*, Sister DeRicci to the Sisters, December 22, 1930.

[4]*Ibid.*

[5]Correspondence with Sister DeRicci, Sister Harriet to Sister DeRicci, December 1930-March 1931, *passim.*

grow between the shoulder bone and the bone in the upper arm did not materialize. Sister DeRicci and Sister Maura went to Rochester to be present for the new surgery on March 19. This proved to be successful and Mother Samuel's progress was steady from that time until her dismissal and return to the Mound on April 30, 1931.[6]

The entry in the Annals of St. Clara Convent for that day describes the happiness with which Mother Samuel was greeted:

> Deferred expectations of welcoming Mother Samuel back from the Rochester hospital kept all anxious during the first three months of this year, and it was not until the eve of St. Catherine's Day that we were finally assured of her coming next morning. Appropriately, she arrived with Sister M. Harriet, nurse, just as dawn was breaking. It was truly a new day for Saint Clara, the mists of fear and anxiety dispelled, the sun of hope and confidence rising. She was able to take her accustomed place in choir that beautiful Feast Day morning for Mass, so joy and thanksgiving filled the Sisters' hearts. . . .[7]

Mother Samuel was still somewhat limited in her mobility after her return to the Mound. Her left arm remained strapped to her side for a time, and only on June 22 was she able for the first time since her fall to dress herself without help. She spent several days in Rochester in October for some "repair" treatment and had therapy for the shoulder in January 1932 in Dubuque, a practice that would recur periodically thereafter.

Despite her long ordeal with the injured shoulder, there was no evidence of any discussion about her not being re-elected at the general chapter in July. On July 11, she received 83 out of the 88 votes cast; the forms for postulation for dispensation from the constitutional limitation on terms were sent to Rome; confirmation was received on August 14. Her diary entries for these days seem to show less agitation on her part than had been the case in the three

---

[6]*Ibid.*, March and April 1931; Sister DeRicci to the Sisters, March 19, 1931.

[7]Annals, St. Clara Convent, April 30, 1931.

preceding elections, though she still expressed feelings of "fears and doubts" known only to God.[8] Her Diary and letters at this time do not show her as having consulted McNicholas, which had been a regular practice at the time of previous elections.

A happier experience during these years, though one to which Mother Samuel seldom, if ever, referred, was the awarding to her by Loyola University on June 8, 1932, of an honorary degree of Doctor of Laws, conferred by Robert M. Kelley, S.J., President of the University. The citation read on that occasion is as follows:

> Mother Mary Samuel Coughlin, as Mother General of the Dominicans of Sinsinawa for twenty-two years, has merited distinction for her great contribution to the education of Catholic youth. During her more than two decades as Superior General she has with marked success carried on the organization of the faculties for more than six score grade schools, high schools and colleges. Twelve hundred sisters, yearly, receive their teaching appointments at her hands.
>
> Among the notable works inaugurated under her inspiration may be mentioned the founding of Rosary College, at River Forest; the establishment of the internationally accredited College for foreign study, at Fribourg, Switzerland, a Junior College and several high schools.
>
> Deprived of the public plaudits that come to great educational administrators, she is called forth today from the recesses of her almost cloistered life for gracious and generous recognition, because she is an outstanding representative of the splendid, magnanimous, and truly devoted service in the interests of God and Catholic womanhood exemplified in the Sinsinawa Dominican Sisters.
>
> Because she is a builder, a skillful administrator and an enlightened and devoted educator, I present MOTHER MARY SAMUEL COUGHLIN for the degree of Doctor of Laws.[9]

As the depression lengthened and intensified through 1932, Mother Samuel instructed the sisters in nearly every general letter she

---

[8]Diary, July 11, 1931.

[9]Honorary Degree, Loyola University, SDA, Papers of Mother Samuel Coughlin, Box 4.

wrote how to respond to the needs of the poor and of the congregation. Her letter of May 15, 1932, had several paragraphs of suggestions, summarized in the following paragraph:

> I cannot stress too strongly our absolute need of practicing community and personal economy for the coming year and as long as God permits our revenues to continue going down steadily. Few, if any, of us truly realize the appalling financial condition around us and our need of saving to meet from our reduced funds the interest on $1,000,000 and payments of $100,000 on principal the coming year. If we each sensed the situation as it is, our loyalty and magnanimity would make us wear patched clothes and old shoes (always polished) and reduce our personal expenditure to a minimum resembling the poverty of our holy Father Saint Dominic. Please give this matter your serious thought. Our finances are very personally every Sister's duty and obligation. I know that your hearts are loyal, your wills devoted. All you need is to realize how much you yourself can help.[10]

In September, her "opening of the school year" letter listed several ways the sisters could economize, such as:

- bi-weekly meetings of superior, business officer, and cook to plan meals and purchase food as economically as possible;
- wear habits two weeks instead of one before laundering;
- avoid lavish foods for feasts, parties, etc.;
- take out extension phones;
- save on stationery and postage by use of light-weight paper, combining letters being sent to the Motherhouse, etc.;
- use plain toilet soap and use salt or soda for cleansing teeth;
- make clothing and shoes last longer by taking good care of them.

To help the pastor save parish funds, Mother Samuel urged the sisters to save on water; economize in the use of gas and coal; reduce costs of electricity by studying by daylight or in the community room at

[10]Mother Samuel to the Sisters, May 15, 1932.

night, and use the radio only for *unusually profitable broadcasts*; and take scrupulous care of the furnishings of the convent and school buildings.[11]

Mother Samuel's practicality in proposing ways of saving money during the times of crisis was matched by her eloquence in pleading for spiritual applications. Early in January 1933, she wrote as follows:

The year 1933 has dawned upon a suffering and depressed world. Everywhere the value of material things grows less and less, as fortunes crumble and opportunities for employment cease. Millions have not enough money to buy the necessities of life, even though abundance of food and clothing at lower prices invite purchase. Other countries less favored than ours are suffering more acutely. One feels the depression as a pall over the whole earth. It would seem that the Hand of God has been extended over the world in reproval for our too great love of earthly and transient goods and our forgetfulness of Him and our eternal destiny. Our Holy Father the Pope and our other great spiritual leaders interpret this universal visitation as a result of sins, especially greed, injustice, luxury, and the ignoring of recognized or recognizable spiritual realities.

Can we who are Catholics and religious be entirely sure that we have had no part in these sins which bring their own terrible chastisement? Is our conduct consistent with our faith? Is God the abiding thought of our lives and His law our constant guide? Do we value money and its equivalents more than we cherish grace and virtue? Is our practice of poverty always so generous that no waste, no petty greed, no habitual ill-ordered self love challenges us as injustice to our Congregation, our individual Sisters, or the poor? Have we wasted or ill-used our time, that precious price of a happy eternity?

We would be remiss in our duty as religious if in this crisis for the Church and the world, we failed to stir up the grace of God within us and like our Holy Mother Saint Catherine offer ourselves as victims of expiation for our own sins first and then for the sins of others.

In this spirit then, dearest Sisters, I ask you in the Name of Our Lord, and His compassionate tender Mother, to recite fervently in community

---

[11] *Ibid.*, September 5, 1932.

daily one extra Rosary, the sorrowful mysteries, that God may lift this depression, as He alone can, and give to His children the world over, faith and charity, peace, plenty and prosperity. . . . If a Sister is absent from this extra Rosary will she please recite it privately, so that our contribution may be about twelve hundred Rosaries daily? Let us each add one special daily act of corporal or spiritual mortification. Hundreds of opportunities offer themselves daily in regard to food, physical comfort, control of tongue or custody of the eyes, ears, etc. But let our one act for this intention be a very definite and deliberate offering. . . .[12]

The inauguration of Franklin D. Roosevelt on March 4, 1933, followed by a vigorous legislative program during his first "100 days" helped place the nation on the road to recovery from the depression. The *relief* measures of those days were succeeded by programs of *recovery* and *reform* that restored stability to the nation and merged with efforts in Europe to improve conditions abroad. The need for economizing in whatever ways possible was by no means over but the grave anxiety that had prevailed since 1930 was mitigated. Mother Samuel could give more of her time and attention to regular duties and long-range interests of the Congregation than had been the case for three years.

Among setbacks of those three years were the limitation on new foundations and cutbacks in staffing of existing missions. In 1929 St. Patrick Grade School in Rockford was opened. Between that date and 1933, only one new grade school was accepted—St. James in Atlantic City (later Ventnor), New Jersey. During that same period, closings of high school departments occurred at Visitation, Kewanee, St. Mary, Champaign, and Eagle Grove, Iowa. The sisters withdrew from the high school ministry in Rockford in 1932-33, though for reasons not entirely due to economic hardship. Following the death of Bishop Muldoon in the fall of 1927, his successor, Edward F. Hoban, chose to replace the coeducational system with two separate schools, the one for the boys to be taught by teaching Brothers. The

---

[12]*Ibid.*, January 23, 1933

process over three years of reorganization and building added to the debt of the diocese and prompted Hoban in August 1932 to offer to sell the convent and the new girls' high school building to the Sinsinawa Dominicans for $160,000. After careful study and prayer, Mother Samuel, Sister Alexia Tighe, the principal, and the members of the General Council, determined that the Congregation could not afford the purchase, given the severity of the depression and other obligations pending. In October Hoban informed Mother Samuel of his decision to sell the properties to the Adrian Dominican Congregation, a transaction that took place during the 1932-33 school year, the final year of the ministry that had begun in 1910.[13]

By 1933, the Congregation was once again being requested to staff parish grade schools, and, as shown in the chart on page 137), at least one was accepted each year through 1940, except for 1937. Another high school, St. Mary, Cheyenne, was also added.[14]

Among the new foundations, some were designed to serve special needs. The Reverend George B. Ford of Corpus Christi Parish in New York City, requested sisters for the organization of a curriculum requiring techniques new to the world of elementary education. Working closely with instructors in the School of Education at Columbia University, the sisters, under the leadership of Sisters Vivian Doran and Joan Smith, provided a laboratory school that was "the talk of the town," open to visitors that came by the dozens. Mother Samuel frequently visited the convent and school and received frequent letters from Father Ford, requesting changes in staffing.[15]

During that same year, 1936, another venture new in character for the Sinsinawa Dominicans was undertaken at Columbia, South Carolina. At the request of the Reverend Thomas L. Weiland, O.P.,

---

[13]Sister Mary Eva McCarty, *The Sinsinawa Dominicans: Outlines of Twentieth Century Development, 1901-1949* (Dubuque: The Hoermann Press, 1952), pp. 368-375. The ministry would be taken up again by Sinsinawa Dominicans in the 1980s.

[14]Book of Foundations, 1933-1940.

[15]McCarty, pp. 326-330; Correspondence with Pastors, George B. Ford to Mother Samuel.

pastor of the Mission of Blessed Martin de Porres, established in 1935 by the Dominican Fathers of St. Joseph Province for African-American Catholics, Mother Samuel and her Council agreed to assign three sisters to teach the first six grades of school—Sisters Andrea Bracken, Marie Therese McGreevy, and Marie Carmel (Marie Therese) Janke, who moved in on September 26, 1936. On Thanksgiving Day, Sister Sean O'Brien arrived to assist with housekeeping duties. The costs of the new mission were covered by the Congregation. The endeavor elicited enthusiastic support in the form of volunteers for staffing, furnishings for school and convent, and monetary donations. The excerpt below from a letter by Mother Samuel to Father Weiland on November 15, 1936, gives some insight into the reasons for her interest in the mission at Columbia:

> While you have few parishioners, dear Reverend Father, you may nevertheless be very hopeful for the future. You are giving these dear people what the metropolitan Dominican churches are giving their parishioners—all the spiritual helps that the Order and the Church provide and permit and Almighty God's blessing must come upon your fidelity and generosity in this spiritual activity. Gradually, I think that through the children's interest in Catholicity, parents will be drawn to come to church and to take an interest in the spiritual life as proposed to them by the Church. It will take time, but even one or two converts a year will mean much for the Church and for Our Blessed Lord, who puts such priceless value upon each soul.[16]

Mother Samuel's interest in ministry for African-American children was further evident in her response to a request by the Reverend James M. Preuss, S.J., pastor of St. Benedict Parish in Omaha for two sisters to begin high school classes at the school taught by the Sisters of Mercy. In 1938 Sisters Emery Tousignant and Martin de Porres Hogan began the first two years of classes while in residence at Sacred Heart Convent, Omaha. A third year was added in 1939 and a fourth in 1940. Attendance was always small

[16] *Ibid.*, pp. 330-334.

because of the attraction of fuller programs in the public high schools. It was a drain for the Congregation to provide personnel for such a small number of students. For these reasons the school was closed in the mid-forties.[17]

Still another school for African-Americans was started in 1940 at St. Peter Claver Parish in Oklahoma City. Sisters Agatha Lyons and Francile Holohan were assigned to teach four grades in the beginning. Though the enrollment was small and the undertaking was beset by problems arising from prejudice, the pastor and the Congregation weathered the storm, adding grades and providing necessary staffing as enrollment increased.[18]

In keeping with her interest in responding to needs identified by the Church, Mother Samuel guided the Congregation in a limited extension of ministry during the 1930s. The teaching of catechism in rural areas during summer vacation continued to flourish. In 1936 another type of service was undertaken for children in a vastly different setting. In collaboration with the Catholic Youth Organization in Chicago, directed by Bernard J. Sheil, Auxiliary Bishop of the Diocese, Mother Samuel began assigning Sinsinawa Dominican Sisters to assist in supervising summer recreational activities for city children, who otherwise would have found it difficult to occupy their time in a beneficial way. The programs included craft classes, gymnasium activities, outdoor sports, singing, story telling, and movies. Formal religious instruction was not given but the presence of the sisters sometimes led to inquiries by parents about the religious upbringing of their children. The Congregation continued its participation in the Chicago program throughout the 1930s and 1940s, assigning as many as fifteen sisters each summer. Similar programs in New York City also were staffed by Sinsinawa Dominicans.[19]

---

[17] *Ibid.*, pp. 387-389.

[18] *Ibid.*, pp. 343-345.

[19] *Ibid.*, pp. 502-506.

Another "summer ministry" that took root beginning in the 1930s was the Catholic Evidence movement. It was associated with the broader activities of the Society for the Propagation of the Faith and was centered at Rosary College where the Reverend Reynold Hillenbrand taught classes to prepare students for participation in the work in "priestless" areas of Oklahoma, North Carolina, and Louisiana. In addition to their speaking to and answering questions from assembled groups, the students and the sisters who served as their chaperones provided religious instruction on a one-to-one basis or in small classes.[20]

Another important extension of ministry during the 1930s was the increase in programs during the school year for religious instruction to children in public schools. In almost all parishes where the sisters served, there were such programs and many small parishes and mission churches that did not have parochial schools were served by programs on Saturdays and Sundays.[21]

The combination of interests held by Mother Samuel personally and among a growing number of sisters of the Congregation during the 1930s—that of concern for ministry to African-American children and their families and participation in catechetical instruction—helps explain the acceptance of a new mission in Cincinnati in 1938. The fact that the request came from Archbishop McNicholas was also a factor. As part of the concern of the Church for evangelization of the African-Americans, the Diocese of Cincinnati had organized a new parish, to be known as Mother of God, for that ministry. There would be no school, but McNicholas wished the sisters to organize a catechetical program for children and also teach some classes for adults. The sisters assigned to the new mission, arriving in late summer, 1939, were: Sisters Kevin Reidy, Borromeo Smith, Vianney

---

[20]*Ibid.*, pp. 477-479; see also Debra Campbell, "Part-Time Female Evangelists of the Thirties and Forties: The Rosary College Catholic Evidence Guild," *U.S. Catholic Historian*, V, Summer/Fall, 1986, 371-383.

[21]McCarty, pp. 501-502.

de Young, and Alain McGillicuddy. In addition to implementing successfully the projects proposed to them, the sisters provided individual religious instruction for adults, held kindergarten classes each weekday morning, and collected and dispensed food and clothing for the poor. They were available at any time of the day or night to provide advice and comfort to people who were hurting.[22]

Another endeavor of a nature different from the regular ministries of the Congregation was the association with the Institutum Divi Thomae, a project proposed and implemented by Dr. George S. Sperti with the support and encouragement of McNicholas in Cincinnati. The stated goal of the Institute was to promote scientific research under the auspices of the Catholic Church that would be rooted in the principles of Catholic philosophy. The basic thesis, as communicated to Mother Samuel, was "that God would reveal the laws of nature imposed by Him more readily to minds and souls nourished daily by His Sacred Body and Blood and by attendance at the Holy Sacrifice of the Mass, than to those who know Him not or who, knowing Him, ignore Him."[23] In the practical implementation of the program, however, the search for a cure for cancer was paramount and the assignment of projects was intimately related to that goal.[24]

After several years of preparation, the Institute was ready to accept sisters in 1936. With vigorous encouragement from McNicholas, Mother Samuel assigned Sisters Veronita Ruddy and Jordan Carroll to the Institute for two years from 1936-1938. At that time they organized a unit at Rosary College to help expand the program. They were replaced at Cincinnati by Sisters Kenneth Loeffler and Basilia Andrus. Mother Samuel was reluctant to undertake the commitment, given what she thought the probable expense would be. McNicholas

---

[22]*Ibid.*, pp. 340-343.

[23]Mother Samuel to McNicholas, June 8, 1938; an extensive study of the project has been provided by Sister Benvenuta Bras, "Rosary College Unit, Institutum Divi Thomae, 1938-1946," October 1986.

[24]Interview with Sister Veronita Ruddy, March 21, 1994.

obtained assurance for her from Father Cletus Miller, a priest of the Archdiocese of Cincinnati, who was Dr. Sperti's assistant, that the investment would be modest.[25] The program was cut short at Rosary following the deaths in June 1941 of Sisters Kenneth and Jordan and the serious injury of Sister Basilia in an automobile accident in Florida. It occurred as they were returning to the Midwest after some weeks in Florida on a research assignment.[26]

Two matters to which Mother Samuel had given considerable attention during the 1920s became the focus of additional attention during the 1930s: consideration of establishing a house in Rome for the Congregation and exploration of ways that American Dominican Congregations might collaborate. In both cases Louis B. Nolan, O.P. continued to promote action; indeed the latter project was initiated primarily by him. McNicholas was interested more in the effort to establish a Roman foundation, but he later became a supporter of collaboration.[27]

During Sister DeRicci's visit to Rome in the fall of 1932, Father Nolan told her about the availability of a 70-room Villa for three million lire at a favorable location. Her reply was that Mother Samuel had not abandoned the idea but could not act upon it given the uncertain financial situation in America.[28]

By the fall of 1934, Nolan was energetically pursuing collaboration plans. He visited Mother Samuel at the Mound in November, meeting with her personally and with the members of the General Council. Out of this dialogue and similar meetings with officers of other Congregations of American Dominican Sisters, Nolan proposed a meeting to be held at the Dominican College of

---

[25]McNicholas to Mother Samuel, September 16, 1935; July 12, 1938. Mother Samuel to McNicholas, September 21, 1935; June 8, 1938; July 15, 1938.

[26]Diary, June 18, 1941.

[27]Correspondence with McNicholas, McNicholas to Mother Samuel from Fribourg, May 12, 1930; from Cincinnati, July 18, 1930.

[28]Correspondence, Sister DeRicci to Mother Samuel, October 25, 1932.

San Rafael, California, beginning January 1. 1935, for the purpose of exploring the organization of a national conference.[29]

Mothers General of twelve American Dominican Congregations responded to the invitation. The goal of the meeting, as expressed by Nolan, was "to explore ways of promoting greater strength, efficiency, and unanimity of spirit and action among their congregations." Assurance was given to the Mothers General that the autonomy and traditions of their congregations would be respected; the goal was to search for unity in spirit and ideal and for uniformity in certain matters. The Conference organized commissions to explore the following topics: uniformity of constitutions; uniformity of ceremonial; uniformity of religious habit; recitation of the Divine Office; training of young sisters; and a house in Rome. The group voted formally for the establishment of the Conference, organized an executive committee of seven mothers general, and elected Mother Samuel as president.[30]

The Conference drew additional support and greater respectability with the interest shown by McNicholas, who, at Mother Samuel's suggestion, hosted the Conference at Cincinnati in July 1935 and preached a pre-Conference retreat. There was some nervousness among the eighteen Mothers General who attended that there might still be some danger of amalgamation, a fear that McNicholas and Mother Samuel tried to dispel in their communications with the Mothers General about the Conference.[31] These fears were ultimately dissipated, and the organization survived, holding meetings biennially except during the war years. It became known as the Dominican Leadership Conference in 1970.[32]

---

[29]*Ibid.*, November 16, 1934; Correspondence, Father Nolan to Mother Samuel, December 2, 1934.

[30]Sister Alice O'Rourke, O.P., *Let Us Set Out: Sinsinawa Dominicans, 1949-1985* (Sinsinawa, Wisconsin: Privately Printed, 1986) p. 112

[31]Correspondence, Mother Samuel to McNicholas, January-July 1935, *passim.*

[32]O'Rourke, p. 208.

Mother Samuel's Diary reflects the cost in energy and worry of the activities during these years. She was often exhausted from her trips and overwhelmed by the duties awaiting her, especially the mail that had accumulated. The letters she received were frequently of a distressing nature, and dictating answers was worrisome and time-consuming. She spent time each day with the sisters at the Mound who were ill and visited the seriously ill elsewhere when she could. The seasons when assignments were being made for summer or fall were extremely burdensome. There were times of peace and consolation, such as during Mass and at Exposition of the Blessed Sacrament on Feast Days, a privilege that would be extended to daily Exposition in September 1940. She made extensive notes about retreats in her Diary.[33]

Among happier entries were those at the time of the ordination of her nephew, Bernard Coughlin, on June 9, 1930, at St. Paul Cathedral and of his First Solemn High Mass the following day in Immaculate Conception Church in Faribault. Other significant events included the dedication of the new school at Holy Rosary, Minneapolis, on September 4, 1932, a building that replaced the one for which she had attended the dedication in 1891; her visit in May 1933 to the old homestead in Faribault where a new house had recently been completed; attendance in May 1935 at the golden anniversary celebration of her graduation from Bethlehem Academy, an occasion that also provided time for visits with her sisters, Angela and Brigid.[34]

The distress that she felt over the illnesses of Sister Benetta is painfully evident in the Diary. Beginning in the summer of 1934, Sister Benetta suffered first a nervous breakdown and later recurring bouts with cancer. Frequently she spent time at Rochester for treatment, including surgery. While she was there, her sisters, brothers,

---

[33]Diary, 1930s, *passim.*

[34]Diary, 1930-1935, *passim.*

Honorary Degree awarded by Rosary College to Marguerite LeHand at the White House, June 10, 1937. Present were: *(seated)* Sister Evelyn Murphy, President of Rosary; Mother Samuel; President Roosevelt; *(standing)* Msgr. Michael J. Ready; Mrs. Roosevelt; Marguerite LeHand; Rev. Maurice S. Sheehy, Assistant Rector of Catholic University, who conferred the degree.

nieces, and nephews visited her. Mother Samuel spent time with her, both at Rochester and in Madison. During the fall of 1936, Sister Benetta was at the Mound several weeks before returning to Rochester. By the end of January 1937 it was evident that there could be no cure. From then until her death on April 25, 1937, she resided at the Mound, generally suffering great pain, as Mother Samuel tearfully recorded. The days of the wake and funeral and the weeks following during which Mother Samuel sorted through Sister Benetta's personal belongings were times of frequent weeping.[35]

A notable event for Mother Samuel in June 1937 was a visit to the White House on June 10 to witness the conferring upon Marguerite LeHand, the personal secretary of President Roosevelt, the degree LLD, Honoris Causis, an honor bestowed by Rosary College. President and Mrs. Roosevelt and about thirty guests were present. Many pictures were taken and reproduced in newspapers all around the nation, much to the embarrassment and annoyance of Mother Samuel.[36]

Mother Samuel's fourth full term as mother general was due to expire on July 9, 1937. She wrote to McNicholas a week or two before that to ask what he thought about her addressing the Chapter on her lack of fitness for reelection. His reply, dated July 7, was as follows:

I think you should remain silent at the Chapter unless it is manifest after the first vote is announced that the choice of the sisters is directed to some one other than yourself. Should this happen, then I would think it well for you to try to make the election of your successor as unanimous as possible.

As I see matters you must not seek the place of honor that belongs to the Office of Mother General; neither must you refuse a burden however great that the Holy Ghost may wish to place upon your shoulders.

We must always guard against interior voices as manifestations of God's will. Personally, we may wish for quiet and retirement in order "to make

---

[35]30 *Ibid.*, July 1936-June 1937, *passim.*

[36]Diary, June 10-15, 1937.

our soul" but our real anxiety must be to do what God wants us to do. This manifestation of the Divine Will comes to us through the ordinary agencies of the Church, especially through official acts. If your Chapter again chooses you as Mother General you may feel that your only duty is to submit and to await the decision of Rome.

All the reasons you give me are not sufficient for you to take the initiative in preventing your election or postulation. Your mature judgment, your experience, your prudence, the confidence the Sisters have in you, mean more to your Congregation than you can realize. The unity of your Congregation is all important. God has, so far as we can judge, been pleased to use you these many years to strengthen this unity.

May the Holy Ghost guide your vocals. May Our Blessed Mother & Saint Dominic protect them and obtain for you many special blessings. I shall say Mass Saturday morning for your Congregation that the Holy Spirit may direct its representatives to do what is best for it.[37]

Mother Samuel's reflections on the day before the election include a comment on McNicholas' letter: "Letter from Abp. McNicholas has advice which makes me peaceful yet fearful. Bishop Griffin came. I have moved to room on second floor. Am Ex-Mother General." The following day her comments were: "I was elected and feared to refuse, but I fail to see God's Will. I am unnerved, and dazed and fearful, but feel new trust in God. Bishop Griffin left. The same general council was elected; the same Bursar General. Tired beyond words." Confirmation of her election came in a letter from Bishop McGavick on July 29, stating that he had received a cable to that effect from the Holy See. Her comment was: "I could wish otherwise. May God have mercy on the Congregation."[38]

McNicholas was pleased with the outcome, as he wrote on September 19, 1937:

. . . I can only thank God that you have been chosen again for the responsibility of directing your Congregation. I beg of you not to attempt

---

[37]McNicholas to Mother Samuel, July 7, 1937.

[38]Diary, July 9, 10, 29, 1937.

the work you did twenty-five years ago. Your physical force is less but your judgment is greater and better. You probably can be more helpful to your sisters than you were ever before by reason of your judgment. We used to say in Rome that when a superior is advanced in years, he gives "high direction" (*alta directio*) to affairs. Whatever your physical force is (which you must never overtax) you must recognize that your value to your Congregation now is in your judgment. Therefore never hesitate to delegate sisters of good sense to perform your tasks (visitations, etc.) which require the endurance of a younger religious. I think Fr. Cormier was 72 or 74 when he took up his duties as master general. He never enjoyed robust health. He rested many times a day in order to be able to do his work better between rests. . . .[39]

There was some unfortunate confusion in communications regarding the approval of the dispensation from the limitation on terms. No official copy came to the Mound until Sister Ruth as secretary of the Congregation wrote to Cardinal Boggiani in mid-October 1937, to question the omission. Shortly thereafter, a copy of the official notice arrived by way of the office of Bishop McGavick, for whom the Vicar General, L. Paschal Hirt, was temporarily acting. At the end of the notice was the stipulation: "provided she shall first send a report of her past term." Mother Samuel was baffled and upset. It was a matter of regular procedure for her to submit a report to the General Chapter as required by the Constitutions, but reports to Rome took the form of quinquennial reports, the most recent of which had been sent just a year previously. It was not until mid-December that the confusion was cleared up, the final resolution being obtained by Louis B. Nolan, acting for Boggiani, who concurred with the opinion that Mother Samuel's report to the Chapter sufficed in conforming with Canon Law.[40]

---

[39]McNicholas to Mother Samuel, September 19, 1937.

[40]Correspondence with Bishops of LaCrosse, L. Paschal Hirt to Mother Samuel, October-December 1937, *passim*.

With her main purpose being to make visitation personally at Fribourg, Mother Samuel visited Europe in the late spring and early summer of 1939. Sister Ambrose Flaherty was her companion. After a fairly comfortable voyage aboard a ship of the Holland-American line, on which they sailed May 2, the sisters spent some days in Paris before traveling to Rome where they arrived on May 18. Sister Reparata Murray, a member of the Rosary College Library Science Department, who had been giving service in the Vatican Library during the preceding year, met them at the station. They were in time to witness the ceremony that day of Pope Pius XII's taking possession of the Basilica of St. John Lateran (Pope Pius XI had died on February 9, 1939).

Mother Samuel visited Cardinal Pizzardo on May 23 and the two of them spoke of their common interest in having the Congregation acquire a house in Rome. The following day, Father Nolan brought the sisters to meet the Master General, who showed them the improvements that had been made at Santa Sabina. The war clouds that would gather in the late summer were not evident in Italy at that time. Mother Samuel described the scene as follows: "Rome is orderly, clean, quiet, and the Church property is improved. People seem natural, very courteous and orderly—200% better than 1920 and 100% better than 1925. Mussolini is a genius and more, I think. His German alliance is hard to understand. We see no American or English papers and know nothing of what is happening."[41]

During the afternoon of that day, they visited Cardinal Boggiani, who had failed greatly since Mother had last seen him. He was interested in developments in the Congregation, including the association with the Institutum Divi Thomae, and asked about Archbishop McNicholas. Their final stop that day was at the new Angelicum, recently restored for Dominican students.[42]

---

[41]Correspondence with Sister DeRicci, Mother Samuel to Sister DeRicci, Rome, May 24, 1939.

[42]*Ibid.*

In what was undoubtedly the highlight of the whole trip, Mother Samuel, Sister Ambrose, and Sister Reparata had a private audience with Pope Pius XII on Sunday, May 28. He spoke English very well, so there was no need for an interpreter. His range of interests on the work of the Congregation was amazing; and he approved Mother Samuel's two petitions: that he permit public and private prayers for the beatification of Father Mazzuchelli and that "he approve and bless a project of the sisters having a house of studies in Rome for training in a deeper appreciation of the Church and its history; and where Sisters may imbibe the spirit of Catholic culture peculiar to Rome alone, and bring the same to enrich the Sisters of our Congregation and other Congregations in the United States." The Holy Father inquired about Boggiani and McNicholas and spoke of his high regard for them.[43]

Mother Samuel and Sister Ambrose left Rome on May 31. They spent two days in Florence, where they were joined by Sister Mary Christ. Their itinerary next included a visit to Siena and stops in Bologna and Milan before reaching Fribourg on June 5. A letter awaiting them there from Sister DeRicci told them of the tragic death on May 21 of Sister Anna Clare Casper from an explosion of a boiler in the basement of St. Basil Convent. The same letter told of the death of Sister Blanche Delaney on May 22. The impact upon Mother Samuel was almost overwhelming.[44]

During her time in Fribourg, Mother Samuel completed her official duties while suffering some health problems. A physician visited the convent to examine her heart and lungs and she took treatments on three separate days at a clinic in the city.[45]

Mother Samuel and Sister Ambrose left Fribourg on June 27, proceeding by way of Paris to LeHavre, where they boarded the *Ile de*

---

[43]Mission Letters, Mother Samuel to the Sisters, Rome, May 28, 1939

[44]*Ibid.*, Villa des Fougères, June 21, 1939.

[45]*Ibid.*

France on June 29. Mother recorded her thoughts as follows on their leaving:

We shall be lonely leaving Sister Rodolpha and our other Sisters so far away. However, I am comforted in knowing that our Sisters from the first have earnestly worked here to maintain the Dominican tradition of seeking truth and sanctity in scholarship and work. When I kneel at our beloved Sister George's grave here, and recall what she and our brave Sister Grace suffered that first year in the heart of war-torn Europe, I think we are justified in believing that God's blessing descended upon the foundation and has produced fruit in fine accomplishment. Each Superior has had crucial trials to meet, however; but the spirit of prayer and holy poverty has kept Fougères safe for God. May it continue so.[46]

Before she mailed the above letter, Mother Samuel received a message from Sister Amata O'Brien, Prioress of St. Robert Convent in Shorewood, Wisconsin, of the death on June 10 of Sister Jeannette Leary. She had stepped off the curb on a busy Milwaukee street into the path of an oncoming car.[47]

The travelers reached New York at 2:00 p.m. on July 5. They spent a few days in New York City, including a visit to the World's Fair, where, among other things, they saw the exhibit on Father Mazzuchelli in the Italian Building. On their return to Chicago, where they arrived on July 9, they stopped to visit McNicholas in Cincinnati.[48]

---

[46] *Ibid.*

[47] *Ibid.*

[48] Diary, July 5-9, 1939

Table V

Missions Accepted by Sinsinawa Dominicans, 1931-1940

Name of Mission	Place	Year Opened	Type of Mission
St. James	Atlantic City, NJ	1931	Parish Gr. School
Aquin	Freeport, IL	1931	Convent Provided
Blessed Sacrament	Madison, WI	1932	Convent provided
St. Mary	Cheyenne, WY	1933	Parish Gr.& H.S.
Annunciation	Green Bay, WI	1933	Parish Gr. School
St. Albert	Minneapolis, MN	1935	Parish Gr. School
St. Cajetan	Chicago, IL	1936	Parish Gr. School
Corpus Christi	New York, NY	1936	Parish Gr. School
Bl. Martin DePorres	Columbia, SC	1936	Parish Gr. School
Holy Rosary	Oklahoma City, OK	1938	Parish Gr. School
St. Benedict	Omaha, NE	1938	Parish H. School
SS. Faith, Hope, Ch.	Winnetka, IL	1939	Parish Gr. School
Mother of God	Cincinnati, OH	1939	Catechetical Cen.
Bl. Martin DePorres	Okla.City, OK	1940	Parish Gr. School
St.Vincent Ferrer	Riv. Forest,IL	1940	Parish Gr. School

Closings:

High School Departments at Visitation, Kewanee; St. Mary, Champaign, Sacred Heart, Eagle Grove—1932;

Bishop Muldooon High School, Rockford—1933;

Parish Grade School, St. Joseph, Sinsinawa,—1934;

St. Catherine Academy, Jackson, NE—1940.

Source: Book of Foundations, Sinsinawa Dominican Archives.

Chapter Seven

The 1940s: World War II and Its Immediate Aftermath

The imperfect settlement at the end of World War I, described at the beginning of Chapter V (see page 79), paved the way for economic, social, and political problems during the 1920s that culminated in the Great Depression. The hardships of this era unleashed further disorder that bred nationalism, militarism, and the demoralization of democracies. A series of aggressive actions were ineffectually handled by the League of Nations or went unchallenged. These included: the Japanese occupation of Manchuria in 1931; the Italian annexation of Ethiopia in 1935-36; the Civil War in Spain, 1936-39; reunification of the Saar with Germany through plebiscite, 1935; Hitler's denunciation of the disarmament clauses of the Treaty of Versailles, 1935; Germany's reoccupation of the Rhineland, March 1936; organization of the Rome-Berlin Axis, 1936; Japanese aggression in China, 1937; German annexation of Austria, 1938; Munich Pact, September 1938; Germany's annexation of remainder of Czechoslovakia, March 1939; Nazi-Soviet Pact, August 1939; invasion of Poland, September 1, 1939; declaration of war on Germany by France and Britain, September 3, 1939.[1]

The hope expressed by Mother Samuel in her letter of September 14, 1939, was one shared by hundreds of thousands—even millions—of other Americans: ". . . On that fatal 1st of September the war began in Europe. The press is already calling this the Second World War. God grant that it will not justify that name, but that peace will come before long . . ."[2]

---

[1]R.R. Palmer and Joel Colton, *A History of the Modern World*, (New York: Alfred A. Knopf, 1965), pp. 817-827. (Copyright now the property of McGraw-Hill, Inc.)

[2]SDA, Mission Letters, Mother Samuel Coughlin to the Sisters, September 14, 1939.

Those old enough to remember 1914-1917, however, had reason to be skeptical, having seen how events had inexorably drawn America into the conflict. A similar dynamic occurred once again. After overrunning Poland in September, Germany and Russia took over the Baltic states in October and invaded Finland in November. The Finns put up heroic resistance but eventually had to capitulate in March 1940. There was little action on the western front during the fall and winter of 1939-40, leading some American journalists to speculate about a "phony" war. This supposition was brutally shattered in April with the German invasion of Denmark and Norway, followed by attacks on the Netherlands, Belgium, and Luxembourg in May. In June, the Germans invaded France, Paris falling on June 13, followed by the full surrender of France on June 22. Mussolini attacked southern France that same month.[3]

By this time, the United States had moved away from its neutrality laws, recognizing that Hitler was the gravest threat in the European war. Ways were found to allow sale of arms to Great Britain, the only major power not dominated by Germany. The success of the British in surviving the air attacks of Germany in the fall of 1940 encouraged the United States to provide more support through the Lend-Lease Program in 1941. Beginning in the fall of 1941 the United States helped to deliver the arms, despite the danger of attack by German submarines. As the United States was moving closer and closer to outright war against Germany, the situation in the Far East became critical. Japan had taken advantage of the collapse of the Netherlands and France to threaten their territories in Southeast Asia. Japanese aggression in China continued. The United States sought to contain these threats through diplomacy. Another development was the disintegration of the Nazi-Soviet Alliance, as Russia pushed into the Balkans, threatening German interests there. Hitler countered the threat with military alliances and occupation. In June 1941, he

---

[3]John M. Blum, et al, *The National Experience*, (New York: Harcourt-Brace-Jovanovich, 1977), pp. 671-672.

invaded Russia. The bombing of Pearl Harbor by the Japanese on December 7, 1941, brought the United States into the war and drew a declaration of war on the United States by Germany and Italy.[4]

Mother Samuel's greatest worry during the early months of the war was for the safety of the sisters in Fribourg. Her fear was magnified when she received word from Sister Rodolpha Rudolph on December 14, 1939, that the upper floor of the Institute had been requisitioned by the Swiss government as an infirmary for soldiers who were convalescing. Though the sisters' privacy was respected and their safety guaranteed, Mother Samuel was afraid that the situation could deteriorate, and she began urging the sisters to return to the United States. Sister Rodolpha arranged passage for Sisters Andreas Goetz and Paulina (Kathleen) Coughlin on the *Manhattan*, which sailed on June 1 and arrived in New York on June 10.[5]

Sisters Rodolpha and Marie Louise Oughton remained for two more years, much to the distress of Mother Samuel, who cabled them periodically and with progressive firmness to "Come home." They finally were able to make the necessary arrangements for passage on the *Gröttingholm*, a Swedish liner that was providing passage for diplomats and was therefore immune from submarine attack. The ship sailed on May 9, 1942 and arrived in New York on June 1. The sisters were able to arrange rental of the Villa by a European congregation of Dominicans.[6]

By this time, the United States had been directly involved in the war for six months during which time the Japanese had overrun the Philippine Islands and other American possessions in the Pacific, as well as occupying the island possessions of European powers and the peninsula of Southeast Asia, and were threatening both India and Australia. The situation was very threatening in Europe also. Mother Samuel's correspondence with the sisters consistently urged prayer,

---

[4]*Ibid.*, 674-680.

[5]Diary of Mother Samuel, December 14, 1939; May 15, June 6, 1940.

[6]*Ibid.*, June 1940-June 1942; Mission Letters, May 5, 1942.

penance, sacrifice, and loyalty to our nation. Her words in a letter of December 15, 1941, are typical: ". . . Our nation is at war. We may have war for several years. Our best contribution to the defense of our four freedoms will be a penitential and self-sacrificing spirit and the keeping of the two great commandments of love of God and love of our neighbor. Let us supplement these by loyalty to our country and our government, in word and in work, complete obedience in making the material sacrifices which will be required of us, tender sympathy for all who must suffer poverty, sickness, desolation and death because of this war; and above all let us pray in season and out of season that God in His mercy may grant the grace of repentance to all those who directly or indirectly precipitated this war." She encouraged sisters who had brothers and nephews and nieces in service to write frequently to them and to their parents, even during the time of Lent. Two of her nephews, Samuel and John E., the sons of her brother John, were called to the Army.[7]

Overlapping concerns about the impact of the war were major developments in areas of Mother Samuel's responsibilities. One such area was the education of the sisters. Under Sister DeRicci's direction since 1930, the sisters worked to complete their degrees during summer sessions and in classes held part-time during the school year. Sister DeRicci also organized a program of supervision of their teaching by assigning highly qualified sisters to undertake that responsibility, usually on a regional basis. In 1940, after Edgewood College had organized its four-year program for a Bachelor of Education degree, ten sisters were released from teaching to spend full-time in study. The following year, eighteen sisters took part in the program. Over the remaining years of the decade of the 1940s, the numbers varied from eight to fourteen. The pressure of assignments

---

[7]Mission Letters, 1941-45, *passim.*

made it made it necessary some times to withdraw a sister from her studies to fulfill a mission need.[8]

In 1940, Mother Samuel and her Council agreed to cooperate with the request of the Commission on American Citizenship at Catholic University for sisters to assist in the preparation of an elementary school curriculum "to integrate religion with all the child's daily activities and in particular with his school activities." Sisters Joan Smith and Nona McGreal were assigned to the project that was directed by the Reverend George Johnson. They produced three volumes entitled, *Guiding Growth in Christian Social Living*, that outlined the curriculum. They also collaborated with sisters of other congregations in preparing the *Faith and Freedom Readers* that implemented aspects of the new philosophy. The Sinsinawa Dominicans promoted this curriculum during the 1940s and 1950s through the Sinsinawa Dominican Education Conference and the educational programs at Edgewood College.[9] Consideration of another project of collaboration with Catholic University began in September 1943 when the Council met to discuss the organization of a summer session of Catholic University classes at Rosary College.[10]

Another project that drew Mother Samuel's direct attention from 1941-45 was the education of the sisters who taught music. The work of these sisters was significant to the Congregation not only for its contribution to culture in general and to the education of the children but also for its financial support of the Motherhouse and of the Congregation as a whole. Sister Edward Blackwell was instrumental in engaging Mademoiselle Nadia Boulanger to conduct summer sessions for the sisters who taught music from 1941 through the summer of 1944. Sister Edward and Sister Ignatia Downey had studied under

---

[8]Sister Mary Eva McCarty, *The Sinsinawa Dominicans: Outlines of Twentieth Century Development, 1901-1949*, (Dubuque, Iowa: The Hoermann Press, 1953), pp. 427-429.

[9]*Ibid.*, pp. 431-432.

[10]Diary, September 26, 1943.

Boulanger at the École Normale in Paris in the mid-1930s. She was a world-renowned conductor and composer, whose reputation drew other famed musicians into her circle of friends and acquaintances, among whom Igor Stravinsky was one of the most prominent. Boulanger spent the months of January to June 1939 in America, conducting at places such as Carnegie Hall and Boston Symphony Hall, lecturing at Radcliffe, Wellesley, and the Julliard School in New York, and teaching students at Harvard, Radcliffe, and other prestigious institutions. Just a year after her return to France, the German Army occupied Paris. She and many of her friends, including Arthur and Georgette Sachs, fled to southern France where they made arrangements to depart for the United States. With the many contacts she had in America, she arranged rather easily for a three-year teaching position at the Longy School in Cambridge, Massachusetts. Due to delays of various kinds, including her efforts to help friends, she did not arrive in New York until November 6, 1940.[11]

Boulanger's affection for Sisters Edward and Ignatia made her receptive to the request made by Mother Samuel at Sister Edward's suggestion that Boulanger hold classes at Sinsinawa during the summer of 1941. Thirty-three sisters took part in the six-week session held in the Academy recreation room. The sisters were in awe of her, almost mesmerized by her talent at the piano and in conducting, and by her efforts to communicate her knowledge and skill. Only a few of the sisters had the ability and experience to profit measurably from her teaching, a situation similar to that at Radcliffe and Harvard.[12] At Mother Samuel's request, Boulanger reported on each student and on the program as a whole. The report was devastating for Mother

---

[11]Leonie Rosenstiel, *Nadia Boulanger: A Life in Music*, (New York: W. W. Norton & Company, 1982), pp. 314-316.

[12]*Ibid.*, pp. 317-319; interviews, Sinsinawa, April 16, 1994, Sister Mary Lourdes Joyce; April 17, 1994, Sister Clara Coffey.

Samuel, since with only two or three exceptions the evaluation was that the sisters needed fundamentals of music.[13]

After further reflection, however, Mother Samuel had a more positive opinion about the experience. She wrote to Boulanger in late August at the home of her friends, Arthur and Georgette Sachs, who had settled in Santa Barbara, California, expressing her appreciation as follows: "What you did for our music teachers and prospective music teachers at Saint Clara this summer can not be expressed in words. Not only your extraordinary knowledge of musical theory and practical theory, but your personality, your courage, your faith, your understanding of human nature and of world problems, gave the sisters a new impetus both artistically and spiritually which will have a lasting effect, I am entirely confident. The Fauré *Requiem* will remain a precious memory for our entire household and the Sisters from our missions who were present."[14]

Mother Samuel's appreciation of Boulanger's gifts was evident in the readiness with which she listened to a proposal formulated by Sister Edward and Boulanger that the Congregation establish a school of music to be taught by Boulanger where sisters who showed the necessary aptitude would study full-time. Classes would continue to be held during the summer for as many music teachers as could be accommodated.[15]

Mother Samuel took an active role in trying to implement the plan. Sister Edward assisted by seeking possible sites among large homes that were up for sale in the Eastern states. Mother Samuel and members of the Council followed up on several of these by visiting the estates and corresponding with diocesan officials to ask permission

---

[13]Correspondence, Mother Samuel Coughlin with Nadia Boulanger, July 1941; Diary, July 26, 1941.

[14]Mother Samuel to Mademoiselle Boulanger, August 23, 1941.

[15]The class was held at Sinsinawa again in 1942. Since space was limited there because of the General Chapter in 1943, the class was moved to Edgewood for a more limited number. The fourth and final session with Boulanger was held again at Edgewood in 1944. See picture on p. 147 of the sisters enrolled that year.

to purchase. One place that seemed to hold promise was that of Daniel C. Mulloney at Magnolia, Massachusetts. Mr. Mulloney was the brother of Monsignor Mulloney, pastor of St. Joseph Parish in Sioux Falls, who let his brother know of the sisters' interest. Negotiations for this property began in December 1942 and continued for several months. The effort came to naught, however, because Cardinal O'Connell would not give permission for the Congregation to purchase the property. His reason was that civic officials were unwilling to allow such properties to be taken off the tax rolls. Similar responses were given by the hierarchy in the dioceses of New York and Brooklyn, where the sisters had located promising real estate.[16]

Though the hope of a school of music conducted by Boulanger was not realized, the communication between her and Mother Samuel about the matter helped to establish a bond of deep affection between them, an affection fostered also by their being together in the summers. Their relationship was strained at times because of their respective strong personalities. One of the episodes that brought tension was Boulanger's determination to provide instruction for Sister Ignatia Downey, whom Boulanger saw as having great potential for helping to preserve the existence of music as part of human culture. In the late summer of 1943 Mother Samuel gave permission to Sister Ignatia to study full-time for a few months with Boulanger at Santa Barbara, California, where she was recuperating at the Sachs' home from her burdensome schedule of teaching and performing. When September came, Boulanger, who planned to remain at Santa Barbara for several more months, prevailed upon Mother Samuel to let Sister Ignatia stay throughout the school year, 1943-44, to continue her lessons. When Mother Samuel told Father George B. Ford, pastor of Corpus Christi Church, New York City, where Sister Ignatia had

---

[16]Correspondence with Boulanger, 1943-45, *passim*; Correspondence with Members of the Hierarchy, 1943-45, *passim*.

Mademoiselle Nadia Boulanger with class at Edgewood College, summer 1944. Men in row 2 are Jean Papineau-Coutre and Richard Johnson; priest in front row is Rev. Elizear Fortier.

taught music in the school for seven years, that she was changing Sister Ignatia's assignment, he objected with great vehemence. Mother Samuel capitulated—temporarily—and reassigned Sister Ignatia to his school. Boulanger reacted with persistent objections and pleas in correspondence that stretched over several weeks. Eventually, Mother Samuel gave in to her and told Sister Ignatia that she might stay in Santa Barbara for the school year. Needless to say, Mother Samuel had to brave the anger of Ford.[17]

The following year, 1944-45, similar contention occurred between Mother Samuel and Boulanger, the latter again getting her way in having Sister Ignatia continue her study. Ford was not involved this time around because he had taken a leave of absence from his duties following an altercation with Archbishop Spellman, a painful period for Ford that ended with the reconciliation of the two men at Christmas time in 1944.[18]

Boulanger had intended to continue her work with Sister Ignatia during the summer of 1945, having made plans to return to France in the fall. The surrender of Germany on May 8, 1945, brought a change of plans that required an earlier departure. This arrangement did not work out and was discarded in favor of the original plan. It was January 1946 when she arrived in France.[19]

Mother Samuel and Boulanger corresponded infrequently during the late 1940s and the 1950s, usually exchanging Christmas greetings. The letters retained a tone of respect and affection.[20]

Among events of consequence during these years, one with the greatest impact was the terrible automobile crash on June 18, 1941, in Florida which took the lives of Sisters Jordan Carroll and Kenneth Loeffler and seriously injured Sister Basilia Andrus, sisters associated

---

[17]Correspondence with Boulanger, August-November 1943; Correspondence with George B. Ford, September-December 1943.

[18]Correspondence with Boulanger, October 1944; Correspondence with Ford, November-December 1944.

[19]Rosenstiel,pp. 329-334.

[20]Correspondence with Boulanger, 1945-1957, *passim*.

with a special research project sponsored by the Institutum Divi Thomae (see page 126). Mademoiselle Boulanger, who had arrived at the Mound the day before, later arranged a program of sacred music in honor of the deceased sisters. Archbishop McNicholas, Dr. George Sperti, the latter the director of the Institutum Divi Thomae, and Father Gustave Brotzge, driver of the car that crashed, visited Sinsinawa on September 3 and 4. McNicholas offered Mass for Sisters Jordan and Kenneth and the men visited the graves in the company of Mother Samuel. Sister Basilia, who had arrived at the Mound on August 22 after several weeks of recuperation at a Chicago Hospital, was present for the Mass. Mother Samuel found the visit "sad but consoling."[21]

There were only four new foundations established during the war years: Resurrection Grade School, Minneapolis, 1941; St. Thomas Grade School, Peoria Heights, 1942; Most Pure Heart of Mary Grade and High Schools, Mobile, Alabama, 1943, and St. Joseph Center, Tuskegee, Alabama, 1944. The latter two served African-Americans, a type of ministry in which Mother Samuel continued to have great interest. At Mobile the sisters assumed responsibility for the schools formerly taught by sisters of another congregation. As had always been the case in similar situations, Mother Samuel was careful to ascertain the willingness of those sisters to withdraw from the schools. The work at Tuskegee first involved visiting hospitals and homes where there was illness; a nursery school and kindergarten was the beginning of what became a fully-graded parish school; Religion classes for both children and adults were also offered.[22]

Transportation during the war proved difficult on many occasions. Sister Louis Bertrand recorded in her Reminiscences of Mother Samuel one such occasion, which also had its humorous aspects:

---

[21]Diary, June 18, July 8, September 3 and 4, 1941

[22]McCarty, pp. 349-358.

There was the time during World War II when we boarded a North Shore train from Milwaukee to Chicago. The coach was almost unoccupied when we entered and whoever brought in our baggage put one suitcase in the rack above our seat and the other in the rack above the seat opposite us. All went well until the train arrived at Great Lakes Naval Station when the whole navy poured in and filled every inch of space in the seats and aisle. As we neared Chicago, Mother expressed concern as to how we ever going to get out, for we were far back in the coach. My anxiety was how we were going to rescue our baggage, and get out. Finally, I asked the young man opposite us if he would take down our suitcase which was in the rack above him. He smiled, blushed *redly*, unfolded at least six feet of navyhood and retrieved my suitcase. Then, pointing, I said 'And we have another one over here.' He had to reach over Mother for that one. At some time during the process, he asked if we were getting off at the next station. I answered: 'No; we want to get off at Belmont but didn't know how we could manage unless we had our bags beforehand.' He nodded understandingly and resumed his seat.

When we were nearing Belmont, I tentatively reached for the handle of my suitcase. Instantly, he was on his feet and, saying 'No,' picked up the two suitcases and stood with them in the aisle close to our seat. As the train was pulling into the station, he took a step backward and leaning toward me said, 'Get out in front of me.' I did. Then he added, 'Take a step forward.' That was easy because he also took a step forward and, at the same time, turned to Mother, saying, 'Get out behind me.' She, chuckling, wriggled her way out into the aisle close behind him.

By that time the train had reached the station and our gallant sailor sang out in a clear tenor voice, 'Gangway ahead!' At that all the men in the aisle threw themselves over the ones in the seats and, amid broad grins and much good-natured laughter, watched the unimpeded progress of the unique procession through the aisle—led by a diminutive Sister followed by a slender, six-foot, baggage-laden sailor making way for the tall, happily smiling Mother General of the Sinsinawa Dominican Sisters.

The grinning conductor doffed his cap as he watched our safe descent to the platform where our charming sailor-boy deposited our bags, graciously acknowledged our thanks, and waving a sailor's farewell, ran to reclaim his place in the coach. (We could only imagine the cheering he received.)[23]

Mother Samuel's diary entries for April and May 1943 show some preoccupation with her age and with the coming General Chapter. She notes her 75th birthday on April 7, when she was visiting Milwaukee, adding: "No one here knows. Mass in St. Gall's church." She records the 75th anniversary of her baptism on April 18 and the 68th anniversary of her first day in school on April 19. On May 11 and 12 she and Sister Louis Bertrand worked on letters and instructions concerning the Chapter, for which she sent letters of convocation to the missions on May 13.

The last ten days of June were occupied with matters related to the Chapter. From June 21 to 24, the Council recorded data from the questionnaires sent in from the missions. A Mass was offered for her intention on June 24: "God's blessing upon our General Chapter and the election of a new Mother General." On June 30 she wrote: "I began my last house cleaning as M.G."[24]

Mother Samuel's expectation that she would not be reelected was further revealed in the entry for July 8: "Retreat closed at 8:30. All well pleased. I completed moving out of the Mother General's rooms to 221, and have left all in readiness for my successor. My authority and office cease tonight. May I never resume them is my earnest prayer." On the following day, the first day of the Chapter, she asked the sisters not to reelect her, a plea that she had wanted to make in 1937 but was dissuaded by McNicholas. This time she did not consult him beforehand. Her diary entry was as follows: ". . . I told the Sisters that my years made it imperative for them not to consider electing the same Mother General, if any had thought of doing so. I hope sincerely to be freed forever from responsibility for the souls of others. . . ." Much to her distress, the electors paid little or no

---

[23]Papers of Mother Samuel, Reminiscences of Sister Louis Bertrand Droege.

[24]Diary, April-June, 1943, *passim*.

attention to her request, voting 97 to 3, to return her to office, pending the necessary dispensation from Rome. Her consternation was evident in the diary entry for July 10: "A hard, puzzling day. The same Mother General was elected. A half hour of . . . fear for me. Mgr. Hirt (Bishop's delegate) confirmed the election, subject to dispensation from the Holy See. I accepted because advised that it was God's will to do so. The burden and fear have returned. . . . I am tired and sad, but have some peace." Sister DeRicci was elected to her sixth full term as member of Council; Sister Januarius, to her third term; Sisters Evelyn Murphy and Amata O'Brien were the third and fourth councillors, respectively.[25]

McNicholas, as always, regarded the vote of the sisters as evidence of the will of God. He wrote as follows in a letter of August 22, 1943:

> . . . You have my sincere sympathy because of the great burden you must continue to carry. I think it is very evident that God wills this immolation of self and the denial of freedom for which you longed. You must so regard it.
>
> I beg of you to delegate more and more of your authority as Mother General. You have able and devoted Sisters whom you can send on delicate and difficult missions both for visitations and for the solution of urgent problems as they arise. This delegation will do much to prepare other Sisters to carry the burden either of Superior General or as a member of the General Council.[26]

The ensuing years of her sixth full term were burdensome for Mother Samuel. In addition to the regular responsibilities of her office, complicated by pressures of war-time conditions, she felt deeply the death of her brother John, who on February 20, 1945, succumbed to a skull fracture suffered from a fall. Sister Januarius' illness in the spring of 1946 was another burden.

---

[25]*Ibid.*, July 8, 9, 10, 1943.

[26]Correspondence with McNicholas, August 22, 1943.

Planning for additional building projects, several of which converged in the mid-1940s, brought added worries. Rosary College engaged an architect for its auditorium; Edgewood began to plan for new buildings to house its College programs and for fund-raising to support the project; the building of a rest home, long postponed, was perhaps highest in priority.

Mother Samuel's diary does not identify any single reason that precipitated her letter to McNicholas on April 2, 1946, exploring the possibility of resigning. For the entire month preceding that date there are no diary entries. The content of her letter, however, shows careful reflection on the matter:

> . . . I am convinced that it is my duty to resign this office of Mother General at the present time, or at least by next July; and for these reasons:
>
> 1. I am seventy-eight years old.
> 2. My health has been considerably impaired the past year; I have had influenza or something similar five times during the year.
> 3. My memory is gradually becoming impaired. This, of course, can be a serious matter.
> 4. My eyesight, too, is not normal.
> 5. My hands have begun to tremble.
> 6. I also am quite crippled by arthritis.
>
> I can honestly say that this conviction does not arise from consideration of myself but because of what is due to our Congregation; a Congregation of nearly fifteen hundred Sisters is too large to be cared for by one so handicapped as I have become.
>
> Our Constitution is not quite plain on the precedure which this resignation precipitates. One paragraph states: 'In case of the death of the Mother General or of her removal from office, the First Councillor shall act as Vicaress General.' Another paragraph farther on states: 'If the Mother General shall die before the third Sunday in May, even if it be in the first year of her office, the Vicaress General is bound to convoke the Chapter for the time of vacancy near the fifth of July. The uncompleted term shall not constitute a term nor part of a term for the new Mother General elected at an extraordinary Chapter, provided that this new election be held after the exact three years from the preceding election; otherwise,

let it be valid for the first term of office although the six years be not complete.'

This year, about the second week of July, is the time for our intermediate assembly; the time for the next General Chapter and Election is three years beyond that date. There is no reference in our Constitution to a Mother General's resignation; but it seems to me that a resignation is practically the same as a death, inasmuch as the Mother General is entirely removed from office by virtue of her resignation.

Sister DeRicci, our First Councillor, is about two years older than I am and I am quite sure she would scarcely be willing, even if it were the proper procedure, to take the place of the Mother General for three years. However, if it is the proper procedure and Sister is willing, shall I simply announce my resignation and have her continue to care for the Congregation? Does it seem to Your Excellency that we should hold an election for next July?

Is it necessary for me to have the permission of the Holy See to make this resignation, since I hold this office under dispensation from the Holy See; or, will it be enough for us to prepare for the election and inform our Ordinary (who by the way, is the new Bishop of Madison) that I have resigned and ask him to preside at the election?

. . . I have prayed for nearly a year very earnestly to know God's will in this matter and it seems to me that I am planning to do what is my duty under the circumstances. I hope for the approval of Your Excellency and your advice on procedures.

Begging Your Excellency's blessing and with profound gratitude for all that you have meant to the Sinsinawa Dominicans and to me, I remain

Yours most respectfully in Our Lady
of the Rosary,[27]

McNicholas responded within a day after receiving Mother Samuel's letter, making suggestions of what procedures would be appropriate. His letter of April 5, 1946, is as follows:

---

[27]Correspondence with McNicholas, April 2, 1946.

It is very hard for me to reconcile myself to your decision to offer your resignation as Mother General. I do so convinced that your reasons are serious and that you have the guidance of the Holy Ghost. You are entitled to a peaceful period during which you can 'make your soul.'

It seems to me you must resign to someone who has the authority of the Church to accept your resignation. Since your Congregation has a Pontifical Character, I do not think that the Bishop of Madison can accept your resignation without authorization of the Sacred Congregation.

I suggest that you write to His Excellency, the Apostolic Delegate asking whether the resignation must be submitted to the Sacred Congregation. If His Excellency gives you a reply in the affirmative you can request that a code message be sent from the Delegation at the expense of your Congregation. You can enclose an offering to His Excellency.

I venture to suggest the resignation by a code message, assuming that you think it wise to hold the election during July 1946. You must be the best judge as to the time of the election. You can tell His Excellency that you have consulted before writing him. You can quote me if you wish.

To me it is very important that there be no undue hurry or excitement about your resignation and that you anticipate the subsequent disturbance among the Sisters of your Congregation who are so sincerely devoted to you.

If the resignation must be accepted by Rome and if you have word from the Sacred Congregation of its acceptance, all will be peaceful.

His Excellency, the Apostolic Delegate will direct you about [notifying] Bishop O'Connor about the petition which you will send through the Delegation to Rome.

In writing to the Apostolic Delegate it may be well to send [him] a copy of your Constitution or at least all the quotations from your Constitution which have a bearing on your resignation.

It is very curious that during the past two weeks the possibility of your resignation many times intruded itself upon me. From no source did I have any intimation of it.

Asking God to bestow his choicest blessings on you, I am,

Fraternally Yours,[28]

---

[28]*Ibid.*, McNicholas to Mother Samuel, April 5, 1946.

Before proceeding any further, Mother Samuel decided to consult the General Council, which she did on April 21, 1946. There is no record of what the council members said, but the fact that the matter was not pursued indicates that they did not approve of her resigning.[29]

The final years of Mother Samuel's last term were dominated by the building projects referred to on page 153, to which was added in 1947-49 a new high school building in Faribault. The continuation of wartime restrictions on building for several years after the end of the war and problems of financing the projects led to the deferment until the 1950s of the plans for new buildings at Edgewood College and Rosary College. Ground-breaking for St. Dominic Villa occurred on April 14, 1948, and by the fall of 1949, the building was ready for occupancy, though the chapel was yet to be completed.[30]

Among more encouraging developments were the return of the sisters to Fribourg in August and September 1946, where they prepared for the reopening of the Institute the following fall, and the organization of the program for Pius XII Institute in Florence, both of which projects owed much to the work of Sister Evelyn Murphy.[31]

Myron Taylor's donation of his Florentine Villa to the Holy See in September 1941 with the proviso that it be used by Rosary College for educational purposes was the culmination of years of correspondence between him and Sister Catharine Wall of the College's art department about a foreign center for the study of art. After Sister Catharine's death in 1938, Mother Samuel continued the correspondence. The war years led to the postponement of the project, although Mr. Taylor proceeded with the legal work of deeding the property to the Vatican on December 18, 1944. After some preliminary negotiations conducted in Florence by Sister Evelyn

---

[29]Diary, April 21, 1946.

[30]Sister Allice O'Rourke, O.P., *Let Us Set Out: Sinsinawa Dominicans, 1949-1985* (Dubuque, Iowa: Hoermann Press, 1986), p. 97.

[31]Annals, Villa des Fougères, Fribourg, 1946; Pius XII Institute, Florence, 1946.

during the summer of 1946, she, Sister Eunice Joy and Sister Marco (Amelia) Giraldi established the sisters' community at Villa Schifanoia in October 1946. The sisters lived for several months in what had been the servants' quarters while renovation and furnishing of the Villa took place. Sister Evelyn was responsible for overseeing negotiations on the contract between the Congregation and the Vatican concerning the respective responsibilities of the two parties, a contract that was completed in August 1947. Sister Evelyn returned to the Mound in October 1947.[32]

Sister Gertruda (Genevieve) Pinion joined Sisters Eunice and Marco that same month to begin her special studies in music. The first students, five in number, arrived in October 1948, accompanied by Sister Matthias Michels, who would be studying art, to be on hand for the formal opening of the Institute on October 10.[33] Postwar conditions, including food shortages and unstable politics due to the threat of Communism, caused hardship for the sisters and students. Mr. Taylor, in addition to his contributions to scholarships and renovations, provided relief funds during these early months.[34]

---

[32] *Ibid.*, pp. 67-68.

[33] *Ibid.*

[34] *Ibid.*, pp. 68-69; Correspondence, Mother Samuel with Sister DeRicci, October 6, 1948.

Villa Schifanoia

Beginning in 1947, new grade school foundations were accepted, including two in California in 1948: All Saints in Los Angeles and St. Leo in Oakland; the others were St. Richard and St. Thomas More in Chicago in 1947 and 1949, respectively, and Queen of Peace, Madison, 1949.

Worry about building projects, concern about the welfare of the sisters in Florence, and many "normal" responsibilities converged in the late summer of 1948 to cause Mother Samuel to suffer nervous exhaustion similar to what she had experienced in the summer of 1922 (see page 95). Under advice from Dr. Strauch of Hazel Green, she entered the health facility at Wedron, Illinois, on September 7, 1948, for several weeks of rest. Sister Ambrose Flaherty spent the first ten days with her, at which time Mother was transferred to St. Margaret Hospital in Spring Valley, Illinois, because the facility at Wedron no longer could accommodate her due to previously scheduled appointments. Sister Antoninus Singleton replaced Sister Ambrose after the move to Spring Valley. Sister DeRicci described the situation in her letter to the sisters of September 7, 1948:

Less than a week ago Dr. Strauch from Hazel Green was summoned to administer to Mother who has been over-fatigued and troubled in recent nights with insomnia, to try to give her relief. His diagnosis was that Mother should have complete rest for at least a month and that she have no contact with her office and responsibilities of any sort; that this amount of rest and change would bring about her recovery; but he urged that the rest be not delayed. . . .

With the help of your prayers I am sure that her health will be restored. You know it is utter fatigue, exhaustion; and as you and I know, it is a wonder that it has not come to her earlier. . . .

The members of Council will try to do whatever is possible in case you need our help. In the meantime, you will help us by your prayers for all the needs of the Congregation.[35]

---

[35]Mission Letters, Sister DeRicci to the Sisters, September 7, 1948.

Though the accommodations at St. Margaret Hospital were very comfortable, Mother Samuel's stay was not as worry-free as her doctor had hoped. Although she refrained from writing general letters to the Congregation, she wrote to Sister DeRicci twice weekly. She worried about the expense of her care and about the extra burden of work that Sister DeRicci had to bear. Her letters showed continuing concern about Congregation projects: progress of construction on St. Dominic Villa; Edgewood College's building plans and fund-raising efforts; progress of planning for construction of Rosary College's auditorium. Of more immediate concern was the impending official opening of the program at Villa Schifanoia on October 10. She was upset at the elaborateness of the opening day celebration to which many high-ranking Churchmen and civic officials were invited, and she wanted Sister Evelyn to be present for the occasion. Sister DeRicci begged her not to require Sister Evelyn to make the trip because she was greatly needed at the Mound. Mother Samuel was deeply grieved upon hearing on September 27 of the death of Father James Dominic Kavanaugh, who had served as Chaplain at St. Clara from 1910 to 1933. Mother Samuel had notified Sister DeRicci of her hope of returning to the Mound on September 27. Sister Antoninus advised against it and Sister DeRicci strongly urged her to stay longer at St. Margaret.[36]

Mother Samuel continued to express disappointment that no one from the Mound would be present at Villa Schifanoia on October 10, noting in her letter to Sister DeRicci on October 6: "We are launched on a big, big undertaking with the 'highest-ups' in Church, State, and finance. May God direct the work and make it contribute to His glory. . . ." Sister Rodolpha Rudolph made the journey from Fribourg to Florence to serve as the official representative of the Motherhouse.[37]

---

[36]Correspondence with Sister DeRicci, September-October 1948.

[37]*Ibid.*, October 6, 1948; Annals, Pius XII Institute, October 10, 1948.

Mother Samuel was greeted warmly on her return to Sinsinawa on October 17, 1948.

Mother Samuel's burden did not get lighter as the New Year, 1949 approached. Word of the injury to her sister Angela, who fell on her way to Mass on December 8 and fractured her hip, was distressing. Early in January, she and the General Council members formulated for the sisters an outline of activities to celebrate the Centennial of the Congregation, planning for which had been under way for more than a year. Mother Samuel's letter of January 11, 1949, announced some of the details. Each convent was to have Mass offered in thanksgiving some time between Easter and June 1. Each mission was to select one of four or five plays written by some of the sisters that told the history of the Congregation to be presented for students and their families. Special commemoration of the Centennial would be a part of the St. Clara Academy Alumnae meeting in early June and of events associated with the General Chapter. The final, central celebration would be held on August 15, 1949, one hundred years from the day the first Sinsinawa Dominicans made their profession. Later correspondence informed the sisters about the presentation of *Centennial Song*: *The Mass at Sinsinawa*, a symphonic drama composed by Sisters Julie Garner, Paul McCabe, and Jeremy Finnegan, and directed by Sister Thomas More (Mary) Hunt, which would be performed by Academy students and novices on various occasions during the summer of 1949.[38]

Mother Samuel had to bear a cross of great weight in the spring of 1949. After several years of failing health—a condition about which Mother Samuel worried continually—Sister DeRicci became critically ill in early April and was hospitalized at Loretto Hospital in Chicago. The doctors recommended exploratory surgery. After spending Holy Week at the Mound, she returned to Chicago on Easter Monday, entering Mercy Hospital where her sister, Sister Mary DePaul, a Sister of Mercy, served as a nurse. Mother Samuel

[38]Mission Letters, Mother Samuel to the Sisters, January 11, 1949; McCarty, pp. 524-526.

was at the hospital when the surgery was performed on April 25. The doctor found cancerous tissue in the tubes leading to the gall bladder and signs of cancer having spread to the liver.

The report was devastating to Mother Samuel, for the person who had shared with her the leadership of the Congregation for thirty-nine years, as well as a close personal relationship, was now facing great suffering. Mother Samuel shared her feelings with the sisters in this letter of May 3, 1949:

. . . While I had been suppressing a vague fear that this condition existed, the realization was a most painful shock. I am sure that it will be the same for you. You know that Sister DeRicci has given herself most generously to the interest and welfare of our Congregation. No one in our history has surpassed her in contributing to the organization and development of our educational policies and programs. The training and professional advancement of each of our teachers has been her personal problem. She has never wearied of helping those in need. She has always inspired courage, because her own heart is brave and anchored in God.

Her piety, spirit of prayer and religious observance have always been edifying.

Remember, dear Sisters, that prayer is all-powerful. Let us beseech God through the intercession of St. Catherine of Siena and St. Dominic to cure Sister by a miracle, giving her more time for merit, even if delaying her eternal reward. Sister DeRicci knows her own condition.

We begin a novena tomorrow, May 4, in honor of St Dominic and St. Catherine for Sister DeRicci. You will please begin a similar novena when you have this letter. Recite the O Spem Miram in English and the prayer to St. Catherine from our Vespers. I know you will pray with fervor and great faith and confidence in God's power and love.[39]

At times during the summer of 1949, Sister DeRicci's condition improved slightly, but there was little hope of full recovery. After spending several weeks in the Infirmary section at the Mound, she

---

[39]Mission Letters, Mother Samuel to the Sisters, May 3, 1949.

was the first patient to enter St. Dominic Villa when it opened on October 17, 1949. Her death came on February 21, 1950.[40]

The most significant event of the summer of 1949 for Mother Samuel was the Eleventh General Chapter of the Sinsinawa Dominican Congregation, held June 14-17, the early date determined by Bishop O'Connor's having scheduled a trip to Rome at the time in July when the Chapter would have ordinarily been held. At the opening of the Chapter, the membership in the Congregation stood at 1,547 professed members, 42 novices, and 59 postulants. The Congregation staffed 92 grade schools with a total enrollment in 1948-49 of 42,486 students; 19 high schools, including four owned by the Congregation, the total attendance being 5,806; the sisters had conducted 77 vacation schools for Christian Doctrine in May and June. At long last, the sisters who had been chosen as electors, allowed Mother Samuel to be relieved of her position of leadership. Elected Mother General in her stead with 67 of the 111 votes cast was Sister Mary Evelyn Murphy. Sisters Mary Benedicta Larkin, Mary Peter Doyle, Amata O'Brien, and Benedict Ryan were chosen as members of Council; Sister Benita Newhouse was elected Bursar General, and Sister Louis Bertrand Droege, Secretary. Among actions of the Chapter of Affairs held on June 16 and 17 was the recommendation that Mother Samuel take a trip to Europe in the fall.[41]

Mother Samuel had written a letter to the Congregation on May 12, which expressed in beautiful, simple terms her peace of mind and soul at this great transition in her life:

Dearest Sisters,

This is the last general letter I shall write you. I therefore take this occasion to thank each of you for your cooperation in our mutual duty of serving God by the observance of our Rule and Constitutions and by our work for the salvation of souls through our teaching in our schools. I pray

---

[40]O'Rourke, p. 97.

[41]SDA, Records of General Chapters, Eleventh General Chapter, 1949.

and I shall continue to pray that each Sister of our Congregation shall aspire daily to perfection; and before death, arrive at the religious perfection which God expects from her.

I now humbly before God ask His pardon and yours for all my sins, faults, omissions, disedifications, unkindnesses in speech or action or by neglects which have injured any Sister spiritually or otherwise, or have lessened the corporate welfare or prosperity or advancement of our beloved Congregation.

May each of you, dearest Sisters, aim to make our Congregation a community of saints and scholars, by having one heart and soul in God, loving and observing the Rule and Constitutions, living in God's presence and loyally obeying and cooperating with your local and General Superior.

When you happen to think of me, please ask God to grant me true contrition for my sins.

Affectionately and gratefully yours,[42]

The sisters at the Chapter addressed the following Testimonial to Mother Samuel:

Testimonial of the Eleventh General Chapter
to The Reverend Mother Mary Samuel, O.P.

Dear Mother Samuel,

Your Sinsinawa Dominican Sisters, united one heart and one soul in God, speak again with one voice in this the eleventh General Chapter of the Congregation of the Most Holy Rosary.

Your Sisters would have no other will than that you who have been their devoted and beloved Superior General for forty years by the Providence of God and the blessing of Holy Mother Church should continue to be their leader and their mother in religious obedience.

You are of another mind, and the obedience of your Sister was never more solemnly, more crucially, and more valiantly exercised than in yielding now to your will, again and again expressed, that the work of your exalted office be undertaken by another.

[42] Mission Letters, Mother Samuel to the Sisters, May 12, 1949.

This historic Centennial General Chapter of 1949 gives us blessed perspective on a unique procession of authority in our Sinsinawa Dominican family. Ours has been a trinity of saintly and gifted leaders. From Father Samuel Mazzuchelli through Mother Emily to Mother Samuel, the Congregation of the Most Holy Rosary of Sinsinawa has known a sustained and unifying heritage of sanctity, scholarship, and zeal for souls.

Sinsinawa is on its knees today. Here at Saint Clara and in a hundred mission Chapels across America and beyond the Atlantic, the Magnificat reverberates as a prayer of gratitude to God for Mother Samuel. Your deeds we shall not review. Their goodness and greatness is known. It is a small thing that you should hear this solemn testimony of our allegiance and love. But we beg leave in your presence one and all, to pledge our fidelity 'to the honor of Almighty God, Father, Son and Holy Ghost, and of the Blessed Virgin Mary, and of the Blessed Dominic, according to the Rule and Constitution.' That will endure. That is the pattern of your governing. That Constitution makes you always *ex-officio* a Mother of the General Council—always our beloved Mother Samuel.

You are kneeling with us as with one voice we call upon the Holy Ghost to bless our Sinsinawa Dominican Congregation of the Most Holy Rosary in the future as He has through a hundred years—with worthy and noble leaders whose only aim will be what yours always has been, dear Mother Samuel—devoted service of Holy Mother Church.

Chapter Eight

Years of Retirement, 1949-1959

With the mantle of leadership having been lifted in the summer of 1949, Mother Samuel looked forward to having leisure for prayer, meditation, and reading; opportunities for visiting family and friends; and responding to assignments from Mother Evelyn that were commensurate with her energy. The latter included serving as honorary member of the General Council, which involved more work than the title implied; teaching classes in the Novitiate and addressing sisters who were preparing for final profession; editing the *Sinsinawa Dominican Newsletter*, which was published quarterly and for which she prepared obituaries of sisters recently deceased. She also maintained an active correspondence with friends, family, and acquaintances among the clergy.

She took an interest in what was happening in world and national affairs, noting in her diary significant events as they occurred and having a sense of their importance. Among these were: the outbreak of the Korean War in June 1950; the discharge of General MacArthur by President Truman in April 1951; the development of hydrogen bombs by both the United States and the Soviet Union; the death of George VI of England in February 1952; the death of Joseph Stalin in March 1953; the crisis in the Straits of Formosa, January 1955; independence for West Germany, May 1955; Geneva Conference, July 1955, one of the first indications of a lessening of tensions between the Western powers and the Soviet Union; the attack by Britain and France on Egyptian military bases on October 31, 1956. She usually commented also on the outcome of national elections in the United States and sometimes on those in Great Britain.[1]

Among the memorable activities of a pleasant nature during the early months of her retirement was the trip to Europe from September to December 1949.[2] Having been encouraged and provided with funds by the General Chapter and assigned by Mother Evelyn Murphy to make visitation at Fribourg and Florence, Mother Samuel and her companion, Sister Mary Nona McGreal, left Sinsinawa on September 3, 1949. They stopped at Cincinnati on their way to New York to visit Archbishop McNicholas, who had been declining in health for several weeks. They boarded the *Mauretania* on September 8, accompanied by Sisters George Lennon and Annora Searfoss, twelve students bound for Fribourg, and one bound for Florence. The trip was generally smooth sailing, but the weather was cloudy and rainy most of the way. The ship docked at Cóbh in County Cork, Ireland, where Sister George and some of the American students went ashore to begin a tour of the British Isles. Four relatives of Mother Samuel boarded the vessel for a visit with her. After arriving in LeHavre, the travelers took the boat train to Paris, where they were met by Sister Rodolpha Rudolph. She handled the transfer of baggage for the sisters and students expeditiously. Mother Samuel, Sister Annora, and Sister Rodolpha departed for Fribourg after two days in Paris, while Sister Nona and two students stayed two more days there.

The two weeks spent in Fribourg before departing for Florence on September 29 included visits with the Master General, the Most Reverend Emanuel Suarez, O.P., and with the Reverend Reginald

---

[1]Diary of Mother Samuel, 1949-1957, *passim*. These events are summarized briefly in R.R. Palmer and Joel Colton, *A History of the Modern World* (New York: Alfred A. Knopf, 1965), pp. 847-902, *passim*. (Copyright now the property of McGraw-Hill, Inc.)

[2] The description of the trip is taken from letters written by Mother Samuel Coughlin and Sister Mary Nona McGreal, dated December 1, 1949, and found in the Mission Letters of the Sinsinawa Dominican Archives; and from the Journal of the trip kept by Sister Nona.

Garrigou Lagrange, O.P., whose work, *The Three Ages of the Interior Life*, had been translated by Sister Timothea Doyle. Sister Nona commented in her Journal on how privileged she felt to be in the company of Mother Samuel as they met so many of her distinguished acquaintances. The two sisters visited the grave of Sister George Adamson, one of the founding sisters, who died on August 20, 1918 (see page 74).

In her letter to the sisters of December 1, 1949, Mother Samuel comments: "It would take the combined work of a poet and a painter to describe Villa Schifanoia." She then describes in detail the magnificent estate donated to the Vatican by Myron Taylor (see p. 156 above) and the changes made to serve the new needs of the property as an educational institution. She hints at the hardships the sisters and the students had to endure during the beginning years.

Mother Samuel and Sister Nona had opportunities to travel to several famous sites during their six-week stay in Florence. On their way to Siena to visit the places with which St. Catherine of Siena was associated, they passed the American Military Cemetery where more than 4,000 American soldiers were buried, their bodies having been brought from the places where they had fought. Mother Samuel described the scene as follows: "Our national flag floats above the rows upon rows of white crosses on the sunny hillside. A few soldiers are stationed there to guard and to supervise the care of the cemetery. We stopped and prayed for our beloved dead." Sister Nona, with Sister Rodolpha as her companion, had the privilege of treading the Via Samuele Mazzuchelli in Milan, which they located with the help of maps and the directions given by a kind passenger on the last of three street cars they took.

The sisters' trip to Rome, November 11-20, included a first stop at St. Peter Basilica, followed over the next several days by visits with Dominican Fathers, including Father Timothy Sparks, who was their guide at Santa Sabina, and sight-seeing at the Forum, the Colosseum, the Catacombs, and San Sisto Vecchio. They spent time with Cardinal Pizzardo, long-time friend of Mother Samuel, who had become Cardinal Protector of the Sinsinawa Dominican Congregation following the death of Cardinal Boggiani on February 26, 1942.

Pizzardo arranged a private audience with Pope Pius XII for Mother Samuel and Sister Nona at Castelgondolpho on November 20. Speaking in English, the Holy Father asked Mother Samuel about the Congregation and gave his special blessing to each sister, to her family and friends and to benefactors of the Congregation. Mother Samuel asked for a special blessing for the sisters who were ill. In her Journal, Sister Nona commented as follows on the experience: "It was over, but the memory never will be. One sees so easily in the Pope the gentleness and fatherliness of Christ, and His love for souls. . . ."

The travelers left Rome on November 21, stopping at Florence for a week before returning to Fribourg on November 27. They left on December 7 for Paris and fitted in a side trip to Lisieux before taking the boat train to Cherbourg for departure on the British liner, the *Queen Mary*, on December 10. They arrived in New York at 2:00 p.m. on December 15. Two days later, after stopping in Dubuque to visit Sister DeRicci at St. Dominic Villa, they arrived at the Mound, to be serenaded by novices and academy students.[3]

Sister Nona completed her Journal with this comment: "What a privilege it has been to spend almost four months in the presence of a great and humble woman, always thoughtful and always ready to find the humor in every situation. I went in awe and some fear, too. But Mother Samuel's greatness overcame all that. In the best sense, 'noblesse oblige.'"

Within the first year of her retirement, Mother Samuel lost to death two of her closest associates, Sister DeRicci Fitzgerald and Archbishop John T. McNicholas, both of whom had been her friends throughout all of her years of leadership. As recounted in the preceding chapter, Sister DeRicci had been diagnosed in the spring

---

[3] Annals of St. Clara Convent, December 17, 1949.

of 1949 as having a terminal illness. She was cared for in the Infirmary at Sinsinawa until her transfer to St. Dominic Villa, newly opened on October 17, 1949. Mother Samuel visited her frequently over the succeeding four months until her death on February 21, 1950.

At Mother Evelyn's request, Mother Samuel prepared a five-page letter to the sisters, describing the funeral and outlining the contributions made by Sister DeRicci throughout her years of service as appointed member of the General Council from 1910 to 1913 and as elected member from 1913 to 1949. From 1919 to 1949 she served as First Councillor.

Selections from Mother Samuel's letter quoted below illustrate her appreciation of and affection for Sister DeRicci:

. . . From 1910 on, no matter what were her duties, her interest in the advancement of our schools was keen and abiding. She dreamed, she thought, she planned for one improvement after another. When as a member of the General Council, she was given chief supervision of our grade schools, she threw herself with great energy into her task, planning help for the teachers, by winter study, by well-organized summer schools, and by careful study of the talents and needs of the individual teachers. Her visits to our schools gave to the teachers an enthusiasm for their sacred calling. She especially aimed to help the young teachers, by teaching classes for them, tactfully correcting faulty methods, and encouraging them to 'pray as if all depended upon God but work as if all depended upon themselves.'

. . . Sister DeRicci was a good religious. Attendance at choir, at Mass, and other community obligations were scrupulously observed. Notwithstanding her heavy responsibilities, she managed to make long visits to the Blessed Sacrament especially since we have had daily Exposition of the Blessed Sacrament here at the Motherhouse. And yet, notwithstanding the edification of her life among us, it pleased God to give her the fiery test of long and excruciating pain in preparation for death. We cannot know till Judgment Day the Divine reason for all the suffering, whether for greater and greater purification and sanctification for her own dear soul, or to win salvation or forgiveness for some of us, or to bring some specially needed help for our Congregation,—or what? But we do know that God is infinitely wise, infinitely more tender and loving than a thousand mothers, and we can confidently hope that our beloved Sister DeRicci is safe in His dear Mercy.[4]

What is not articulated in the letter but is evident in the reams of correspondence between the two sisters is Mother Samuel's dependence upon Sister DeRicci for assistance in the daily tasks of leadership and for emotional and spiritual strength in bearing the burdens of her office.

Mother Samuel's acquaintance with McNicholas spanned almost the same period of years as that with Sister DeRicci. She had first met him when Mother Emily had invited him to give a retreat at the Mound in August of 1909. He had been her spiritual advisor for all of her years as Mother General. As indicated in their correspondence over the years, he was influential in convincing her that she should accept the office of Mother General if chosen by her sisters.[5]

Mother Samuel and McNicholas engaged in frequent correspondence during the last two years of his life. One of their joint interests was encouraging Pope Pius XII to instruct priests throughout the world to offer Mass for the remission of sins on a day determined by the Holy Father. Mother Samuel had made similar suggestions through the Cardinal Protector of the Congregation to Pope Benedict XV during World War I and to Pope Pius XII during World War II, both of which were honored. In February 1948, McNicholas consulted Cardinal Stritch of Chicago and the Apostolic Delegate about such a proposal, both of whom encouraged it. Over the succeeding months of 1948, McNicholas engaged in correspondence with authorities in Rome, particularly Monsignor Tardini, Under Secretary of State to Monsignor Montini (later Pope Paul VI).[6] Tardini's response was usually encouraging, but delays ensued because

---

[4]Mission Letters, Mother Samuel to the Sisters, March 2, 1950.

[5]Correspondence, Mother Samuel Coughlin with Archbishop John T. McNicholas, 1910-1949, *passim.*

[6]McNicholas to Mother Samuel, February 16 and April 9, 1948.

Pope Pius XII wished to incorporate the proposal into a more extensive document explaining its significance.

Eventually, the suggestion was implemented in conjunction with the celebration on April 3, 1949, of the Pope's fiftieth anniversary of ordination to the priesthood. Among the reasons for his complying was his gratitude to American bishops for their contribution in 1948 of $400,000 to the Holy Father for works of charity, a project proposed by McNicholas as chairman of the administrative board of the National Catholic Welfare Conference, an office he held from 1945-1950.[7]

Mother Samuel was delighted with the outcome, but also became increasingly worried about McNicholas' health. Her invitation to him to preach at the Centennial Mass on August 15, written to him on May 18, 1949, and repeated in a letter of June 21, had to be declined. His response on June 29 was as follows:

> . . . May I send you a belated thanks for your gracious invitation to preach at the centenary of your foundation on August 15. It would give me great happiness to have the privilege of interpreting this occasion for the Dominican family of the United States and for the Sisterhoods of our country. I regret therefore, with all my heart, that I must say very frankly that I cannot attempt to preach the sermon. My physician has excluded all sermons. My preaching now is restricted to funerals of priests and to celebrations in the Diocese. I rarely speak longer than three or five minutes. . . .[8]

While he did not exclude at this time the possibility of attending the celebration, that, too, became necessary.

In her letter of June 21, Mother Samuel had informed McNicholas of the election of Sister Mary Evelyn Murphy at the General Chapter held in June. She added this comment and request:

---

[7]McNicholas to Mother Samuel, May 16, July 18, November 11, 1948; January 31, February 12, February 13, 1949.

[8]McNicholas to Mother Samuel, June 29, 1949.

. . . You have met Mother Evelyn in Fribourg and no doubt at Rosary College or elsewhere. I am confident that with God's help she will be an excellent Mother General. Very many problems await her, but she is prudent and prayerful and God's help will not be wanting. May I ask a remembrance at the Altar for her and for our Congregation? . . .[9]

McNicholas' response to that part of Mother Samuel's letter is quoted below:

Let me unite with you in thanking God that you are freed from the great responsibilities of office, after forty years of administration that have been epochal in the Dominican family of the United States. God has blessed you and your work in a degree rarely given to Superiors. It is hard for me to think of the Sinsinawa Community without Mother Samuel as its guiding Superior.

Please convey to Mother Mary Evelyn my congratulations, good wishes, and assurance of prayers. I shall write her in the near future. She may be assured, as you can be, that she and you and your Congregation are in every Mass that I say.[10]

The Reverend Edward McCarthy, Secretary to McNicholas, kept Mother Samuel informed of the Archbiship's condition, which became critical on September 16, 1949, when he suffered an embolism in the brain. He recovered to some degree over the next few months, being able on March 10, 1950, to append to McCarthy's letter what was probably his last written message to Mother Samuel: "God bless you, the Mother General, and all the members of your Congregation. Progress seems to move slowly—God's will be done. I hope you are reasonably well."[11]

His death came on Saturday, April 22, 1950, at 7:03 p.m. During the day he had offered Mass, conducted some business relating to the

---

[9]Mother Samuel to McNicholas, June 21, 1949.

[10]McNicholas to Mother Samuel, June 29, 1949.

[11]Edward McCarthy to Mother Samuel, March 10, 1950.

canonical approval of the Glenmary Home Mission Sisters, and visited briefly with Bishop Edward C. Daly of Des Moines, Iowa, his nephew, Father Tim McNicholas, and Dr. George Sperti of the Institutum Divi Thomae. Also present at the end, following the anointing by his nephew, was Monsignor Maurice E. Reardon, later the editor of the book, *Mosaic of a Bishop*, a collection of sermons and addresses by McNicholas, who had been in attendance on the Archbishop during the final days.[12]

Accompanied by Mother Evelyn, Mother Samuel attended the funeral of Archbishop McNicholas, held at St. Monica Cathedral in Cincinnati, where his body lay in state on April 26, and the Pontifical Mass was offered on April 27.[13] It was not until the end of May that Father McCarthy wrote the letter cited above, which included details of the Archbishop's comments on death during his last few days on earth. McCarthy closed his letter with the following comment that must have eased the grief felt by Mother Samuel:

> You know, I am sure, Mother, that His Grace was deeply devoted to you and always spoke of you in words of highest esteem. I trust that in a high place before the glorious throne of God he continues to remember you and all the members of your Community.[14]

Another burden of grief experienced by Mother Samuel during the early 1950s was the illness of Mother Evelyn. Early in her term, she began suffering from cancer. Between October 1951 and November 1952, she spent several periods of time at Rochester, often for tests and surgery. Between those times, she received treatments at St. Dominic Villa. From December 1952 to January 1955, her health was better than usual. During that month, however, there was a recurrence of malignancy. After some improvement in March 1955, she was able to return to the Mound.

---

[12]Edward McCarthy to Mother Samuel, May 29, 1950.

[13]Diary of Mother Samuel, April 25-27, 1950.

[14]*Ibid.*

On August 19, 1955, Mother Benedicta Larkin, who had been elected Mother General in July, informed the sisters of the progression of the illness: "It grieves me, dear Sisters, that this first general message to you must carry the word of our beloved Mother Evelyn's failing strength. On August 8 she went to Mercy Hospital in Dubuque. The following Saturday, August 13, the doctors permitted her to transfer to the Villa. Mother is suffering from a notable advance of the malady in spite of which she labored heroically to carry on in the service of the Congregation. . . ."[15] She was anointed at the Villa on September 4. Her death came at 5:40 p.m. on Friday, September 9, fifteen minutes after Mother Samuel had arrived for one of her frequent visits.[16]

Mother Evelyn's body was taken to the Mound on September 11, where the wake was held in the Community Room. The sisters at St. Clara and others from the Missions whose duties permitted them to come were in attendance day and night, saying the Office of the Dead and reciting the rosary continuously. On September 13, the early Mass of Requiem, which was to have been a Solemn Mass, had to be a low Mass instead because a storm had caused the interruption of electricity, forcing the use of candles only. During the prayers of the burial service after the Mass, the lights came on. The Solemn Requiem Mass was held at 11:00 a.m., at which the Very Reverend Edward Hughes, O.P., Provincial of the Province of St. Albert the Great, was celebrant and Bishop William P. O'Connor, the Bishop of Madison, preached the sermon and gave the last blessing. The Mass was attended by about seventy Monsignori and priests, twenty-seven sisters of other Congregations, and scores of Alumnae, other friends, and Superiors of the Sinsinawa Dominican Missions.[17]

Among other sisters and friends who died in the early and mid-fifties were: Mrs. Charles Kallal on March 7, 1951, the twenty-fifth

[15]Mission Letters, Mother Benedicta Larkin to the Sisters, August 19, 1955.

[16]Diary, 1951-1955, *passim.*

[17]Obituary for Mother Mary Evelyn Murphy, September 9, 1955.

anniversary of the death of her husband; Sister Paschala O'Connor, October 8, 1955; and on October 10, 1955, Mother Mary Joseph Rogers, Superior of the Maryknoll Congregation, whom Mother Samuel had known for forty years. Mother Benedicta Larkin and Mother Samuel attended the funeral at Maryknoll, New York, on October 13, where Francis Cardinal Spellman acted as celebrant.[18]

Mother Samuel had more time to be with her brothers and sisters and their children than had been the case during her years of congregational leadership. All of her brothers and sisters, except Sister Benetta, who had died on April 25, 1937, and her brother, John, who succumbed to an injury due to a fall on February 20, 1945, were living when she retired in 1949: Joseph, Angela, Brigid, and Daniel. Daniel's wife, Blanche, died on July 8, 1941; he married Lucille Malone Dugan (Molly) on August 12, 1947. John's wife, Anna, died on October 29, 1946.

Mother Samuel's nieces and nephews included eight in John's family: Daniel Martin (usually called Martin); Mary, married to Vincent Hunt; John E., married to Grace Kleven; Father Bernard; Ellen, married to Ray Deegan; Catherine, married to John McBride; James, married to Cleone Hauge; Samuel, married to Joan Clover.

Daniel and Blanche had one son, Bertrand, who married Barbara Temm. Joseph and his wife, Marie, had a daughter, Mary, who died in infancy, and a son, Thomas, who died at age 21.

The member of the family who most frequently came to visit Mother Samuel during her years of retirement was Bernard, who spent most of his priestly career at St. Thomas College, St. Paul, Minnesota, as teacher, Dean of Students, and Director of Activities. He regularly visited in late April to commemorate with Mother Samuel the anniversary on April 25 of Sister Benetta's death. An October visit was also regularly on his calendar. He usually stayed two or three days. She offered the responses at his Masses, and the two of them visited Sister's grave.

---

[18]Diary, March 1951; October 1955.

John Coughlin

Brigid, Daniel, Angela

Mary Hunt's family: ***top row:*** **Robert Vincent, Emily Jeanne, Elizabeth Louise, Mary Ann, William Coughlin;** ***bottom row*****: Mary Hunt, with James, Vincent with Kathleen.**

Nephew, Father Bernard Coughlin; Grandniece Kathleen Hunt

Nephew, Bertrand, wife, Barbara, son and daughters

Her brother Dan and his second wife, Molly, and her sisters, Brigid and Angela, frequently corresponded with Mother Samuel. Several deaths within her family were the occasions of visits to Faribault: her brother Joe's death on July 2, 1952; and the deaths of Vincent Hunt, husband of her niece Mary Coughlin, in March 1955; Marie, wife of Joe, January 1956; and Angela, September 18, 1956. When her brother Dan was diagnosed in the spring of 1957 as having cancer, she visited him in the hospital in Minneapolis where he had had surgery. He recovered sufficiently to return to Faribault in June, where with assistance from Brigid, Molly was able to care for him until the recurrence of cancer that led to his death on March 19, 1959.[19, 20]

Among Mother Samuel's greatest joys was having her grand-niece, Kathleen Hunt, daughter of Mary Coughlin, who had attended St. Clara College from 1916-1920, enrolled at the Academy for the last three years of her high school work, 1956-1959. Mother Samuel had opportunity for monthly visits with Kathleen, if not more frequently, and watched with pride her accomplishments in curricular and co-curricular activities.[21]

Kathleen's brother, William, took an interest in Mother Samuel, beginning with his enrollment at St. Paul Seminary in 1956. After his visit with her at the Mound in January 1957, he wrote her periodically of his studies and of the prospect of his being assigned to the four-year program at the North American College in Rome. He visited her in September 1957 before he left for Rome and kept her informed by letter of his experiences in Rome. Several Sinsinawa Dominican Sisters had opportunities to visit him on trips to Rome, including Mother Benedicta Larkin and Sister Bernadetta Duffy in December 1957.[22]

---

[19]Correspondence with Members of the Family, 1950s, *passim*; Diary, 1952-1959, *passim*.

[20]Molly died in July, 1994.

[21]Diary, 1956-1959, *passim*.

[22]Correspondence with members of the family, 1957-1958, *passim*.

Until early 1959, Mother Samuel was able to continue with most of the duties she had assumed early in her retirement. Her instruction of the novices included sessions biweekly or monthly on the Rule and Constitution, on the history of the Order and of the Congregation, and on the lives of St. Dominic and Father Samuel Mazzuchelli. She faithfully edited the quarterly issues of the Newsletter, though with increasing assistance from novices assigned to help her. The writing of obituaries remained one of her more important services. She also continued to attend meetings of the General Council.[23]

As had been the case during her years as Mother General, Mother Samuel frequently experienced illnesses and infirmities, occasions of which became more frequent as the decade of the 1950s advanced. She often felt pain or weakness for two or three hours at a time, requiring bed rest at various times during the day. Some of the problems were due to arthritis and to the recurring effects of the injury to her left shoulder in December 1930. For several years, she suffered from an umbilical hernia, which was finally relieved by surgery in August 1957. Occasionally, she experienced heart problems, such as auricular fibrillation, and was subject to frequent colds.

A significant change came in March 1959. Mother Benedicta reported to the sisters about the incident that seemed to trigger Mother Samuel's decline in health:

On Holy Saturday afternoon as she was leaving the confessional, she fell and is suffering today from the pain of a wrenched back. Dr. Strauch was called and gave us assurance that there was not a fracture of any kind. . . . She is cheerful and full of courage. She is eager, as usual, to resume as soon as she can the complete round of Community exercises. Her favorite expression, one she has been saying over long years—almost an ejaculation—is, 'I wish we were all in heaven.'[24]

---

[23]Diary, 1950-1958.

[24]Mission Letters, Mother Benedicta Larkin to the Sisters, March 29, 1959.

Mother Samuel suffered another fall in her room on July 14, and on August 25 experienced a period of great weakness, on both of which occasions she was anointed. Her nephew, Father Bernard, came from St. Paul to visit her at the end of August. Dr. Strauch attributed the weakness to slight strokes to which he said she would probably continue to be subject.[25] From this time on, sisters were in constant attendance upon her in her room at the Mound.

On October 13, a message came for her from Joseph Cardinal Pizzardo, Cardinal Protector of the Congregation and long-time friend of Mother Samuel, with a special blessing from Pope John XXIII and a rosary and medal blessed by him. The medal with an image of the Holy Family on one side and the likeness of Pope John on the other was attached to the chain around Mother Samuel's neck on which hung her relic of the True Cross. The white rosary was entwined around her right forearm. She seemed aware of what was happening and was able to respond with the ejaculation, "Hail Mary," and to request that the sisters pray that "God may forgive me all my sins," for "the intentions of the Holy Father," and "for the conversion of sinners."[26]

On Thursday morning, October 15, Mother Samuel seemed aware of the significance of the day as being the Feast Day of her patroness, St. Theresa. She also showed some response on the following day when told it was the fiftieth anniversary of the death of Mother Emily Power. Father Walker anointed her that evening of October 16. Her last word was spoken on Saturday morning, October 17, her "Yes" in response to Sister Mary Camillus Harney's question whether she would like to receive Holy Viaticum. Her death came at 11:35 a.m., shortly after the sisters in attendance had sung the *Salve Regina* and the *O Lumen*, and had begun the Litany for the Dying.[27]

---

[25]Obituary, Mother Mary Samuel Coughlin, October 17, 1959, p. 1.

[26]*Ibid.*, pp. 1-2.

[27]*Ibid.*, p. 3.

On this day of Mother Samuel's death, her sister Brigid wrote the following note to Mother Benedicta:

My dear Sister Benedicta,

Your letter reached me about an hour ago, and I am very grateful to you for it.

I cannot feel that a visit to Mother now would benefit either her or me. Dr. Samuel thought that she did not recognize him at his second visit.

It is a comfort to know that she is receiving the best possible spiritual and physical care, and we must leave the rest to God, who has done so much for her in her long life.

Gratefully,
Brigid[28]

The section below, taken from the obituary, describes the funeral services.

It was arranged to have Mother's remains taken to St. Dominic Villa on Saturday evening in order that the Sisters nearest to her in age, and all the sick not confined to bed might look upon her countenance in death and pray at her bier. About nine o'clock Sister Bernadetta Duffy, Sister Thomas Kellogg, Sister Amata O'Brien, and Sister Mary Enos Patrick then accompanied her mortal remains from Dubuque in a final Homecoming to St. Clara. The Sisters carrying lighted candles waited on the steps leading to the convent entrance while novices lined the walk, all praying the rosary.

Day and night vigil was kept by a guard of two Sisters. The rosary was prayed from hour to hour Saturday night, Sunday, Monday, and Tuesday and until the time of the eight-thirty Mass on Wednesday. Many priests, Sisters of other communities, and lay friends from near and far came to pay their respects. Scores of Sisters from the less distant missions also came to watch, to pray, to touch the hands wherein their own had been laid when making the divine engagement of their vows.

---

[28] Correspondence with Close Relatives, October 17, 1959.

Vespers and the first Nocturn of Matins of the Office of the Dead were recited Tuesday afternoon. At eight-thirty in the evening in the chapel the second and third Nocturns of Matins were said, followed by Lauds.

On Wednesday morning, October 21, at eight-fifteen, Sisters carrying lighted candles formed the Libera procession for the transfer of the coffin from the community room to the chapel. At eight-thirty the Reverend Bernard Coughlin of St. Thomas College, St. Paul, Minnesota, nephew of Mother Samuel, celebrated the Requiem High Mass, which was sung chorally. The St. Clara Community, novices, postulants, academy students and the members of the Coughlin Family were present. The Very Reverend J.B. Walker, Chaplain, gave a consoling and inspiring sermon. Office of Burial according to the Dominican Rite followed with its notes of promise and triumph. . . .

At eleven o'clock the Dominican Solemn Requiem Mass was offered by the Very Reverend John Alexius Driscoll, O.P., American Socius to the Master General of the Order of Preachers, celebrant; the Very Reverend Donald G. Sherry, O.P., Vicar Provincial of St. Albert Province, deacon; the Very Reverend Leo T. Dolan, O.P., St. Rose Priory, Dubuque, sub-deacon. The Reverend W.J. Aldridge, O.P., Chaplain at Trinity High School, River Forest, and the Reverend J.B.Schneider, O.P., St. Pius Priory, Chicago, acted as acolytes. His Excellency, the Most Reverend Bishop O'Connor, presided in the sanctuary, delivered the sermon, and gave the absolution. Present in the sanctuary also was the Very Reverend Dom Philip O'Connor, O.C.S.O., Abbot of Our Lady of New Melleray, Dubuque. About thirty Monsignori were in attendance with nearly one hundred priests; many Religious of other Communities; ninety Superiors from our Mission Houses, and a group of twenty or twenty-five lay guests.

The members of the Coughlin Family included Miss Brigid Coughlin of Faribault, the sole survivor of Mother's immediate family; Mrs. Daniel Coughlin; Mrs. Mary Coughlin Hunt, a niece; a grandniece, Kathleen Hunt; Mr. and Mrs. Martin Coughlin; Mr. and Mrs. John Coughlin; Mr. and Mrs. John McBride (Catherine Coughlin); Sophia Coughlin, grandniece; Mr. and Mrs. W. Moudry, cousins; Sister Mary Patrick, O.S.F., of Winona, a cousin, and Sister Mary Helen, O.S.F., Sister Richard Barden's niece.

John Coughlin, John McBride, Julius Loosbrock, Francis O'Connor, Odilo Conlon, and Doctor Henry Willits served as pall-bearers. (Titles, except 'Doctor' are eliminated.)

The procession formed to escort the coffin from the chapel to the cemetery. Along the Green Road, St. Clara Academy students stood in blue and white uniforms, a reverent guard of honor. It was a day of autumnal glory, maple trees flashing gold and oaks bronzed against the blue October sky. The postulants in a black line girded the first section of the cemetery from the gate along the north and west novices following the cross bearer as far as the great crucifix then circled round in the section to the south opposite to the postulants and close to the hedge. The professed Sisters in turn moved around Mother Emily's grave, passed Mother Evelyn's, and on to places in serried black and white rows in front of the postulants.

Dominican Sisters from Columbus, Springfield, Kenosha, Racine, Adrian, Maryknoll, Sisters of Mercy, of the Visitation, of the Presentation, Franciscans, and Sisters of Charity of the Blessed Virgin Mary were in the aisle to the east; lay guests to the south behind the Crucifix; Dominican Fathers, Monsignori and other members of the clergy came last into the aisle to the west; the Mother General, the Prioress of Saint Clara Convent, and the members of the General Council, followed by the mourners in the Coughlin Family, stood close to the grave. His Excellency, Bishop O'Connor, the ministers of the Mass and clerical assistants took their station on the walk at the foot of the Crucifix next to Mother Emily's headstone, at the foot of the new grave.

Bishop O'Connor blessing Mother Samuel's grave, October 21, 1959.

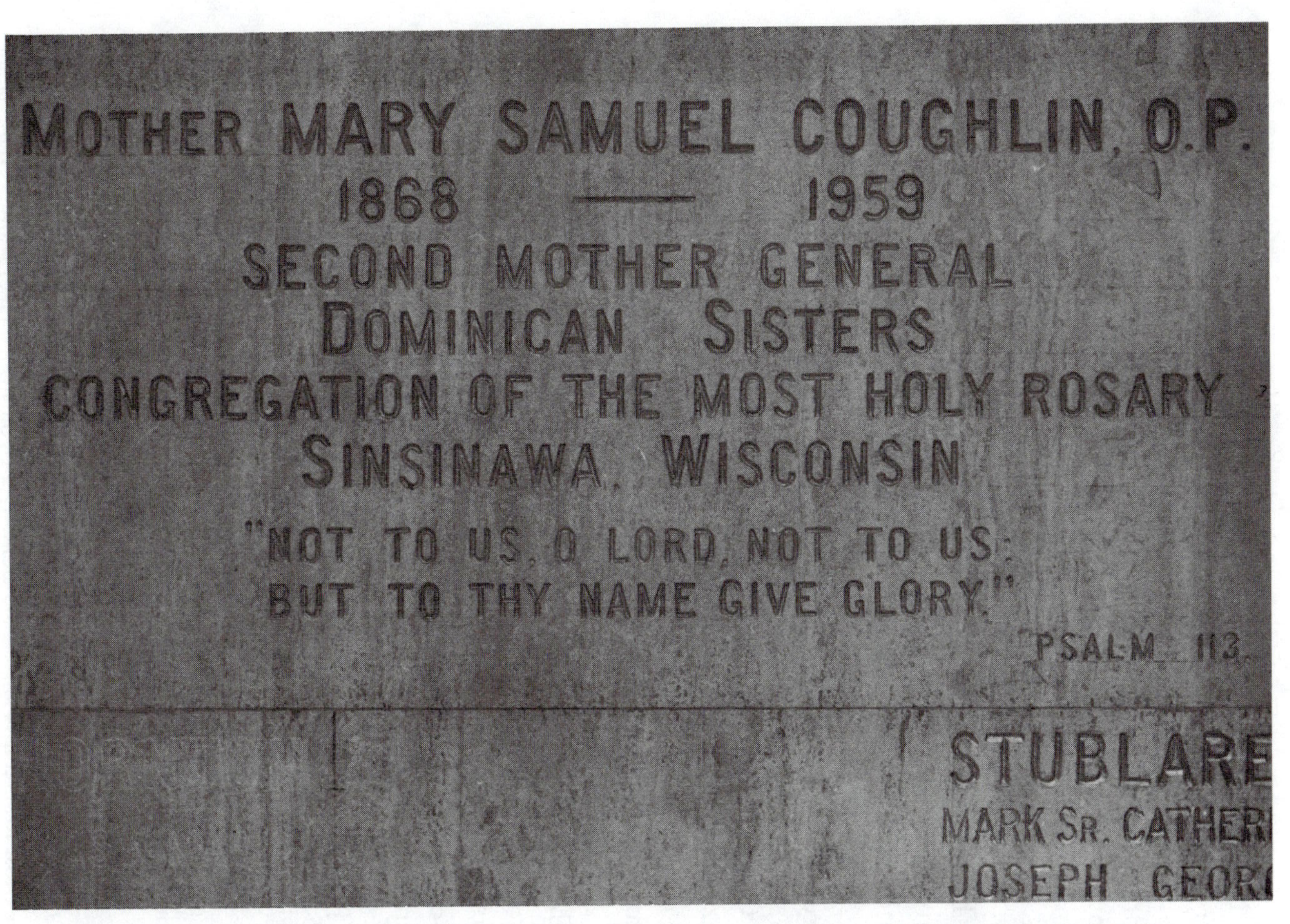

Mother Samuel's Memorial Tablet, Shrine of the Immaculate Conception, Washington, D. C.

Mother Samuel often spoke with awe of the cemetery as a holy place. Her precious body was interred there to the chant of the Benedictus to await God's hour for resurrection in the company of Mother Emily, Mother Evelyn, her own sister, Sister Mary Benetta, and the seven hundred of our dear departed Sinsinawa Family—all but a few of whom Mother had known in life and saw go before her signed with the sign of faith.

Requiescant in peace.[29]

Bishop O'Connor's sermon was a magnificent tribute to Mother Samuel, a deep consolation to the sisters and to the members of her family, and valuable documentation for historians.

Among the characteristics of Mother Samuel that he stressed were:

One who had imbibed the spirit of the Reverend Samuel Charles Mazzuchelli, Founder of the Sinsinawa Dominican Congregation;

a stately, quiet, modestly humble, energetic and efficient leader of this great community of Sisters;

a deeply spiritual woman who sought strength from Our Divine Savior in the tabernacle;

one who wanted her sisters to learn to bear the Cross, to take Mary as their model, and to base their lives upon a strong, basic, interior life;

one who hoped to prepare teachers who were not only good but learned.[30]

His concluding paragraphs were ringing accolades:

Who can ever measure the service rendered by this woman who with rare vision and rare sagacity, rare astuteness, saw where she could best place these educated and trained young Sisters so that they might do the greatest amount of good for Holy Mother Church and the Kingdom of God?

---

[29] *Ibid.*, pp. 3-4.

[30] The Most Reverend William P. O'Connor, Sermon at Funeral of Mother Mary Samuel Coughlin, October 21, 1959.

Thousands and thousands of souls have been saved and will be saved because of her service and the service of the holy women, educated and trained women, that she has helped to prepare here at Sinsinawa.

While it is natural for the Sisters to feel the pangs of separation, I am sure that there is a certain joy also in their religious souls at the passing of Mother Samuel. She turns a page in your history, a glorious page, a golden page—but you are writing another one. If she had an opportunity to stand here this morning, I think she would say: "Remember your Dominican ideals; remember what St. Dominic said: 'I leave you a modest humility; I leave you a love of poverty; and I leave you a Divine charity.'" She would say that to you. Keep alive the traditions and the ideals which were established here by Father Mazzuchelli and which have been continued by Mother Emily, and later Mother Samuel, Mother Evelyn, and now Mother Benedicta. Be loyal to these ideals. Every day on your knees thank God for your vocation. Thank God for the great privilege that He has given you, the privilege to live a life of spirituality, a life of learning, and a life of service to God and to mankind.

May God bless you and may God bless her. May God keep her in His loving care. May God love you. May God love her forever.[31]

The hundreds of tributes that came from clergy, religious, former students, civic leaders and other lay people across the land and abroad echoed many of the themes expressed by Bishop O'Connor. Dozens of letters also came from Sisters of the Congregation who had not been able to attend the funeral because of limitation on space or obligations to their ministry. One letter typifying the sentiments expressed by the Sisters is the one below, sent by Sister Avellina Buckley, then at Sioux Falls:

My dear Mother Benedicta and the Council Members:

We just heard Sister's report of Mother Samuel's funeral. The occasion is one of grief to all of us but especially to you. I will not attempt to eulogize her—much has been said and will be said in her praise. If we said

---

[31]*Ibid.*, p. 3. The full text of the Sermon is given in the Appendix.

nothing, the very stones would cry out and the reverberations [would] go on through the ages. What I shall attempt to write is this.

To us who loved Mother Samuel, it has been the greatest comfort to know that in her failing years she was in the midst of such kindness and understanding. Never for a moment could she feel unwanted or that her words of wisdom were unheeded. It gave us implicit trust in you, and the feeling that many of the gifts given to her through nature and Grace were simply being transferred into other channels. May she continue to direct you from her well-earned place in heaven. My prayers and loving sympathy go to you.

In St. Dominic,
Sister M. Avellina[32]

---

[32]Sister M. Avellina Buckley, Letters of Tribute to Mother Samuel, October 22, 1959.

Chapter Nine

Her Legacy

Mother Mary Samuel Coughlin was a woman of her time, favored by natural ability and family circumstance to emerge as a leader. Her companions recognized her gifts and designated her for positions of authority. Mother Mary Emily Power was the one most responsible for calling Mother Samuel to use her gifts. In keeping with her vow of obedience made to Mother Emily on August 15, 1887, for three years, and on August 15, 1890, for life, Mother Samuel had cheerfully responded to her assignments to Lemont, Illinois, in 1888-89, to Holy Rosary, Minneapolis, 1889-1901, to St. Clara in 1901 as instructor in English for Academy and College and as Bursar-General of the Congregation, a position conferred upon her by the diffinitory of the General Chapter of 1901.

Her life changed dramatically and forever in July 1904. On July 9, Mother Emily asked Mother Samuel to meet with her in the Bay Window Room outside the Chapel on the third floor of the 1882 Academy and College Building. There, overlooking the countryside where the three states of Illinois, Wisconsin, and Iowa intersect, Mother Emily told Mother Samuel that she intended to appoint her, Mother Samuel, prioress of St. Clara, a position that carried with it the responsibilities of directress of Academy and College. The General Council proceeded with the notification on August 24, 1904. The two dates, July 9, and August 24, 1904, henceforward were regarded by Mother Samuel as the "most awful days of my life," as "the anniversary of the beginning of my big worries."[1]

Her "yes" at this time, given, no doubt, as conscious assent under her vow of obedience, committed her to duties that she thought she could not possibly discharge. Having said "yes" to this position in the

---

[1]Diary, Mother Samuel Coughlin, *passim.* The latest recorded reference of this sort was July 9, 1957.

summer of 1904, she found it impossible to refuse other positions as these were put before her over the years. She accepted a position as member of the General Council in August 1907; and an appointment by Mother Emily as Vicaress of the Congregation in June 1908. By virtue of this appointment and of her position as prioress of St. Clara, she served as acting-Mother General upon Mother Emily's death. Her other "yeses" included her acceptance of election to the three-years of Mother Emily's uncompleted term in August 1910 and to the six terms of six years each that followed.

With sincere conviction she deemed herself unworthy of and unequal to the tasks she nevertheless felt bound to accept. The diary entries quoted in this text on the occasion of the elections are striking proof of her reluctance and her suffering in face of these burdens. Her reason for accepting always came down to the belief, fostered by John T. McNicholas, that the will of the sisters expressed through election was the will of God.

Her consciousness of the burden she carried was ever vivid to her, rather than something that troubled her only occasionally. Physical weariness was a constant challenge. The seasonal duties of preparing summer and fall assignments and providing substitutes throughout the year were demanding. Visitation of convents on a biennial schedule or annually, as in the case of St. Vincent Sanitorium in Denver, Colorado, required absences from the Motherhouse of several days, even weeks at a time. The mail that piled up when she was away was one of her most exhausting tasks. Telephone calls and visits from priests seeking commitments for staffing their schools or from pastors requesting changes in staffing and visits from bishops making courtesy calls or conducting business of a special nature expanded her business responsibilities.

Her physical weariness wore down her resistance and subjected her to illnesses of various kinds. She suffered frequent spells of heart trouble, flu-like symptoms, and nervous disorders. On several occasions she was forced to spend weeks in extended recuperation from maladies, injuries, and surgery, at which times Sister DeRicci acted as vicaress.

Day after day, her diary entries contain expressions concerning worry, tiredness, fear, humiliation, disappointing mail, and illness. Her worries extended to her own family members and the family members of the sisters. Among her greatest burdens was her concern for sisters who were ill, especially those suffering mental illness with which the Congregation was not yet prepared to cope adequately.

Her lifeline throughout all these trials was her rootedness in the spiritual life, especially her devotion to the eucharistic presence of Christ. Sister Louis Bertrand recalls in her reminiscences that Mother Samuel's first visit on arriving at a Mission was to the convent chapel, "There to salute the 'Master of the House' and beg His blessing on the purposes of her visitation." When she was leaving, she would open the chapel door and kneel for a brief farewell to the Lord.[2] In addition to being present for regular times of prayer unless urgent business prohibited it, Mother Samuel spent additional time in chapel for holy hours and other times of adoration. One of her greatest moments was the occasion on September 12, 1940, when Bishop Griffin of LaCrosse granted the privilege of daily exposition of the Most Blessed Sacrament in St. Clara Chapel.[3] Her general letters to the sisters continually stressed the importance of prayer, especially the rosary, and called for novenas at regular times throughout the year and for special needs. She found further comfort in the practice of reading daily from Holy Scripture, completing the entire Bible almost every year.

Despite, or perhaps because of, the suffering endured by Mother Samuel, she maintained an effective administration and governed with steadiness and vision. Most important to the future of the Congregation was her ability to maintain unity, a trait appreciated by the sisters and one of which Archbishop McNicholas was conscious throughout her administration. She commanded the respect of all with whom she worked: fellow council members, superiors, the sisters

---

[2]Reminiscences of Mother Samuel Coughlin, Sister Louis Bertrand Droege, p. 5.

[3]Diary, September 12, 1940.

in general, pastors, bishops, Roman hierarchy, business men. In difficulties involving pastors and the sisters on the missions, Mother Samuel worked skillfully to defuse tension and reach decisions that respected all parties involved. There were few "scolding" letters among those she received from bishops and pastors. At the same time, she insisted upon proper deference from the sisters towards the priests and proper respect for school and convent properties. Personally and through the superiors and principals, she carefully upheld Church doctrine and moral standards such as those in dress and behavior on the part of the students. She kept constant vigilance in calling forth the sisters' obedience to the Rule and Constitutions.

Of all that Mother Mary Samuel Coughlin hoped that her sisters would accomplish, nothing was more significant than the combination of holiness and learning. She wanted the Congregation to be one of saints and scholars. That is the phrase she used in her final message as Mother General: "May each of you, dearest Sisters, aim to make our Congregation a community of saints and scholars, by having one heart and soul in God, loving and observing the Rule and Constitutions, living in God's presence and loyally obeying and cooperating with your local and General Superior" (see page 164).

Building on programs for the education of the sisters begun under Mother Emily, Mother Samuel and Sister DeRicci worked tirelessly to provide higher education for the sisters: the colleges, the Institute at Fribourg, summer sessions, Saturday classes during the school year, released time for university education at Catholic, public, and private universities. Other forms of education, such as the organization of study groups by discipline for high school teachers and the establishment of the Sinsinawa Dominican Education Conference for grade school teachers further promoted the education and personal development of the sisters.

Mother Samuel's legacy included on-going development in programs of inter-congregational activity, especially with the Dominican Mothers General Conference but including also programs for the initial formation of sisters. These activities were encouraged by Pope Pius XII during the 1950s and resulted in tangible outcomes such as the organization of the Conferences of Major Superiors of Men and of Women, and the establishment of Regina Mundi in Rome in 1956 by the Sacred Congregation of Religious to prepare directors of formation. Though this institution did not fully conform to the dream Mother Samuel had held for decades of "a house in Rome," it met some of her initial goals.

Mother Samuel's leadership as Mother General in two other areas of activity helped provide links to developments associated with Vatican Council II. These were diversification of ministries and revision of constitutions. During the last twenty-five years of her administration, beginning with the organization of vacation catechism programs in the mid-twenties, the Congregation had diversified its services in formal ways; and it continued to provide help in informal ways to the children and their families whenever the need arose. Many of these services would later become the focus of formal programs.

Next to her disappointment regarding not obtaining a house in Rome, the failure to achieve an appropriate revision of the Constitutions of the Congregation was perhaps Mother Samuel's greatest disappointment. The experience gained in the effort documented in Chapter Five (pp. 85-86; 88-89; 92-94) was not a total loss, however. The episode had provided for the raising of awareness on the part of all of the sisters of ways in which our Constitutions could be improved. The identification of the parts that would be suitable to change—matters related to ritual and discipline as contrasted with the essentials of religious life—would be instructive when Vatican Council II called for the reopening of such questions.

As the Sinsinawa Dominican Congegation of the Most Holy Rosary looks forward to the celebration in 1997 of the sesquicentennial of its founding, it has one more part of Mother Samuel's legacy to honor: her appreciation of the worthiness of Father Samuel for beatification. Very soon after she was elected Mother General, she authorized the translation and publication of his *Memoirs.* At every chance she had, she encouraged the copying of documents by and about Father Samuel, including especially those in Roman archives. Mother Samuel carefully guided the process for studying the possible canonization of Father Samuel, working in collaboration with the Dominican Fathers and appropriate Church officials. Building step-by-step on Mother Samuel's contributions, the process, guided in its final stages by Sister Mary Nona McGreal, culminated on July 6, 1993, with the declaration of Father Samuel Mazzuchelli as Venerable.

The title of this biography, *Your Will Be Done*, reflects the reality of her deep suffering freely and fully accepted and offered for the honor and glory of God and the salvation of her soul. How fortunate for the sisters whom she led for forty years, the people whom the sisters served, and those who continue to benefit from her legacy!

Appendix A
Ancestry and Family Relationships

John Coughlin—Mary O'Brien
Timothy Coughlin—Mary Mehigan

Jeremiah O'Mahoney—Murray
Jeremiah O'Mahoney—Honora Burns

Daniel Coughlin—Ellen O'Mahoney

Mary Ann (died in infancy)
John Patrick—Anna Muldown
- Daniel Martin—Elizabeth Blackwood
- Mary B.—Vincent Hunt
  - Mary Ann
  - Emily Jeanne
  - Elizabeth Marie
  - Robert Vincent
  - William Coughlin
  - Kathleen
  - James
- John Eugene—Grace Kleven
  - John Patrick
  - Anne Elizabeth
- Fr. Bernard J.
- Ellen Gertrude—Ray Deegan
  - Paul Joseph
  - Daniel David
- James P.—Cleone Hauge
  - Julie Anna
- Catherine Elizabeth—John McBride
- Samuel Thomas—Joan Clover
  - Sophia Marie
  - Joseph John
  - Lester Thomas
  - George Patrick

Ellen Theresa (Mother Samuel)
Mary E. (Sister Benetta)
Joseph—Marie Dusterhoff
- Thomas J.

Angela C.
Brigid A.
Daniel D.—
(1st)-Blanche Abbey;
(2nd) Lucille Malone Dugan (Molly)
- Bertrand Daniel—Barbara Temm
  - Barbara
  - Blanche
  - Bertrand Daniel, Jr.

The O'Mahoneys—Brothers and Sisters of Mother Samuel's Mother

Mary O'Mahoney—John Kelly
Four sons: Pat, John, Robert, Jerry
One daughter: Margaret (Sister Samuel)

Michael O'Mahoney—Jude Collins
Three sons: Jerry, John, Mike
One daughter: Catherine

John O'Mahoney—Anne O'Neil
Two sons: John, Robert
One daughter: Mary

Catherine O'Mahoney—John Coughlin

Jeremiah O'Mahoney—Julia Stack
Three sons: James, John, Joseph
Two daughters: Honora, Mary Ellen

(Marie Mahoney Fitzgerald of South Dartmouth, Massachusetts, who provided the above information, is descended from Michael O'Mahoney.)

Appendix B

Funeral Sermon for Mother Samuel Coughlin

By the Most Reverend William P. O'Connor, Ph.D., D.D.,
Wednesday, October 21, 1959, Saint Clara Chapel
Sinsinawa, Wisconsin.

Right Reverend, Very Reverend, Reverend Fathers, devoted and bereaved Sisters, relatives and friends:

In the Name of the Father and of the Son and of the Holy Spirit, Amen.

At the end of a very long life and a remarkable career in religion, Mother Samuel might well have made her own those beautiful and comforting words of the Psalmist: 'In peace in the selfsame I shall sleep, and I shall rest, for Thou, O Lord, has strengthened me singularly in hope.'

It is not necessary for me to tell anyone who is here who knows the story of Mother Samuel that she was a great woman, that she was a great person, that she was a good religious. It is not necessary for me . . . to attempt to utter a eulogy of this woman—her life has been her eulogy, for seventy long years a dedicated daughter of St. Dominic in dedicated service of her Divine Master and the Master of St. Dominic; forty of those seventy years spent as the Mother General of this community—an extraordinary term of office. . . . Not an easy thing to be mother to such a great family! No other mother in the world, no natural mother, had the trials and the tribulations, and the cares and the consolations that this woman had during her long religious career.

Coming here as a young girl from Bethlehem Academy in Faribault, she learned something of the spirit of the zealous missionary who founded this community, Father Mazzuchelli. With great vision and with that energy which was chracteristic of the man, he planned an Order of Religious Women, who might dedicate themselves to the ideals of spirituality, of learning and of service. The spirit that was enkindled here followed him to Benton where he set up this academy for girls which saw the beginnings of this life of spirituality and of learning and of service. Then there was the coming back to this sacred spot, the Mound, which is so revered and so loved by every young girl who has come here to dedicate her life to the high ideals of the Dominican Sisters. When Mother Samuel came as a young girl she felt at home and never felt homesick again.

I had the privilege of knowing Mother Samuel a long time; in fact, I knew her predecessor, Mother Emily. I made the first speech I ever made, when I was about six years old, to Mother Emily at old St. John's Cathedral School. Perhaps Mother Samuel was there—I can't remember, it is so long ago. But I can remember the first time I met Mother Samuel, after my ordination, when I was a young priest at St. Rose's in Milwaukee, with the impression that she made upon me—stately, quiet, modestly humble, the energetic and efficient leader of this great community of Sisters.

Mother Samuel believed, above all, that every religious must be *religious.* She believed with Dom Chautard that the soul of the apostolate is the apostolate of the soul. She believed that first of all she must become deeply religious if she were to educate and train other religious. She was a deeply spiritual woman. She sought strength from Our Divine Saviour in the tabernacle. She began the beautiful devotion, daily adoration of the Blessed Sacrament here at the Mound which continues even to this day. She wanted the Sisters to realize that in the Blessed Sacrament would they find the sources of their dynamism, of their energy, the spiritual energy that would be indispensable for the fulfillment of their vocation. She wanted them to learn, furthermore, to meditate upon the Passion here in the presence of the Eucharistic Saviour that they too might be able to face the crosses, the trials, the weaknesses, the defeats and the frustrations of everyday life, the things that come not only to every human being but come to a religious, sometimes in a peculiarly acute way. She wanted them to learn to bear the cross because she knew that they had to bear the cross and that others who came after her would have to bear the cross. Above all things, Mother Samuel sought to turn the minds and hearts of her Sisters to that valiant woman, Mary, asking them to take her as their model in so far as they could. Particularly, she asked them to hold the beads of her rosary in their hands day and night. She asked them to walk side by side with Mary through their everyday tasks and to fear nothing so long as Mary was at their side.

It is tremendously important in our own day for religious to realize that their lives must be founded upon a strong, basic interior life. It is becoming more and more difficult for them to think of supernatural truths. Our minds are so deeply immersed in the material that it is difficult to draw them away from the attractiveness of things to the importance of truth, and goodness, and beauty and holiness. Our minds are not exercised sufficiently on the supernatural, and the spiritual and the metaphysical. We have become dull in these tremendously important approaches to the understanding and comprehension of reality. God has faded into the distance of unexplored space. Men are so engrossed in the things that surround them that they have lost their vision of the better things. Men sometimes are so steeped in the physical, even in the evil physical, that they can't see God, for no man sees God clearly though sin-stained eyes.

Mother Samuel held fast to the ideal of personal spirituality and of passing on this ideal to those whom God in His goodness had committed to her care. Here at the Mound she caught the ideal of learning. Here she came to realize, as St. Dominic realized when he began fashioning the community at Prouille and the Third Order and the Order of men, that the world needed teachers who are not only holy but are also learned. St. Alphonsus says somewhere that the world needs *good* teachers. If these teachers be holy, well and good, but they must also be learned, lest they be like soldiers without arms. That is important in our day when so much attention is being paid to the cultivation of the intellect.

It is important for our spiritual leaders to be persons of learning. Mother Samuel was. She was a learned woman. She not only believed in her own personal cultivation, but she believed in giving to those entrusted to her care opportunities to acquire personal culture.

You know of Rosary College (who doesn't in the Midwest or throughout the country). You know of Edgewood College where such splendid opportunities are being given to the young novices to acquire a college education and culture for their future work on the missions. You know of Fougères in Switzerland and the Villa Schifanoia in Italy, (I was there a few weeks ago), a beautiful spot, so beautifully fitted for the task in which it is engaged, the promotion of the fine arts.

Mother Samuel believed not in any kind of learning but in Christian learning—and there is a Christian learning. There is a Christian attitude toward things and persons which is very, very important. Someone has said that the most important task of all for a person is to know how to get along with other persons and to know how to communicate with other persons. Our Christian learning must be learning of a kind that enables us to understand the importance of personal relations in our own lives and in the lives of others, personal relations with other persons who are made in the image and likeness of God, even as we are, personal relations with the Divine Persons, with God the Father, God the Son, God the Holy Spirit.

In the Book of Deuteronomy you read about the greatest and first commandment: it is to love God with your whole heart, your whole soul, your whole mind and with all your strength. The second is like to this: thou shalt love they neighbor as thyself—in personal relations. This is at the heart of Christian learning. We believe that unless we stand in right relations with the Second Person of the Most Holy Trinity become incarnate, that we can not know the truth because He is Incarnate Truth; we can not know the way; we can not know the life to lead, for did He not say, 'I am the way, the Truth and the Life?' There is a Christian learning which must grow in modest humility of intellect not only in knowledge of those truths that can be seen by the natural light of the human mind, but of those which are received through the goodness of the Incarnate Truth, the Truth of His revelation.

Mother Samuel believed not only in learning for its own sake. She believed in Christian learning for the soul's sake, for the sake of mankind and the salvation of souls. Mother Samuel found here at Sinsinawa the ideal of service to others. There are many priests here this morning and they are here because the Dominican Sisters have been rendering service to their parishes across the years. From New York to San Francisco, from the deep South to the far North, these Sisters are spread across the land, dedicated and consecrated to one single task, the task of serving others through teaching in our elementary schools, our secondary schools and our colleges. This is rather unique among the Sisterhoods in the United States. We of the Dominicans of Sinsinawa are teachers.

Who can ever measure the service rendered by this woman who with rare vision and rare sagacity, rare astuteness, saw where she could best place these educated and trained young Sisters so that they might do the greatest amount of good for Holy Mother Church and the Kingdom of God? Thousands and thousands of souls have been saved and will be saved because of her service and the service of the holy women, educated and trained women, that she has helped to prepare here at Sinsinawa.

While it is natural for the Sisters to feel the pangs of separation, I am sure that there is a certain joy also in their religious souls at the passing of Mother Samuel. She turns a page in your history, a glorious page, a golden page—but you are writing another one. If she had an opportunity to stand here this morning I think she would say: 'Remember your Dominican ideals; remember what St. Dominic said, I leave a modest humility; I leave you a love of poverty; and I leave you a divine charity.' She would say that to you. Keep alive the traditions and ideals which were established here by Father Mazzuchelli and which have been continued by the first Mother, Mother Emily, and later Mother Samuel, Mother Evelyn and now Mother Benedicta. Be loyal to these ideals. Every day on your knees thank God for your vocation. Thank God for the great privilege that

He has given you, the privilege to live a life of spirituality, a life of learning, and a life of service to God and to mankind.

May God bless you and may God bless her. May God keep her in His loving care. May God love you. May God love her forever.

Bibliography

Archival Records

Sinsinawa Dominican Archives
- Diary of Mother Mary Samuel Coughlin
- Papers of Mother Mary Samuel Coughlin
  - Mission Letters (Letters of Mothers General to all of the Sisters)
- Correspondence:
  - with the Holy See;
  - with Bishops;
  - with Diocesan Officials
  - with Pastors;
  - with Dominican Fathers;
  - with Nadia Boulanger;
  - with other Laity;
  - with Sister DeRicci Fitzgerald
  - with Superiors;
  - with individual Sisters;
  - with Sisters of other Congregations;
  - with Family Members.
- Annals of St. Clara Convent
- Annals of Local Missions
- Book of Foundations
- Records of General Council Meetings
- Records of General Chapters
- Records of Dominican Mothers General Conference
- *Sinsinawa Dominican Newsletter*, 1920-1959
- Obituary Records

Minnesota Historical Society
- Records of Rice and Steele Counties

Wisconsin Historical Society
- Map Room Documents

Official Records

Catholic Directory, 1835-1993. Published under various titles: *United States Catholic Almanac; Metropolitan Catholic Almanac; Sadlier's Catholic Directory; Official Catholic Directory.*

Records of Rice County, County Courthouse, Faribault, Minnesota.

Books and Articles

Bethlehem in Fairbault, 1865-1915. Minnesota, Jubilee year, 1915.

Blegen, Theodore C. *Minnesota: A History of the State*. Minneapolis: University of Minnesota Press, 1963.

Boo, Mary Richard, O.S.B. *House of Stone: The Duluth Benedictines*. Duluth, Minnesota: St. Scholastica Priory Books, 1991.

Bras, Sister Benvenuta , O.P. "Rosary College Unit, Institutum Divi Thomae, 1938-1946," October 1986.

Campbell, Debra. "Part-Time Female Evangelists of the Thirties and Forties: The Rosary College Catholic Evidence Guild." *U.S. Catholic Historian*, V, Summer/Fall, 1986, 371-383.

Condon, William H. *The Life of Major-General James Shields: Hero of Three Wars and Senator from Three States*. Chicago: Blakely Printing Co., 1900.

Connors, Joseph B. *Journey toward Fulfillment: A History of the College of St. Thomas*. St. Paul, Minnesota: College of St. Thomas, 1986.

Documents of American History. Edited by Henry Steele Commager. Seventh Edition. New York: Appleton-Century-Crofts, 1963.

Dictionary of American Biography. New York: Scribner's, 1964.

Folwell, William Watts. *A History of Minnesota, 1833-1929*. Four Volumes. St. Paul: The Minnesota Historical Society, 1921-1930.

Garnier, Charles Marie. *A Popular History of Ireland*. Translated and Adapted by Hedley McCay. Baltimore: Helicon Press, 1961.

History of Rice and Steele Counties, Minnesota. Compiled by Franklyn Curtiss-Wedge. Two volumes. Chicago: H. C. Cooper, Jr. & Co., 1910.

Kantowicz, Edward R. *Corporation Sole: Cardinal Mundelein and Chicago Catholicism.* Notre Dame, Indiana: U. of Notre Dame Press, 1983.

Lernoux, Penny. *Hearts on Fire: The Story of the Maryknoll Sisters.* Maryknoll, New York: Orbis Books, 1993.

McCarty, Sister Mary Eva, O.P. *The Sinsinawa Dominicans: Outlines of Twentieth Century Development, 1901-1949.* Sinsinawa, Wisconsin: St. Clara Convent, 1952.

McGreal, Sister Mary Nona, O.P. *Samuel Mazzuchelli, O.P., a Missionary to the United States: A Documentary Account of His Life, Virtues, and Reputation for Holiness.* (Rome, 1989)

The Memoirs of Father Samuel Mazzuchelli, O.P. Translated by Sister Maria Michele Armato, O.P., and Sister Mary Jeremy Finnegan, O.P. Chicago: The Priory Press, 1967.

Mosaic of a Bishop: An Autobiographical Appreciation of His Grace, the Most Reverend John T. McNicholas, O.P. Compiled by Maurice E. Reardon, S.T.D. Cincinnati: Archdiocese of Cincinnati, 1957.

Mohnihan, James H. *The Life of Archbishop John Ireland.* New York: Harper & Brothers, 1953.

O'Connell, Marvin R. *John Ireland and the American Catholic Church.* St. Paul: Minnesota Historical Society Press: 1988.

O'Connor, Sister Mary Paschala, O.P. *Five Decades: History of the Congregation of the Most Holy Rosary, Sinsinawa, Wisconsin, 1849-1899.* Sinsinawa, Wisconsin: The Sinsinawa Press, 1954.

O'Hanlon, Sister Mary Ellen, O.P. *Three Careers: Highlights and Overtones.* Edited by Sister Benvenuta Bras, O.P. Sinsinawa, Wisconsin, 1994.

O'Leary, Johanna M. *Historical Sketch of the Parish of the Immaculate Conception.* Faribault, Minnesota, 1938.

O'Rourke, Sister Alice, O.P. *The Good Work Begun: Centennial History of Peoria Diocese.* Chicago, Illinois; Privately Printed, 1977.

———. *Sown on Good Ground: Centennial History of St. Mary Cathedral Parish.* Gaylord, Michigan: Privately Printed, 1984.

———. *Let Us Set Out: Sinsinawa Dominicans, 1949-1985.* Dubuque, Iowa, Privately Printed, 1986.

Portraits and Memories of Rice County, Minnesota. Rice County Historical Society, 1987.

Reardon, James Michael, P.A. *The Catholic Church in the Diocese of St. Paul: from Earliest Origin to Centennial Achievement.* St. Paul, Minnesota: North Central Publishing Company, 1952.

Rosenstiel, Leonie. *Nadia Boulanger: A Life in Music.* New York: W. W. Norton, 1982.

Shannon, James P. *Catholic Colonization on the Western Frontier.* New Haven: Yale University Press, 1957.

Swanberg, L. E., Editor. *Then and Now: A History of Rice County, Faribault, and Communities.* Rice County Bicentennial Commission, 1976.

Sweeney, David Francis. *The Life of John Lancaster Spalding: First Bishop of Peoria, 1840-1916.* New York: Herder and Herder, 1965.

Interviews

Sister Mary Benedicta Larkin, O.P., St. Dominic Villa, Dubuque Iowa, August 4, 1993.

Mary Ann Randall and Kathleen Hunt, North Oaks, Minnesota, August 19, 1993.

Sister Veronita Ruddy, St. Clara Convent, Sinsinawa, Wisconsin, March 21, 1994.

Sister Mary Lourdes Joyce, St. Clara Convent, Sinsinawa, Wisconsin, April, 15, 1994, regarding classes taught by Mademoiselle Boulanger.

Sister Clara Coffey, St. Clara Convent, Sinsinawa, Wisconsin, April 16, 1994, regarding classes taught by Mademoiselle Boulanger.

Index

(Note: Except for Mother Mary Samuel Coughlin, religious names of Sisters are given first, followed by their family names.)

Adrian Power, 46
African-American, 122-123, 125
Agatha Lyons, 124
Alain McGillicuddy, 126
Aldridge, W. J., O.P., 184
Alexia Tighe, 122
All Saints, Los Angeles, 159
Amata O'Brien, 136, 152, 163, 183
Ambrose Flaherty, 134, 135, 159
American Military Cemetery, 169
Anaconda, Montana, 47
Andrea Bracken, 123
Anna Clare Casper, 135
Annora Searfoss, 168
Annunciation, Minneapolis, 97
Anti-Catholicism, 80, 81
Anti-Foreignism, 80
Antoninus Singleton, 159
Apostolic Delegation, 41-42
Arbre Croche, 7, 8
Arcola, Illinois, 49
Arms Race, 54
Aurora, Illinois, 14
Australia, 141
Austria-Hungary, 42, 54, 55
Avellina Buckley, 189-190

Baltimore, Diocese of, 5
Baltimore, Third Council of, 38
Baraga, Frederic, 8
Barnabas McTighe, 83
Basilia Andrus, 126, 127, 148, 149
Belgium, 42, 140
Benedict Ryan, 163
Benedict XV, 85, 91, 172
Benedicta Kennedy, 87
Benedicta Larkin, *ix*, 163, 176, 177, 180, 181
Benedictine Monastery, Einsiedeln, 83
Benetta Coughlin, 19, 39, 94, 100, 129-131, 177
Benita Newhouse, 163
Benton, Wisconsin, 11, 12, 17
Benvenuta Bras, 126n
Benvenuta McCullough, 17, 20
Bernardus Fitzgerald, 50
Bethlehem Academy, *x*, 12, 19-21, 22, 23, 49, 129
Blanche Delaney, 135
Blessed Martin de Porres Mission, Columbia, South Carolina, 123
Bloomington, Illinois, 49
Boggiani, Thomas Cardinal, 81, 89-94, 99, 101-106, 133, 134, 135, 170 (death)
Bologna, 83, 135
Bolshevik Revolution, 79-80
Bonaventure Tracy, 46
Borromeo Smith, 125
Bosnia, 54
Boston Symphony Hall, 144
Boulanger, Nadia, 143-148
Brotzge, Gustave, 149
Brown, Joseph R., 1
Burns, Honora, 13
Bursar General, 37, 43

Cahensly, Peter Paul, 42
Camillus Harney, 182
Camp We-Ha-Kee, 97
Cannon River, 4
Canon Law, 58, 84, 93, 133
Carnegie Hall, 144
Carroll, Bridget, 49
Castelgondolpho, 170
Catacombs, 169
Catharine Wall, 64, 104, 106, 107, 156
Cathedral High School, Duluth, 110
Catholic Church, 5-7, 37, 124, 135
Catholic Evidence Guild, 125
Catholic University, 38, 41, 143
Catholic Youth Movement, Italy, 108

Catholic Youth Organization, Chicago, 124
Catholic Women's League, 64
Cause of Father Samuel Mazzuchelli, 12, 135, 195-196
Causse, Jacques, 56
Centennial, 1949, 161, 173
Centennial Song, 161
Central Powers, 55
Champaign, Illinois, 49
Charles Borromeo, 10
Chaska, 6
Cherbourg, 107
Chicago, 14, 43, 63, 124, 136, 150
Chicago Builder's Association, 82
China, 55, 139
Chippewa, 1, 8
Cincinnati, Diocese of, 7, 125, 127
Cincinnati, Ohio, 7, 8, 126-127, 128, 168
Civil War, 4, 37
Clara Conway, 11
Clare Urel, 78
Clemente Davlin, *x*
Clover, Joan, 177
Cobh, County Cork, Ireland, 168
Colonization, 3
Colosseum, 169
Colton, Joel, 113
Columbia University, N.Y., 122
Columbia, South Carolina, 122
Communism, 79
Conferences of Major Superiors, 194
Congress, 3
Conlin, Emma, 22, 25
Conlon, Odilo, 185
Constantia Leamy, 61
Constitutions of the Congregation, 37, 48, 58, 67, 83-94, 101, 107, 195
Cork County, Ireland, 1, 12, 13, 49, 107, 168
Corpus Christi, N.Y. City, 122
Cortaux, Mathilde, 83
Coughlin, Angela, 19, 40, 129, 161, 178
Coughlin, Anna, 177
Coughlin, Barbara Temm, 177, 179
Coughlin, Bernard, 110, 129, 177, 182, 184
Coughlin, Bertrand, 179
Coughlin, Bertrand Daniel, 179
Coughlin, Blanche, 179
Coughlin, Blanche Abbey, 177
Coughlin, Brigid, 13-14, 19, 24, 40, 129, 177, 178, 180, 183
Coughlin, Daniel, Sr., 13-14, 19, 40, 100 (death), 178
Coughlin, Daniel Martin, 110, 177
Coughlin, Daniel, Jr., 19, 40, 177, 180
Coughlin, Ellen (Mother Samuel's mother), 13-14, 19, 24-25, 40
Coughlin, James, 177
Coughlin, John, 13, 19, 24, 40, 152 (death)
Coughlin, John E. (Nephew), 142, 184, 185
Coughlin, Joseph, 19, 40, 177, 180 (death)
Coughlin, Martin, 184
Coughlin, Mary (Benetta). *See* Coughlin, Benetta
Coughlin, Mary Anne, 14
Coughlin, Mary Samuel, iv
- ancestry, 13-14, 19
- attitude toward school, 29-30
- autobiography, 27-36
- birth and early childhood, 19, 23, 27-28
- character of father, 28
- character of mother, 27-28
- death and funeral, 181-190
- education, 23-25, 29-30, 44-45
- entrance into Congregation, 26, 30-31
- illnesses and injury, 76, 94-95, 100, 116-117, 135, 159-161, 181, 192
- instructions to the sisters:
  - on World War I: 56-58
  - on the Great Depression: 114-115
  - on World War II: 139

legacy, 191-196
prioress of St. Clara Convent, 45, 48
relationship with Nadia Boulanger, 143-148
relationship with Mother Emily, 33, 45
relationships with Roman authorities, 58, 81, 83-94, 99, 102-106, 108, 133, 152, 154, 155, 169-170, 172
resignation proposed, 153-156
responsibilities of, 37, 43
Coughlin, Molly, *ix*, 177, 180, 184
Coughlin, Patrick, 14
Coughlin, Samuel (Nephew), 142, 177
Coughlin, Sophia, 184
Coughlin, Thomas, 177
Coughlin, Timothy, 13
Cram, Ralph Adams, 63, 64
Cretin, Joseph, 5, 6, 7, 14
Crowley, Jim, 111n
Czechoslovakia, 139

DaVinci, 83
Daly, Edward. C., 175
David O'Leary, 97
Deaths, 48-49, 77, 89, 100, 106-107, 135, 136, 152, 160, 170-175
Deegan, Ellen Coughlin, 177
Deegan, Ray, 177
Delehanty, Julia, 22, 25
Denmark, 140
DePaul University, 60
DeRicci Fitzgerald, *ix*, 49, 67, 68, 78, 82, 87, 88, 94-95, 100, 106, 116-117, 127, 135, 142, 152, 154, 159, 160, 161-162, 170-172 (death)
Dhough, 13
Dolan, Leo T., O.P., 184
Dominican College of San Rafael, 127
Dominican Leadership Conference, 128
Dominican Master General, 10, 134, 168
Dominican Mothers General Conference, 127-128, 194
Dominican Order, 10, 12, 26
Dominican Sisters, Adrian, 122, 185
Dominican Sisters, Columbus, 185
Dominican Sisters, Kenosha, 185
Dominican Sisters, Racine, 185
Dominican Sisters, Springfield, 185
Driscoll, John Alexius, O.P., 184
Dublin, 107
Dubuque, Iowa, 8, 17, 31, 59, 76
Dubuque, Diocese of, 5
Duluth, Minnesota, 110
Dunmanus Bay, 12
Dusterhoff, Marie, 177, 180

Eagle Grove, Iowa, 121
East Dubuque, Illinois, 59
École Normale, 144
Edgewood Academy, 63
Edgewood College, 109-110, 142, 156, 160
Edgewood High School, 105, 109
Education of the Sisters, 46-47, 142-143
Edward Blackwell, 143, 144, 145
Elections, 37, 45, 48-49, 53, 77-78, 101, 117, 118, 131-132, 151-152
Emery Tousignant, 123
Engelbert Dilger, 97
England, 42, 106
English Overlords, 12
Enos Patrick, 183
Esser, Thomas, O.P., 81, 83-84, 90
Ethiopia, 139
Eunice Joy, 157
European Trip, 1949, 168-170
Evangeline Cleaveland, 97
Evans, Mary, 14
Evelyn Murphy, 74, 83, 94, 104, 130, 152, 156-157, 160, 163, 167, 168, 173, 175-176 (death and funeral)
Exposition of the Blessed Sacrament, 129, 193
Eymard Keating, 65-66
Facists, 108
Faenza, 7

Faith and Freedom Readers, 143
Far East, 37, 55, 140
Faribault, Alexander, 3, 4
Faribault, Jean Baptiste, 3-4, 6
Faribault, Minnesota, *ix*, 3, 4, 14, 16-17, 19, 27, 49, 129
Farley, Cardinal, 171
Fenwick, Edward J., 7, 8
Fidelia Delaney, 71-72
Fitzgerald, John, 49
Fitzgerald, Marie Mahoney, *ix*
Flint, Edith Foster, 44
Florence, Italy, 87, 135, 156, 159, 160, 168, 170
Florida, 127
Ford, George B., 122, 146, 148
Fort Crawford, 1
Fort Snelling, 1, 6
Fortier, Elizear, 147
Forum, 169
Founder's Day, 12
Four Horsemen, 110
Fowler, Major, 17, 19
France, 5, 7, 54, 79, 139, 148, 167
Francile Holohan, 124
Francis Ferdinand, 54
Franciscan Sisters, 185
Frank, Glenn, 109
Freeport Catholic High School, 97
Freeport, Illinois, 58
Fribourg, Switzerland, 58, 72-74, 83, 87, 88, 106, 134, 135, 136, 141, 168, 170
Fund-raising, 60, 153, 160

Galena, Illinois, 8, 59
Galtier, Lucien, 5, 6, 7
Garrigou-Lagrange, O.P., 168-169
Gasparri, Pierre Cardinal, 102
General Chapter, 37, 45, 48, 58, 84, 94, 101, 133, 151-152, 163-165 173, 181
General Council, *ix*, 58, 62, 63, 65, 66, 143, 156, 161, 167, 181
Geneva Conference, 1955, 167
George Adamson, 67, 69, 73, 74, 83, 136, 169
George Lennon, 168
George VI of England, 167
German Immigration, 8, 10
Germany, 42, 54, 79, 139, 140, 141, 148
Gertruda (Genevieve) Pinion, 157
Gertrude Power, 17, 20, 21, 23, 31
Glenmary Home Mission Sisters, 175
Grace James, 69, 83, 109, 136
Grace, Bishop Thomas L., 14-17, 25
Great Britain, 54, 80, 139, 167, 168
Great Depression, 113-115, 118-121
Green Bay, Wisconsin, 7, 97, 98
Griffin, William R., 132, 193
Guiding Growth in Christian Social Living, 143

Harriet Donoghue, 115-116
Harvard College, 144
Hauge, Cleone, 177
Hazel Green, Wisconsin, 58, 159
Hefferan, Mrs. William, 82
Hefferan, William S., 64
Hines, Mrs. Edward, 82
Hirt, Paschal, 133, 152
Hitler, Adolph, 139, 140
Hoban, Edward F., 122
Holy Rosary, Minneapolis, 26, 37, 43, 129, 191
Honorary Degree, Marguerite LeHand, 130, 131
Honorary Degree, Mary Samuel Coughlin, 118
House in Rome, 102-106, 127, 134, 135, 195
Hoyle, 63
Hughes, Edward, O.P., 176
Hunt, Elizabeth, 178
Hunt, Emily Jeanne, 178
Hunt, James, 178
Hunt, Kathleen, *ix*, 178, 179, 180, 184
Hunt, Mary Coughlin, 77, 110, 180, 184
Hunt, Robert Vincent, 178
Hunt, Vincent, 177, 178, 180
Hunt, William Coughlin, 178, 180
Hyacintha Finney, 78, 96
Hyphenated Americans, 55

Ignatia Downey, 143, 146, 148
Ignatia Fitzpatrick, 11

Illinois, 3, 5, 8, 10, 43
Imelda Hertzog, 17
Immaculate Conception Church, Faribault, 20, 21, 129
Immaculate Conception School, Faribault, 20, 21, 24
Immaculate Conception Church, Chicago, 81, 96
Immaculate Conception School, Waukegan, 49-50
Immigration, 8, 12, 38, 42-43
India, 141
Industrial Revolution, 37
Influenza epidemic, 58
Institutum Divi Thomae, 126-127, 134, 149
Iowa, 5, 10
Ireland, 1, 42, 106
Ireland, John, 25, 38, 39, 47
Irish immigration, 3, 38
Italy, 43, 55
James II, 12-13
Januarius Mullen, 152
Japan, 139-141
Jean McSweeney, O.P., *x*
Jeannette Leary, 136
Jeremy Finnegan, 13n, 161
Jersey City, New Jersey, 13
Jesuit Order, 5, 7
Joan Smith, 122, 143
John XXIII, 181
Johnson, George, 143
Jordan Carroll, 126, 127, 148
Josephine Cahill, 11, 17
Julie Garner, 161
Julliard School of Music, 144

Kallal, Charles W., 64, 106-107 (death)
Kallal, Mrs. Charles W., 176-177 (death)
Kavanaugh, James B., O.P., 160
Kaye Ashe, O.P., *x*
Keating Family, 65
Keller, Rev. George, 16-17, 19, 20, 21
Kelly, Robert, 107
Kelley, Robert M., S.J., 118
Kenneth Loeffler, 126, 127, 148
Kevin Reidy, 125
Kleven, Grace, 177
Korean War, 167
Ku Klux Klan, 80

LaBatte, Mary, 97
LaCrosse, Diocese of, 48, 98
Lake Superior, 8
Land Ordinance of 1785, 3
Laserian Doran, 74, 83
"Last Supper," 83
Lateran Treaties, 109
Laurenti, Camillus, 93, 101
Layden, Elmer, 111n
League of Nations, 79, 139
LeHand, Marguerite, 130, 131
LeHavre, 5, 82, 88, 135, 168
Lend-Lease Program, 140
Leo XIII, 42
Lernoux, Penny, 71-72
Lewis, William H., 110
Lilly, Michael, O.P., 26
Lincoln, Abraham, 14
Liturgical Practices, 35
Liverpool, 107
London, 106
Long Branch, New Jersey, 13
Longy School, 144
Loosbrock, Julius, 185
Loras, Mathias, 5, 7, 9
Loretto Hospital, Chicago, 161
"Lost Generation," 81
Louis Bertrand Droege, 96-97,149-150, 163, 193
Louisiana, 125
Lourdes, 88, 107
Loyola University, 118
Lucerne, Switzerland, 42, 83
Lusitania, 55
Luxembourg, 140

MacArthur, General Douglas, 167
Macarius Murphy, 16-17
Mackinaw Island, 7
Madison, Wisconsin, 61
Magnolia, Massachusetts, 146
Malavogue, 13
Mallory, Hervey F., 44

Manchuria, 139
Marco Giraldi, 157
Maria Michele Armato, 13n
Marie Carmel (Marie Therese) Janke, 123
Marie Louise Oughton, 141
Marie Therese McGreevy, 123
Marie Thomas Keating, 65-66
Marinette, Wisconsin, 97
Mariola Dobbin, 104
Marise Barry, *x*
Marita Fitzgerald, 50
Marquette, Diocese of, 8
Martin de Porres Hogan,123
Mary Christ, 97
Mary DePaul Fitzgerald, 161
Mary Emily Power, 33, 39, 44, 45, 46-47 (death and funeral), 172, 182, 191-192
Mary Eva McCarty, *ix*, 74, 96
Mary Helen, 184
Mary John Kallal, 64
Mary Joseph Rogers, 68, 71-72, 177 (death and funeral)
Mary Nona McGreal, 143, 168-170, 196
Mary Patrick, 184
Mary Peter Doyle, 163
Maryknoll Congregation, 71-72, 177
Matthias Michels, 157
Maura Cotter, 74, 76, 100, 115, 117
Mayo Clinic, 100
Mayo, Charles, 100
Mazzuchelli, Samuel, 181
  Cause, 12, 135, 195-196
  Dominican Sisters, founding of, 11, 14, 17
  educational efforts, 11-12
  death, 12
  German and Irish immigrants, 8, 10
  Italian origins, 7
  legacy, 12, 136
  Sinsinawa Mound, purchase of, 10
  St. Charles Borromeo, province of, 10, 11
  St. Thomas Aquinas, College of, 11
  work with Bishop Loras, 5, 10
  work in Michigan and Wisconsin, 7-9
McBride, Catherine Coughlin, 177, 184
McBride, John, 177, 185
McCabe, Francis X., 60-61
McCarthy, Edward, 174, 175
McGavick, Alexander J., 101, 133
McGuinnis, Edward S., O.P., 48
McManus, Mary, 22, 25
McNicholas, John T., 69, 103, 110, 128, 134, 135, 136
  early acquaintance, 48
  and elections, 53, 77-78, 131-132, 151-152
  and Fribourg venture, 70, 72
  illness and death, 172-175
  and Institutum Divi Thomae, 126-127, 149
  and Maryknoll Foundation, 71-72
  and Mother of God mission, 125
  and Mother Samuel's possible resignation, 153-156
  as spiritual advisor and confidant, 53, 78, 84, 192, 193
McNicholas, Timothy, 175
Meagher, Raymond, O.P., 73
Mehigan, Mary, 13
Memoirs, 10
Mendota, Minnesota, 1
Mercy Hospital, Chicago, 161,
Mercy Hospital, Dubuque, 76
Messmer, Sebastian G., 61, 110
Mexican War, 3
Mexico, 55-56
Michigan Territory, 7
Middle West, 3
Milan, Italy, 7, 10, 83, 135, 169
Miller, Cletus, 127
Miller, Don, 111n
Milwaukee, Wisconsin, 43, 98, 136
Minnesota, 1, 2, 3, 4, 5, 6, 24
Minnesota River, 1
Missionary Areas, 9
Missionary Groups, 5
Missions (Tables I-V), 51, 52, 75, 112, 137
Mississippi River, 1, 7, 31
Mistress of Novices, 94

Mobile, Alabama, 5
Montini, Giovanni Battista, 109, 172
Morocco, 54
Most Pure Heart of Mary, Mobile, Alabama, 149
Mother Emily Power Memorial Hall, 96
Moudry, W., 184
Mound, 23, 31, 32, 35, 43
Muldoon, Peter J., 47, 85, 98, 121
Mulloney, Daniel C., 146
Mundelein, George Cardinal, 63-66, 69, 81, 96, 103
Munich Pact, 139
Murphy, Mr, and Mrs. Daniel, 19
Mussolini, Benito, 108, 134

National Catholic Welfare Conference, 98, 173
Native Americans, 1, 3
Nazi-Soviet Pact, 139-140
Netherlands, 140
Neutral Rights, 55
New Year's Resolutions, 111
New York City, 87, 124, 136, 141, 170
Nolan, Louis B., O.P., 92-93, 104, 106, 127-128, 133, 134
North American College, Rome, 180
North Carolina, 125
Northwest Ordinance of 1787, 3
Norway, 140
Novitiate, 33
Nuyts, Herbert J., 17

O'Brien, Mary Jane, 22, 25
O'Connell, William Cardinal, 146
O'Connor, Dom Philip, O,C.S.O., 184
O'Connor, Francis, 185
O'Connor, William P., 176, 184-185, 186, 188-189
Oklahoma, 125
O'Mahoney Clan, 12-13
O'Mahoney, Catherine, 13
O'Mahoney, Count Daniel, 13
O'Mahoney, Ellen, 13-14
O'Mahoney, Jeremiah, 13
Oak Park, Illinois, 64
Omaha, Nebraska, 61, 62, 98
Oregon School Case, 81
Ottoman Empire, 54
Our Lady of Mercy, N.Y., 112
Our Lady of Refuge, N.Y., 97, 112
Oxford, 107

Padua, 83
Palermo, 104
Palmer, A. Mitchell, 80
Palmer, R.R. 113
Paris, 55, 107, 134, 135, 168, 170
Parle, 6
Paschala O'Connor, 50n, 176
Paul VI, 109
Paul McCabe, 161
Paulina (Kathleen) Coughlin, 141
Pauline Ingram, *x*
Pearl Harbor, 141
Pelamourges, Anthony, 5, 6
Peoria Diocese, 38
Peter Connor, 61, 77
Petiot, Remigius, 5
Philippine Islands, 141
Pierz, Francis, 3
Pius X, 91
Pius XI, 91, 101, 105, 108,134, 172
Pius XII, 91, 134, 135, 170, 172, 194
Pius XII Institute, 156-157
Pizzardo, Joseph Cardinal, 81, 90, 102, 105, 108, 169-170, 181
Platteville, Wisconsin, 59
Plattsmouth, Nebraska, 47
Poland, 42, 139, 140
Postulancy, 33
Power, Louis, 46
Prairie du Chien, 1, 6
Premonstratensian Fathers, 97
Presentation Sisters, 185
Preuss, James M., S.J., 123
Prioress of Motherhouse, 45, 48
Prohibition, 80
Prouille, 88

Queen of Peace, Madison, 159
Quigley, James E., 61, 63

Rachel Conway, 11
Radcliffe College, 144
Railroads, 59-60
Randall, Mary Ann, *ix*
Ravoux, Augustine, 5, 6, 7
Ready, Michael J., 130
Reardon, Maurice E., 175
Recollect Priests, 5
Regina Mulqueeny, 17
Regina Mundi, 195
Reginald Kean, 47, 50, 77
Reilly, Thomas à Kempis, O.P., 69, 73
Rempe, Francis, 81
Reparata Murray, 134, 135
Rescript on Constitutions, 93
Resignation Proposed, 153-156
Resurrection, Minneapolis, 149
Reville, Emile, O.P., 21
Rhode, Paul, 97
Rice County, 3, 4
Rice, Grantland, 111
Rice, Henry Mowrer, 1
Richard Barden, 77, 82, 94
River Forest, Illinois, 66
Rochester, Minnesota, 100, 115, 117, 129
Rockford, Diocese of, 98
Rodolpha Rudolph, 136, 141, 160, 168, 169
Roman Officials. *See* Coughlin, Mary Samuel; relationships with Roman Authorities
Rome, 10, 42, 71, 83, 104, 134, 152
Rome-Berlin Axis, 139
Roosevelt, Franklin D., 121, 130, 131
Roosevelt, Mrs. Eleanor, 130
Rosary College, 63, 81, 125, 134, 143, 156, 160
Rosary College Auxiliary, 82
Rosary College Building Project, 87, 90, 94, 95
Rosary House, 76, 82
Rosati, Bishop Joseph, 8
Rose McSweeney, 32
Rosemary Crepeau, 74, 83, 104
Rule of 1860, 12
Russia, 43, 54, 79, 140, 141
Ruth Devlin, 67, 68, 71, 78, 82, 94, 95, 96

Sachs, Arthur & Georgette, 144, 146
Sacred Congregation of Religious, 81, 84, 86, 89, 155
Sacred Heart, Omaha, 123
Sacred Heart, Washington, D.C., 94
San Domenico, 83
San Sisto Vecchio, 169
Santa Barbara, California, 144, 148
Santa Sabina, 134, 169
Sarajevo, 54
Sault Ste. Marie, 8
Scandinavia, 42
Scannell, Richard, 61, 62
Scheve, Clement, 21
Schneider, J. B., O.P., 184
Schools and Convents Established (Tables I through V) 51, 52, 75, 112, 137
Schwebach, James, 48, 72, 89 (death)
Sean O'Brien, 123
Serbia, 43
Sheehy, Maurice S., 130
Sheil, Bernard J., 124
Sherry, Donald G., O.P, 184.
Shields, General James, 3, 4
Sibley, Henry Hastings, 1
Siena, Italy, 135
Sinsinawa Dominican Congregation, *iii*, *ix*, *x*, 1, 7, 11, 21, 26, 47, 79, 83, 89, 113, 124, 132
Sinsinawa Dominican Education Conference, 143
Sinsinawa Dominican Newsletter, 167
Sinsinawa Dominicans, 1, 11, 14, 24, 38, 43, 49
Sinsinawa Female Academy, 11, 43
Sinsinawa Mound, 10, 23, 31, 32, 35, 43, 59, 144
Sioux, 1
Sioux Wars, 4
Sisters of Charity, B.V.M., 60, 185
Sisters of Mercy, 123, 185
Smith, Joseph, 10

Society for Propagation of the Faith, 10, 125
Somerset, Ohio, 8, 11
South Dartmouth, Massachusetts, *ix*
Southeast Asia, 141
Soviet Union, 167
Spain, 139
Spalding, John Lancaster, 38, 39, 41-42
Spanish-American War, 37
Sparks, Timothy, O.P., 169
Spellman, Francis J., 148, 177
Sperti, George, 126-127, 149
Stalin, Joseph, 167
St. Anthony de Padua, 83
St. Basil Convent, Chicago, 135
St. Benedict, Omaha, Nebraska, 123
St. Bernard, Wauwatosa, 97
St. Brendan, Chicago, 50
St. Cecilia, Omaha, 76
St. Clara Academy, 11, 43, 45, 59, 64, 191
St. Clara Alumnae Association, 46, 60
St. Clara College, 43, 45, 48, 60-61,77
St. Clara Convent, 31, 45-46, 117
St. Dominic Convent, Denver, 46, 76
St. Dominic Villa, Dubuque, Iowa, 156, 160, 163, 170, 175, 176, 183
St. James Church, Jersey City, N.J., 13
St. James, Atlantic City, N.J., 121
St. James, Kenosha, Wisconsin, 50
St. James, Rockford, 26
St. Jarlath, Chicago, 81
St. Joseph Province, 11, 73
St. Joseph Sisters, St. Paul, 17
St. Joseph, Sioux Falls, 76
St. Joseph, Tuskegee, Alabama, 149
St. Leo, Oakland, California, 159
St. Louis, Missouri, Diocese of, 8
St. Malachy, Geneseo, Illinois, 97
St. Margaret Hospital, Spring Valley, Illinoism 159-160
St. Mary, Appleton, Wisconsin, 50
St. Mary, Champaign, Illinois, 121
St. Mary, Cheyenne, Wyoming, 122
St. Patrick, Imogene, Iowa, 76
St. Patrick, Lemont, Illinois, 26, 191
St. Patrick, Rockford, Illinois, 121
St. Paul, Minnesota, 3, 14, 129
St. Paul, Diocese of, 7, 16, 17, 25
St. Peter Claver School, Oklahoma City, 124
St. Peter, Oshkosh, Wisconsin, 46-47,76
St. Richard, Chicago, 159
St. Robert, Shorewood, Wisconsin, 115, 136
St. Theresa of Lisieux, 108
St. Thomas High School, Rockford, Illinois, 96
St. Thomas More, Chicago, 159
St. Thomas the Apostle, Chicago, 76
St. Thomas, Peoria Heights, Illinois, 149
St. Thomas College, St. Paul, 177
St. Vincent Sanitorium, Denver, 76, 192
Stock Market Crash, 113
Stone Constitutions, 107
Strauch, Dr., 159, 181
Stravinsky, Igor, 144
Stritch, Samuel Cardinal, 172
Stuhldreyer, Harry, 111n
Suarez, Emanuel, O.P., 168
Submarine Warfare, 55-56
Sussex, 55

Tardini, Monsignor, 172
Taylor, Myron, 156-157, 169
Temm, Barbara. *See* Coughlin, Barbara Temm
Teresians, 71
Teresita Hessian, 74, 83, 87
Third International, 80
Third Order of St. Dominic, 11
Thomas Aquinas O'Neill,109
Thomas More (Mary) Hunt, 161
Three Ages of the Interior Life, 169
Timothea Doyle, 169
Toormore Bay, 12
Transportation problems, 59-60, 150-151

Treaty of Traverse de Sioux, 4
Trinity High School, 76, 105, 107, 109
Triple Alliance, 54, 55
Triple Entente, 54
Truman, President Harry, 167
Tudor Monarchy, 12
Turkey, 55

United States, 37, 79, 80
University of Chicago, 44
University of Notre Dame, 110, 111
Universiy of Wisconsin, 44, 110

Vacation Religion Study, 98
Vatican, 134, 169
Vatican Council II, 195
Venice, 83
Veronica Power, 17, 20
Veronita Ruddy, 126
Versailles, Treaty of, 79, 139
Vianney de Young, 126
Vicaress General, 46, 49, 67
Villa Schifanoia, 156-157, 158, 160, 169
Villa des Fougères, 70-74, 83, 141
Visitation, Chicago, 76, 96
Visitation, Kewanee, 97, 121
Visitation Sisters, 185
Vivian Doran, 122
Walker, J. B., O.P., 184
Walsh, James, 71
War Guilt Clause, 79
Wardell, 13
Wedron, Illinois, 159
Weiland, Thomas L., O.P., 122-123
Wellesley College, 144
West Germany, 167
White House, 130, 131
William of Orange, 13
Willits, Dr. Henry, 185
Wilson, President Woodrow, 55, 57, 79
Winifred Mary Carmody, 83
Wisconsin, State of, 1, 5
Wisconsin Territory, 8, 10
World War I, 54-58, 80, 139
World War II, 139-142

Y.W.C.A., 105

Zacchaeus Ryan, *ix*